International Money and Banking

International Money and Banking
The Creation of a New Order

A. W. Mullineux
Lecturer in Money and Banking
University of Birmingham

NEW YORK UNIVERSITY PRESS
Washington Square, New York

First published in the USA in 1987 by
NEW YORK UNIVERSITY PRESS
Washington Square, New York, N.Y. 10003

© A.W. Mullineux, 1987

Library of Congress Cataloging-in-Publication Data

Mullineux, A.W.
　International money and banking.

　Bibliography: p.
　Includes index.
　1. Banks and banking, International.　2. International finance. I. Title.
HG3881.M815　1987　　　　332.1'5　　　87-12393
ISBN 0-8147-5436-8

Printed in Great Britain

All rights reserved

THE HARVESTER PRESS PUBLISHING GROUP
The Harvester Group comprises Harvester Press Ltd (chiefly publishing literature, fiction, philosophy, psychology, and science and trade books); Harvester Press Microform Publications Ltd (publishing in microform previously unpublished archives, scarce printed sources, and indexes to these collections) and Wheatsheaf Books Ltd (chiefly publishing in economics, international politics, sociology, women's studies and related social sciences).

To Joe

Contents

Preface ix
Abbreviations xi

1 Supervisory Aims and Objectives 1
2 Banking Supervision in the UK 12
3 Banking Supervision in the US 27
4 Supervision of the International Banking System 50
5 The Latin American Debt Problem 67
   5.1 The origins of the problem 67
   5.2 The Mexican Crisis 69
   5.3 The aftermath 70
   5.4 1985: The turning point? 73
   5.5 The Plaza Agreement, the Baker Plan, OPEC III and GATT 81
   5.6 Alternative solutions 93
6 European Monetary Integration 113
   6.1 The Present arrangements 113
   6.2 Future prospects 118
7 Reforming the International Monetary System 138
   7.1 The problems 138
   7.2 The proposals 149
8 Do we need a World Central Bank? 165

Appendix A. The Secondary Banking Crisis 176

Appendix B. The Johnson Matthey Affair 182
Appendix C. The Continental Illinois Crisis 187

References 193
Index 201

Preface

This book had its origins in a course taught to students taking the Money Banking and Finance degree at the University of Birmingham (UK). The degree programme produced its first graduates in 1985. The book covers only part of the course, entitled 'Comparative banking and financial systems', which undertakes a comparative study of banking systems and discusses various domestic (UK) and international financial issues. The book is designed to serve as a text for students taking similar courses and should also be of interest to students of international economics. Given the topicality of the issues discussed, it is hoped that it will have a wider appeal and attract interest from people wishing to learn more about some of the burning issues of today.

I would like to thank my students, who seemed to enjoy the lecture course on which the book is based, for their comments and questions which have helped to guide me in my writing. I would also like to thank Sheena Hutton for typing the various drafts of the book. Finally I must thank my wife Judith for her support and my children, Ruth and Joe, for not using the manuscript for their drawing.

September 1986

Abbreviations

BIS	Bank for International Settlements
CBI	Confederation of British Industries
CCC	Competition and Credit Control
DTI	Department of Trade and Industry
EC	European Communities
ECU	European Currency Unit
EEC	European Economic Community
EMCF	European Monetary Cooperation Fund
EMF	European Monetary Fund
EMU	European Monetary Union
ERM	Exchange Rate Mechanism
FDIC	Federal Deposit Insurance Corporation
FDIS	Federal Deposit Insurance Scheme
FER	Floating Exchange Rate
FFCS	Federal Farm Credit System
FHLBB	Federal Home Loan Bank Board
FOMC	Federal Open Market Committee
FRB	Federal Reserve Board
FRN	Floating Rate Note
FRS	Federal Reserve System
FSLIC	Federal Savings and Loan Insurance Corporation
FSLIS	Federal Savings and Loan Insurance Scheme
G5	Group of Five
G7	Group of Seven
G10	Group of Ten
G24	Group of Twenty-Four
G30	Group of Thirty
GATT	General Agreement on Trade and Tariffs

GNP	Gross National Product
IADB	Inter-American Development Bank
IBRD	International Bank for Reconstruction and Development
IFC	International Finance Corporation
IIE	Institute of International Economics
IIF	Institute of International Finance
IMF	International Monetary Fund
JMB	Johnson Matthey Bank
LA	Latin American
LDC	Lesser developed country
LDT	Licensed deposit taker
MCRS	Multi-currency reserve system
MDB	Multilateral development bank
MIGA	Multilateral Investment Guarantee Agency
MYRA	Multi-year rescheduling agreement
OCC	Office of the Comptroller of Currency
OECD	Organisation for Economic Cooperation and Development
OPEC	Organisation of Petroleum Exporting Countries
SDR	Special Drawing Right
SLA	Savings and Loan Association
SSDS	Supplementary Special Deposit Scheme
UK	United Kingdom
UN	United Nations
UNCTAD	United Nations Conference on Trade and Development
US	United States

1 Supervisory Aims and Approaches

The purpose of prudential supervision of the banking and financial system is to protect the depositors, investors and shareholders in financial institutions from various risks and thereby to reduce their losses. In particular it aims to eliminate bad practice and fraud as sources of risk and to isolate the effects of any losses incurred by a particular institution by preventing 'knock-on' or 'domino' effects damaging other institutions dealing with it.

Depositors are regarded as the most vulnerable because of the prohibitive cost individuals would incur in the process of collecting and analysing the information necessary to assess the risk of loss from what they are encouraged to believe is a safe refuge for their often small deposits. The regulation and supervision of banks and other deposit taking in institutions and the establishment of deposit insurance schemes are primarily designed to protect depositors in those institutions. They do, however, have other uses, since they contribute to the reduction of domino effects by helping to isolate the problems that do occur. This is important because banks have become increasingly interdependent through interbank, Eurocurrency and Eurobond markets. Consequently, banks may not be fully cognisant of the risk undertaken by the final link in the credit chain and failures could potentially send shock waves throughout the banking system. A deposit insurance scheme helps to localise the effects of a failure because it reduces the incentive to withdraw deposits from a bank in trouble, which would probably cause its rapid demise. This in turn affords indirect protection to banks known to be dealing with the troubled bank from a run on their own deposits. Deposit insurance schemes have the further benefit that they may reduce the tendency towards concentration in banking. This is especially true where the schemes, as they commonly do, cover deposits only up to some maximum amount. This should encourage potentially large depositors to spread their deposits around the banking system. In the absence of deposit insurance, the tendency would be to make deposits in the larger banks which, because of their larger and more diversified portfolios of assets and liabilities,[1] are less likely to fail.

The case for investor protection is similar to that for depositor protection, namely the protection of consumers of financial services against loss through fraud or malpractice. The argument is for protection of small investors, for simliar reasons to those given above, rather than institutional investors. Many people hold their savings outside the banking system in the form of investments: in insurance and pension funds, in unit trusts, in investment funds, and in building societies and stocks and shares, for example. A framework for investor protection, based on self-regulatory bodies overseen by the Securities and Investments Board, was introduced in the UK in 1986.

Shareholders are expected to bear some of the risk undertaken by the companies in which they invest. But they too should be protected from bad practices such as insider dealing and domino effects. Shareholders are to be regarded as investors in the new framework of UK investor protection mentioned above. Shareholders in financial institutions, by implication, take a share in the risks which financial institutions undertake as an integral part of their business. Shareholder protection provides another justification for the supervision and regulation of the banking and financial system because at the root of prudential banking is sound capitalisation, which depends on shareholders' willingness to invest and, therefore, on the perceived risk of their investments.

It should be noted that responsibility for regulation and supervision of the banking system need not necessarily lie with the central bank. A distinction should be drawn between regulation and supervision. Regulation entails the imposition of rules and restrictions whilst supervision entails the monitoring of the banking and financial system to ensure that the rules are adhered to. When rules are contravened the supervisors should be able to set in motion procedures which will require the recalcitrant institutions to account for their actions, perhaps in a court of law, and appropriate bodies should exist to impose sanctions. Commonly the supervisors are not responsible for establishing regulatory systems although they may use moral suasion to impose certain restrictions. Finance or trade and industry ministries are usually responsible for formulating and revising regulations and ensuring compliance. Regulatory reforms are, however, commonly devised after full consultation with the supervisors, who may well have drawn attention to the need for reform in the first place. Supervisory authority is, however, usually delegated. The degree of delegation varies between countries and supervisory responsibilities may be delegated to more than one institution. The Ministry of Finance in Japan, for example, is heavily involved in regulation and shares supervisory responsibility with the central bank, the Bank of Japan. In the UK supervision of the recognised banking system has been primarily the responsibility of the central bank, the Bank of England. In the US responsibility for supervising the banking system is shared between a number of authorities, including the central banking system, the Federal Reserve System. The degree of independence of the supervisory authorities also varies. The Bank of Japan and the Bank of England are directly accountable to their finance ministries. The US regulators enjoy more independence and are empowered to make judgements on the interpretation of existing banking laws, although their judgements can be and frequently are challenged in the courts by interested parties.

There is a general choice between an informal and a legislative approach to supervision. In the UK, where the central bank is the chief bank supervisory authority, the Bank of England has forged special relationships with banks and other city institutions. It has encouraged self-regulation, for example, in the stock market and the Lloyds insurance market. This system of supervision, which has been likened to a club arrangement, came under strain with increasing competition in the 1970s and 1980s and as a result of the deregulation and technological innovation that occurred in the latter period. Following the 1977 EC banking directive,[2] which aimed to harmonise the supervision and regulation of banks and deposit-taking institutions in the EEC, the 1979 UK Banking Act imposed more rigorous registration rules on banks and deposit-taking institutions and made provisions for the establishment of a deposit isurance scheme. Also consistent with the directive have been guidelines, issued by the Bank of England, concerning liquidity ratios, capital ratios and foreign currency exposure.[3] This tendency for the supervision of the banking system to be backed by more statutory regulation is likely to continue in the UK in the wake of the 1984 Johnson Matthey affair;[4] the implications of which we shall discuss in Chapter 2. The new arrangements for investor protection in the UK are based on self-regulatory organisations overseen by a specially created agency, with statutory backing, which will have power delegated to it by the Department of Trade and Industry. The US system of regulation has been considerably more formal, in both the banking and wider financial system. The US banking supervisory arrangements will be discussed in Chapter 3. In the US, investor protection is overseen by the Securities and Exchange Commission (SEC), which has strong legislative underpinnings.

Revell (1975) discusses the appropriate form of prudential supervision with particular reference to the UK. He draws attention to the link between liquidity and the willingness of a central bank to act as lender of last resort. He also observes that liability management, through the interbank and Eurocurrency markets, can increase liquidity, but that it only does so at the cost of raising the risk of insolvency. This is because, in crisis, funds flowing through the interbank market will dry up rapidly for all but the most creditworthy. In the case of such a crisis he argues that the central bank might have to consider direct intervention as lender of last resort to the interbank market. At present the UK interbank market is, however, an unsupported market, and so are the Eurocurrency markets. In Revell's terminology, liquidity relates to the day to day running of a bank in normal circumstances, whilst solvency relates to a bank's long term viability, encompassing crisis conditions.

In principle central banks should be willing to extend funds to troubled banks, in their capacity as lender of last resort, in order to prevent a bank's liquidity shortage developing into an insolvency crisis. The problem is that if the banking system thinks it can rely on the central bank to bail it out then market discipline will be weakened. This is known as the 'Bagehot Problem'.[5] Further, the Continental Illinois crisis, discussed in Appendix C, illustrated the need for bank supervisors to pay more attention to the practice of liability management by banks. Liability management is the practice of actively seeking out loans and other liabilities and then securing finance for this business. The finance is commonly sought in the interbank and Eurocurrency markets. As mentioned above this practice appears to increase the liquidity of banks. The case of Continental Illinois, however, illustrated the point that when a bank is judged to have serious problems the supply of wholsesale funds through these markets to the bank in question can rapidly dry up and a liquidity problem can develop into an insolvency crisis. In the case of Continental Illinois the fears were largely due to the bank's heavy exposure to the troubled oil sector. The Continental Illinois crisis highlighted the need for banks to have diverse sources of funds and, in particular, the risks involved in relying too heavily on the wholesale money markets for funds and in developing overconcentrated loan portfolios. The fact that Continental Illinois could not rely on a sound base of retail deposits was a result of the severe restrictions on branching in the state of Illinois.

In the absence of speculation and rumour the Continental Illinois liquidity problem would probably not have developed into a crisis. This observation has been used to support the case for greater disclosure of information by banks. The cost to some banks might be a downgrading of their credit rating, but the benefits would be to reduce the risk of collapse as a result of rumours and speculation. It would also lead to a strengthening of market discipline and force banks to hold an appropriate quantity of liquid assets in the light of the risks involved in their balance sheets. Further, the presence of deposit insurance should reduce the reliance of banking systems on the lender of last resort. This is because if depositors are adequately insured then the risk of a run on the bank is reduced. If assets could also be insured, then worries about loans to sectors of the economy, or countries, facing problems would be alleviated but the profitability of banking would be reduced by the amount of the insurance premium. We shall discuss deposit insurance schemes more fully below.

Revell (1975) also draws attention to the problems of conflict between regulation and competition. If, following the traditional British route, a banking club with rules is founded, then entry is likely to be restricted and competition with it. Under such a situation there exists the additional problem of 'moral hazard', since overreliance on support, from the Bank of England might encourage excessive risk taking. The central bank might try to introduce a counterforce to this moral hazard by imposing market discipline so that banks are encouraged to seek maximum profits and are confronted with the risk of failure. It is, however, difficult to apply this discipline to large and small banks alike, since the consequences of the failure of a large bank are so much greater. This in turn will reinforce any tendency towards concentration in the banking industry. In most countries banking is a highly concentrated industry, the US being an exception. The US authorities have been more willing to allow failures amongst the smaller banks than the larger ones. However, because of the hitherto severe restrictions on branching in the US, this has not led to a marked change in the level of concentration in the USA. Thus the conclusion seems to be that informal controls lead to cartelization, whilst market controls lead to oligopoly, in banking, unless strict branching restrictions are in force.

The form of supervision advocated by Revell (1975) is one of preventive medicine applied through 'vicarious participation in management' by the monetary authorities.[6] The aim is to ensure that risks of insolvency are reduced to the point where failures are rare. Revell observes that the insurance schemes in operation are for retail, rather than for wholesale, deposits. The need for wholesale deposit insurance schemes would, however, appear to be implied by growth of liability management, through the interbank and Eurocurrency markets, as a source of liquidity. He advocates that insurance should also be extended to cover assets, as well as liabilities. Revell argues that supervisory policy is an integral part of the financial policy of the monetary authorities and that it should not be hived off to a quasi-independent agency.

Maisel (1981) addresses the problem of assessing the capital adequacy of banks. It is argued that the emphasis should be placed on the appropriate measurement of risk and capital adequacy and that a bank's capital requirements will depend on the risk undertaken. He argues that the supervisory process could be markedly improved by a more thorough application of the ideas developed in portfolio theory.[7] He advocates that net worth, which is the difference in valuation of assets and liabilities, be appraised taking due account of the risks involved. To achieve this the Federal Deposit Insurance Scheme (FDIS), in the USA, should be replaced by a system in which insurance premiums vary according to net worth and risk. Maisel believes that the risk-related insurance scheme could be provided either by an independent public agency, or through the private sector, so long as it is separate from the monetary authorities. This is to enable the possible conflict between lender of last resort and monetary supply control to be avoided. He also argues that the agency should be run as a true insurance business; covering its own costs and perhaps even making a profit. 'Free riders'[8] should be eliminated by making membership of the scheme, or one of a number of competing schemes, compulsory. This would also eliminate the problem of 'adverse selection'.[9] It is observed that the nature of a bank is to take risks and that a bank should be able to insure, at the appropriate price, against the risks undertaken. Hence, there should be no need for any failures, except through mismanagement. The US supervisory and regulatory system of the early 1980s was judged, by Maisel, to be inadequate because arbitrary capital ratios were imposed which were unrelated to portfolio risks, and because the fixed rate insurance scheme presented a 'moral hazard' problem, by encouraging banks to undertake risks in excess of that justified by the flat rate premium. A flexible rate insurance scheme is advocated, but the problems remain of deciding which risks should be insurable, and implementing practical methods of classifying portfolio risks into various bands and making appropriate insurance charges.[10]

A major issue concerns whether banks should be forced to join insurance or other joint protection schemes. One argument is that if it were in the banks' own interests to participate in deposit, and perhaps asset, protection schemes, they would set them up themselves. There is not much evidence of this in banking history. The major German banking groups do, however, operate schemes which commit them to help troubled banks but they have not gone so far as to set up deposit insurance funds voluntarily. Voluntary participation would leave the insurance system open to 'adverse selection' and the larger banks might well opt out. An alternative view is that government intervention is required because this is an example of market failure involving significant externalities. The major beneficiaries of such schemes are not just the banks, who benefit as a group through the reduction of the risks of domino effects, but the depositors and shareholders and the economy as a whole. Further, the payments transmission system has become an essential part of the infrastructure of modern economies and its smooth functioning should be assured.

The large US banks have complained that they are effectively subsidising the smaller banks through their participation in the FDIS. This is because they hold larger and more diversified portfolios and are consequently less subject to the risk of insolvency. Whilst there is some merit in this view, it should not be taken as a case for reducing the coverage of the scheme. Instead it can be used in support of the argument for risk-related premiums. The fact that smaller banks face higher risks and would consequently pay proportionately larger premiums might, however, act as an inducement to increased concentration in the banking industry.

The Continental Illinois crisis apparently confirmed that large depositors enjoyed *de facto* insurance beyond the maximum limit provisions of the FDIS. The bank supervisors have been trying to ensure that this will not be the case in the future. This is important if one of the major benefits of deposit insurance is to be realised, namely the encouragement of potentially large depositors to hold smaller deposits in a large number of banks, rather than to concentrate them on a particular bank. The concentration of large deposits by single depositors in individual banks raises the risks of insolvency in times when these banks face liquidity shortages, since large withdrawals can severely exacerbate the problem.

It has been argued that there may be a conflict between the lender of last resort and monetary control roles of a central bank.[11] It should be noted that the provision of crisis lender of last resort services, 'at a price',[12] need not be inflationary provided the central bank can reign back the funds when the liquidity crisis passes. This is because in a pure liquidity crisis the increase in the monetary base (cash and bank deposits) permitted will be, if finely judged, matched by an increase in the demand for cash by the public and the banks. If the central bank took no compensatory action the rise in demand for liquidity could lead to a multiple credit contraction, which would result in a reduction of the money supply. Thus, provided the central bank can adjust its supply of funds to the system, when the demand for cash subsides as the crisis eases, it should be able to continue to hit its monetary targets. In this light, lender of last resort and monetary control roles are complementary rather than conflicting, so long as the central bank has sufficient control over the supply of cash and reserve assets.

It is probably easier, however, to achieve a balance between lender of last resort action and monetary control if intermediate monetary targeting rather than monetary base control is being pursued. This is because the relationship between the monetary base and monetary aggregate chosen for control is probably least reliable in abnormal times.[13] In the depression period of 1929-33 it was found that in the USA the monetary base rose but the money supply fell catastrophically.[14] This illustrates the point that in a crisis the central bank should feel free to inject as much liquidity as required. Even a rise in the money supply in such crisis periods of depression might not be inflationary, because the velocity of circulation of money is likely to fall.

If, as in the case of Continental Illinois, the banking crisis occurs in a period of economic expansion and appears localised, then the central bank should consider allowing the interest rate to rise to squeeze out any potential inflationary consequences. If, however, there are fears that the crisis could potentially spread throughout the banking system, then the rise in interest rates could exacerbate the problem by making bank funding more costly. During the Continental Illinois crisis the Federal Reserve Board (FRB) allowed interest rates to rise.

We have also noted that there might be a conflict between the crisis lender of last resort and supervisory roles of a central bank. This has been dubbed the 'Bagehot Problem'. Since Bagehot (1873) many economists have regarded the lender of last resort function, in its crisis and rediscounting forms, as the primary one of a central bank. Bagehot advocated that central banks should lend freely, 'at a price', in a crisis in order to prevent a generalised collapse of the system. He did not advocate the support of banks that had little or no chance of recovery, however, and argued that appropriate charges should be made to discourage over-reliance of the facility. The problem is that if the banks feel that the central bank can be relied upon to perform this role, and if when it does so it does not charge sufficiently penal rates, then the banks might exploit the situation by taking on unduly risky business under the assumption that the central bank will bail them out if problems arise. In order to avert this moral hazard problem, central banks do not lay down any hard and fast rules concerning their lender of last resort role. This is because they do not want to excite a general expectation of intervention and encourage abuse of the system. The Bank of England's understanding of its crisis lender of last resort function can, however, be gauged from its actions in, and commentary on, the 'secondary banking crisis' and the 'Johnson Matthey affair'; see Appendices A and B.

NOTES

1. The larger the portfolio the greater is the pooling of risk and the lower the average risk; *see* Coghlan (1980, Chapter 8) for example.

Diversification can lead to the reduction of the risk on a portfolio of assets below that associate with each of the individual assets; see Coghlan (1980, Chapter 6) for example.
2. Commission of the European Communities (1977).
3. See Chapter 2 for further discussion.
4. See Appendix B.
5. See Hirsch (1977).
6. Facilitated by regular meetings between a bank's management and representatives of the central bank's supervisory division.
7. See, for example, Francis and Archer (1971) or Levey and Sarnet (1982).
8. Those that utilise a good or service without paying for it.
9. This is commonly experienced by voluntary insurance schemes. The people most likely to take out insurance cover are those most at risk and, therefore, more likely to claim. The larger the incidence of claims, however, the greater is the premium required. Larger premiums are more likely to deter low risk insurers and the insurance company is left with a larger proportion of high risk insurers.
10. Classification of portfolio risks would appear to be a natural extension of the service performed by US credit rating agencies, such as Moody's and Standard and Poors, and could perhaps be undertaken by these agencies, for a commission, on behalf of the insurers, whose task would then be simplified to that of setting appropriate insurance premiums.
11. See Congdon (1981), for example.
12. As advocated by Bagehot (1873).
13. Most monetary economics textbooks contain a section on the relationship between the monetary base and the money supply, or the credit or money multiplier; see Coghlan (1980, Chapter 9) for example. The stability of the credit multiplier over time and its interest rate sensitivity are the subject of much debate. To the extent that a fairly stable money multiplier exists, however, it will depend on the prevailing monetary payments technology and arrangements. In times of crisis and lack of confidence the payments system is normally disrupted and consequently the previously observed relationship between the monetary base and the money supply no longer holds.
14. See Friedman and Schwartz (1963).

2 Banking Supervision in the UK

Following the 1977 EC banking directive,[1] which aimed to harmonise the supervision of banks and deposit-taking institutions in the EEC, and in the wake of the 'secondary banking crisis' (see Appendix A) the 1979 UK Banking Act was passed. It imposed more rigid registration rules on banks and deposit-taking institutions[2] and made provisions for the establishment of a deposit insurance scheme. Also consistent with the directive have been the guidelines issued by the Bank of England concerning liquidity and capital ratios and foreign currency exposure.

The liquidity guidelines[3] apply to all deposit-taking institutions. Their purpose is to ensure that they are able to meet their obligations as they fall due. Such obligations include deposit liabilities, commitments to lend, and unutilised overdraft facilities. To ensure adequate liquidity, banks should hold liquid reserves, avoid inappropriate mismatching and maintain adequately diversified portfolios. The Bank did not set rigid liquidity ratios since it acknowledged that the appropriate reserve ratio depends on the risk of being 'caught short', and that this in turn depends, at least in part, on the degree of mismatching and the degree of diversification of exposure. The Bank outlined the method by which it would measure liquidity, taking the above-mentioned factors into account. It aimed to relate its measurement of liquidity to the reality of the circumstances of each bank after holding discussions with individual banks. It thus adopted a case by case approach. Whenever it was deemed appropriate, the Bank declared that it would like to deal with the consolidated accounts of banks and their subsidiaries. It should be noted that the liquidity ratio finally judged to be appropriate is set for prudential reasons alone. It has no monetary policy connotations, as liquidity ratios had prior to 1981.

New liquidity proposals were announced in 1986, following a period of consultation with the clearing banks. The 'club money' arrangement introduced in 1981, which requires banks to hold a proportion of their liabilities as money at call in the discount market, is to be terminated as part of the restructuring of the UK financial markets made necessary by the 'Big Bang'—the reform of the Stock Exchange which came into effect in October 1986. The new regime will reintroduce minimum liquidity ratios but retain the case by case approach to the determination of supplementary liquidity requirements. A two-tier system is proposed. The eleven major clearing banks will be required to hold their own liquid assets whilst the secondary banks will be allowed to choose between maintaining deposits with the primary liquidity banks and holding their own liquid assets. The system is to be finalised following consideration of the responses to the proposals.

Concerning foreign currency exposure,[4] the Bank sets out the basis on which it will monitor, measure and discuss, with recognised banks and licensed deposit takers, their exposure to movements in exchange rates. These arrangements are to be included in the regular process of supervision and are within the scope of prudential interviews between individual institutions and the Bank. Guidelines are set down concerning the relation of a bank's dealing position to its capital.

With respect to the measurement of capital,[5] the Bank discusses two methods of assessing the adequacy of banks' capital. Again no firm rules are laid down; the appropriate ratios are to be determined, on a case by case basis, following discussions with individual banks. It is recognised that a sufficient flow of earnings is essential as a first line of defence against losses and as a fresh source of capital to allow the business to grow, or even to maintain its scope of operations in times of inflation, and to attract further interest from the stock market, so that further capital can be raised when it is needed. Thus a capital reserve ratio is not judged to be all important in assessing capital adequacy, which is to be assessed on a consolidated account basis, taking account of a bank's subsidiaries and operations worldwide. The Bank's approach to consolidated supervision was spelt out more formally in a notice issued in 1986.[6] This was as a response to the 1983 EC directive[7] and the revised Basle Concordat, which is discussed in Chapter 4.

The Bank's interest in capital adequacy stems from its desires to ensure that the capital position of a bank is regarded as acceptable by depositors, other creditors and shareholders, and that capital reserves are adequate in relation to risks of losses. Different measures of capital are designed for each purpose. For the former, the 'gearing ratio' is used. This is a ratio of 'free resources' to 'liabilities'. The 'free resources' are the capital base, which is the total value of capital assets at market prices less the value of assets such as buildings and equipment. The idea is to measure the value of readily saleable capital assets. For the latter the 'risk asset ratio' (RAR) is used. This is also calculated by relating 'free resources' to liabilities. In this case, however, the buildings are counted, along with the free resources used in calculating the gearing ratio, and the assets are assigned weights from zero for cash to two for buildings, according to their designated liquidity. The aim is to take account of the eventuality that, in case of liquidation, the full market value is unlikely to be recovered on buildings and other non perfectly liquid assets. The weights are designed to take account of the fact that, in case of liquidation, some credits will not be redeemable. Hence investment risk, which is the risk that the marketable value of claims or directly held assets may decline, will be incurred. Having calculated these ratios for each institution their adequacy is judged in the light of the risks undertaken, in the form of mismatching and in connection with the degrees of diversification or concentration in exposure, on a case by case basis. Larger institutions with more diversified portfolios would be expected to be able to operate with smaller prudential capital ratios.

Following the onset of the Latin American debt crisis,[8] central banks around the world urged banks with exposure to country risks to raise their capital ratios, which had by the early 1980s fallen to historically low levels due to the rapid expansion of their loan business and the increased recourse to liability management. The Bank of England was no exception. In this connection the central banks also encouraged banks to bolster their bad debt provisions. In addition, as a result of deregulation banks were moving into new and potentially more risky business and were beginning to pay increasing attention to asset management.

In 1985 the Governor of the Bank of England expressed concern at the practice being adopted by international banks of making loans in the form of securities which could be traded by banks, as did the President of the German Bundesbank. Traditionally commercial banks make loans which stay on their books. Large loans to the Latin American countries had commonly been provided by syndicates of banks. Increasingly, however, banks were making loans which could be bought and sold so that banks can swell or shrink their loan portfolios as required. The process has become known as 'securitisation'. The stimulus to this process was the desire to introduce more flexibility into bank balance sheets following the Latin American debt crisis. The risk is that if banks are forced to sell then only the best quality loans will be saleable and even then at a significant discount and banks will be left with loan portfolios of severely reduced quality, which may raise questions about their liquidity and solvency. To the extent that 'securitisation' adds to risk then more capital will be required. Similarly, off balance sheet risks, such as contingent liabilities in the form of interest rate swaps, note issuance facilities, and forward rate agreements, which the banks are increasingly undertaking, should be covered by boosting their capital bases.

As a result of the concern expressed by a number of bank supervisory authorities the Cooke Committee of international bank supervisers undertook a study of the implications of the growth of off balance sheet exposures.[9] Its report, in March 1986, attempted to identify the major sources of risk and assess their importance. It stopped short of prescribing precise capital requirements, leaving this to the discretion of the supervisory authorities. The committee did, however, express its concern about the lack of information available and the extent to which banks had become involved in financial innovation. It felt that the information supplied by banks was insufficient to give their shareholders and depositors a reasonable picture and that consequently more disclosure of information was required. In the same month the Bank of England published a paper outlining criteria from which it expected to develop formal new proposals on capital adequacy by the end of the year. It had, in May 1985, imposed an interim capital requirement on note issuance facilities of half that applied to loans.

In 1985 UK banks turned to the floating rate note market[10] as a source of funding and as a means of reducing their reliance on the Eurocurrency markets. The Bank of England had warned the UK banks in 1984 that notes and other debt issued by other UK banks could not be included in a particular bank's capital base and, to the extent that it was, that bank would have its own capital reduced by the commensurate amount for prudential purposes. The aim was to guard against the risks involved in increased bank interdependence.

In December 1984 the Bank issued a discussion document which introduced new proposals concerning capital adequacy. These proposals were formulated without consulting the banks, which had been the practice in the past, and the banks were unhappy about this development. The proposals covered conditions under which bank debt issues could be counted as primary capital. In particular perpetual floating-rate notes (FRNs),[11] it argued, should only be counted if they carried the provision that they could be converted to ordinary shares if a bank got into trouble. The banks felt that this was unnecessarily restrictive and that perpetual FRNs subject to these conditions would be virtually unsaleable. They were understandably frustrated because they felt that they had found a relatively easy and cheap route to raise capital in response to the Bank's promptings. They also felt that the Bank could have put their case to the Chancellor more forcibly prior to the 1984 Budget,[12] which had handicapped their attempts to raise their capital ratios and bad debt provisions and that undue 'arm twisting' had been used to encourage them to contribute to the indemnity package for the Johnson Matthey bank (see Appendix B), which was likely to prove costly to them. FRNs are cheaper than equity, in part due to a tax anomaly. Equity dividends are paid out of tax income whilst interest on FRNs is chargeable against taxable profits.

In the event, the Bank and the banks reached a compromise in 1985, following the issue by Lloyds of a perpetual FRN which was convertible into preference, rather than ordinary, shares which the Bank recognised as primary capital. The other major clearers subsequently boosted their capital by issuing similar convertible perpetual FRNs. The banks are now required to match every £1 of such loan stock, in their primary capital base, with £2 of equity. This led some banks to make rights issues of ordinary shares to meet this requirement and to raise extra funds for their expansion into the new business open to them through deregulation, especially following the reform of the Stock Exchange in October 1986.

The Bank has thus effectively authorised an international market in risk capital. In the event of crisis the contingent liability is higher on FRNs than ordinary shares because they will be converted to preference shares and their holders will rank ahead of the ordinary shareholders in priority for reimbursement. The risk of a crisis in an individual bank sparking a general UK banking crisis has been contained by the proviso that UK banks cannot hold each other's FRNs as primary capital but this does not extend to the increasingly globalized banking system. The attraction of UK banks' FRNs to non-UK international bank investors is that their safety is seemingly assured given the belief that the Bank will not allow a major UK bank to fail. Hence FRNs are judged to be virtually as safe as gilt-edged securities. It should be noted, however, that the Bank is only formally committed to standing behind depositors, not capital suppliers. But the feeling seems to be that the Bank extends *de facto* cover to capital suppliers because it would need to contain the potential international consequences of a crisis. The US bank supervisors had, after all, in 1984 taken the unprecedented step of guaranteeing all of Continental Illinois debts and deposits in an attempt to protect the US banking system and to contain potential international consequences. The separation between domestic and international bank supervision is, therefore, breaking down as domestic banks in the major financial centres are becoming increasingly international and a global banking market is developing. We shall discuss international banking supervision more fully in Chapter 4.

Another contentious issue has been the treatment of bad debt provisions. Specific provisions are made to cover known bad debts and general provisions are precautionary in nature. The UK banks were prompted to raise both their general and specific provisions during the domestic economic recession in the early 1980s as a result of the Latin American debt crisis. Unlike many countries the UK has no fixed rules about the tax treatment of provisions against losses on loans to Third World countries. The matter is a subject of negotiation between the banks and the Inland Revenue. If allowed, these provisions count as an expense, which is deductable for tax purposes. Under these arrangements it appears to be the case that general provisions come out of after-tax earnings in the UK and take a slice of profits whilst specific provisions come out of pretax earnings and reduce profits. Banks have been permitted to count general provisions as part of capital because they play a similar role in meeting losses.

The Bank has, however subsequently argued that some of the general provisions are 'earmarked' for expected losses and as such are not dissimilar to specific provisions. The Bank, therefore, suggested that general provisions should not be counted as capital. In the US and in some other countries they are counted and this change would have imposed a small handicap on UK banks. A compromise appears to have been reached between the Bank and the banks, entailing the increase of specific provisions relative to general. It seems likely, however, that provisions are inadequate. Latin American debt has, for example, been trading at a 20 per cent discount whilst provisions by the major UK banks are estimated to be about 3 per cent of their loan exposure. This is because banks tend only to make provisions they can afford, retaining profits for distribution to shareholders, boosting capital and making equity (especially rights) issues attractive. Shareholders would perhaps be wise to accept lower dividends and profits at the expense of more healthy bad debt provisions, especially specific ones. The classification of general provisions as primary capital gives the banks at least some incentive to build up general provisions. Tax concesssions on general provisions could also be considered as an additional incentive.

Apart from the EC directive of 1977, another major influence on the 1979 UK Banking Act was the 'secondary banking crisis'. The crisis was partly the result of the growth of a fringe banking sector which was, somewhat loosely, supervised by the Department of Trade and Industry (DTI), rather than by the Bank of England. The Banking Act aimed to rectify this situation by extending the supervisory responsibilities of the Bank to cover some of these secondary or fringe banks.

The UK Deposit Protection Fund came into effect in February 1982 and the Deposit Protection Board met its first claim in connection with the liquidation of a licensed deposit taker (LDT) in May 1982. The 1979 Banking Act provided for the establishment of the scheme to which both recognised banks and LDTs were required to contribute, in relation to their deposit base and subject to minimum and maximum levels of contributions. In the event of the insolvency of a contributory institution, each depositor will receive compensation from the Fund to the extent of 75 per cent of the 'protected deposit'. The maximum 'protected deposit' for each depositor was £10,000 sterling. The building societies, Trustee Savings Banks and the National Savings Bank and National Girobank were excluded from the arrangement because they were judged to be satisfactorily regulated and supervised under statute.

The Bank of England acknowledges that the banking system is an essential part of the monetary mechanism in the UK and consequently argues that it must be regulated to ensure that cheques, and some of its other liabilities, are readily accepted as means of exchange, and that there is no interruption to normal economic activity. The Bank points out that it performs two separate roles.[13] As supervisor its primary responsibilities are to depositors and as auditor its primary responsibilities are to bank shareholders. In the absence of regular bank inspections the Bank has had to rely heavily on auditors' reports in pursuing its supervisory role. It does not have the general power to appoint auditors or to change the auditors approved by shareholders, although it can request a special audit. Under this system there is no mechanism for a bank's auditor to convey unease to the supervisory authorities, unless the problems are concrete enough to merit a qualification in the accounts. A direct dialogue between the Bank and a bank's auditors is not possible. It is prevented by the confidentiality of the client–auditor relationship and the 1979 Banking Act, which required the Bank to treat information supplied by banks confidentially. The Bank of England was, however, in receipt of plentiful supplies and banking statistics and held regular supervisory interviews with bank managements and it was believed that it was in principle able to identify the need to appoint independent auditors, except perhaps in cases of fraud.

The 'Johnson Matthey affair', discussed in Appendix B, highlighted the inadequacies of the UK practice of relying on independent auditors reports without provision for a dialogue between the Bank and its auditors, who are appointed by the shareholders. In June 1984 the auditors had presented an unqualified report on the Johnson Matthey Bank and yet on 1 October 1984 the Bank of England felt obliged to put together a rescue package for the bank. It also brought attention to problems involved in supervising banks which are part of larger groups of companies. Johnson Matthey Bank was part of a larger non-financial group of companies. Deregulation and the trend towards the formation of financial services groups containing banks and other subsidiaries providing specific financial services is likely to make the problem of regulating banks which belong to conglomerates more common. It is, therefore, not sufficient to look at a bank's financial strength in isolation. Instead the financial strength of the group as a whole must be considered. The Bank believes that the principle of consolidated supervision, hitherto applied to banks and their subsidiaries, should be extended to cover the new relationships formed by banks and should complement supervision on an unconsolidated basis.[14]

It was also becoming increasingly apparent that the separation of recognised banks and licensed deposit takers, introduced in the 1979 Banking Act, was no longer appropriate. This was because the breakdown of traditional barriers between the types of business they undertook, due to deregulation and technological innovation, made this distinction irrelevant. The distinction detracted from the creditworthiness of LDTs, many of whom were in fact more creditworthy than recognised banks, and exposed them to discriminatory regulation. This was illustrated by the fact that the Johnson Matthey Bank (see Appendix B) was in fact a recognised bank.

In many countries, bank supervisors and auditors work quite closely. The US has official bank examiners. The Belgian Banking Commission appoints auditors. The Swiss have a special licensing system for auditors, as does the Federal Banking Commission in Germany. Auditors are often much more familiar with the operations of a bank and the management of a bank than are the supervisors but may become too close to the management to act as agents for supervision. In order to overcome this risk, a mandatory rotation of auditors or the appointment of two auditors, to get a second opinion, could be considered. Alternatively, or additionally, greater disclosure could be required. A halfway-house measure would be to require auditors only to report gross violations of bank regulations or situations where the bank deposits seem to be in jeopardy.

On 17 December 1984, following the Johnson Matthey affair, the Chancellor announced an investigation of the bank supervisory system by the Treasury and Bank Review Committee. The committee of inquiry's report[15] prompted the Chancellor to propose the following changes in bank supervision on 20 June 1985. The two-tier system of recognised banks and LDTs would be replaced with a single authorisation to take deposits, and the 1979 Banking Act would be amended accordingly. A regular dialogue would be permitted between the Bank and the bank's auditors. This would initially require the agreement of authorised institutions but future legislation should remove confidentiality constraints. The Bank would also be given new power to obtain information. In August 1985 the Bank issued a consultative paper developing the recommendations of the Treasury and Bank Review Committee. It recognised that supervisors, auditors and managers of banks should maintain their separate functions but discussed several ways in which supervisors could obtain information from auditors without undermining the auditor's primary duty to the banks. These included: regular meetings between the Bank and the bank's auditors with bank representatives present, periodic auditing of banks' quarterly returns to the Bank at the request of the supervisor, *ad hoc* requests for information from auditors and provisions for the auditors to initiate discussions with supervisors. The paper also discusses how the proposals could be given legislative effect.

The Chancellor also proposed that exposure to a single or related borrowers should not exceed 25 per cent of a bank's capital except in exceptional circumstances, and exposure over 10 per cent of capital should require greater capital resources than otherwise required. Further, the Bank's supervisory staff should be increased and given commercial banking experience, and more accountants should be hired. Also banks should be encouraged to strengthen their internal control and reporting requirements and to seek 'letters of comfort' pledging support from shareholders owning more than 15 per cent of a bank.

In response to the findings of the Treasury and Bank Review Committee and the Chancellor's proposals for changes in bank supervision a White Paper entitled *Banking Supervision* was published in December 1985.[16] It announced the government's intention to bring in a Banking Bill to reform the 1979 Banking Act as soon as possible in the light of the Johnson Matthey affair and the rapid changes occurring in the financial markets. Its main recommendation was the formation of a Board of Bank Supervisors to help the Bank's Governor in his banking supervisory duties. This has been interpreted as an attempt by the Treasury to subject the Bank itself to a measure of supervision and increase the accountability of the Governor. The annual report to the Chancellor, which is made by the Bank under Section 4 of the Banking Act and laid before Parliament, will include a separate section by the Board giving an account of their work and expressing their views on current issues within the field of banking supervision. It also recommended that the distinction between recognised banks and LDTs be replaced by a single authorisation criteria, which is outlined. It stated that auditors would be required to play a greater role in supervision and empowered the Bank to require supervised institutions to appoint a second firm of accountants if it was not satisfied with the work carried out by the original auditors. Further, confidentiality constraints on both supervisors and auditors would be removed to the extent necessary to facilitate the proposed supervisory arrangements. In order to bolster the Bank's ability to collect accurate prudential information promptly, it was proposed that it should be made a criminal offence to provide false or misleading information to supervisors. Statutory backing for the Chancellor's proposed guidelines on exposure to individual customers was also to be given. Banks will be required to notify the Bank of exposures to individuals in excess of 10 per cent of their capital base. Exposure in excess of 25 per cent of capital base will require prior notification to the Bank. These proposals stop short of advocating the creation of an all-embracing regulatory regime and aim to preserve as much as possible the flexibility of the UK supervisory system, which is deemed to be its strength. The proposed reforms are also designed to complement legislation which aims to introduce a system of investor protection and achieve regulatory reform of the building societies.[17] It is essential that an understanding develops between the Bank and the new financial supervisory authorities that will emerge as a result of the investor protection legislation. Supervisory responsibilities must be allocated in such a way that all institutions are adequately supervised whilst overlapping supervision is eliminated. Problems of supervisory allocation will be particularly acute in the case of the emerging financial conglomerates involving institutions undertaking both banking and other financial business.

Prior to the White Paper, in September 1985, the Bank had established a Bank Supervisory Committee consisting of the Deputy Governor, who is to be the Chairman, and four senior directors with specific responsibilities. One is to be responsible for banking supervision, another for Basle Committee coordination,[18] another for home finance and the fourth for securities and general supervision. In addition the Banking Supervisory Division is to have its staff increased to 120 and the staff are to receive additional training. In May 1986 the Chancellor approved five nominations by the Bank for members of the independent Board of Banking Supervision foreshadowed in the White Paper. The Board will advise the Governor of the Bank and report separately to the Chancellor each year. The Governor is free to ignore its advice but must report to the Treasury if he does so. The Board's first monthly meeting was in June 1986.

The government's attempts to eradicate fraud in the City have involved the establishment of a fraud investigation group at the Department of Public Prosecutions office and the involvement of auditors in the fraud detection process. The fraud investigation group was set up to coordinate efforts on major fraud cases using lawyers and accountants from the Department of Trade and Industry and working in close contact with the City police fraud squad. Concerning the role of auditors, the government had been considering, in both the Financial Services Bill[19] and the Banking Supervision White Paper, imposing a statutory duty on auditors to act as watchdogs for fraud and to detect inadequate management control systems. These proposals caused unease both among management and within the accountancy profession. In June 1986 the Department of Trade and Industry (DTI) gave the professional bodies of the accountancy profession twelve months to define the circumstances, such as suspicion of fraud, in which they should bypass clients and report directly to supervisory bodies. The DTI reserves the right to lay down its own rules if those proposed by the profession are inadequate. Given the desire to coordinate banking supervision with that of the rest of the financial system it seems unlikely that the forthcoming banking legislation will impose statutory obligations on auditors. The auditors fear that statutory requirements will disturb their relationships with their clients and leave them open to law suits concerning breach of confidence, and to those concerning negligence if they fail to report suspicions to regulators.

The overall picture is not, therefore, one of deregulation. It is rather one of regulatory reform involving a move towards more professional banking supervision. This trend started after the secondary banking crisis in the mid 1970s (see Appendix A) when there were only thirteen officials concerned with bank supervision. The 1979 Act formally empowered the Bank to supervise the banking system on behalf of the Treasury and raised the number of staff in the Bank Supervisory Division to eighty. In the wake of the Johnson

Matthey affair (see Appendix B), and with the breakdown of traditional barriers between the business undertaken by banks and other financial institutions and the internationalisation of banking operations, it has become necessary to increase the staff of the Bank Supervisory Division to at least 120. Taken together the forthcoming investor protection and banking legislation will mean that there will be more supervisory bodies and possibly more regulation. The challenge has been to devise a regulatory and supervisory structure that is well coordinated, to ensure full coverage whilst avoiding wasteful overlap, and yet sufficiently flexible to cope with the rapidly changing financial environment. It is hoped that flexibility combined with rigour in supervision will attract business to London, rather than divert it to less regulated offshore centres where there will be more freedom but also more risk. London has become the adventure playground of the international financial system and the regulators are trying hard to ensure that there are no major accidents. This situation has been brought about by the removal of restrictive practices and trends in international banking, rather than through deregulation. As far as restrictive practices are concerned, the major events have been: the elimination of the interest rate cartel operated by the major clearing banks in 1971,[20] the collapse of the interest rate cartel operated by the building societies in the early 1980s, and the decision[21] to eliminate a number of restrictive practices being operated in the Stock Exchange, culminating in the Big Bang in October 1986. The result has been a general increase of competition between banks and building societies in the retail and housing finance markets, and a trend towards the transformation of the major merchant banks into investment banks, akin to those in Japan and the US, and of the major clearing banks into universal banks, akin to those in continental Europe and especially Germany. The trends in international banking had their influence through the development of the largely London-based Euromarkets, and the development of global bank networks, which have further increased competition in UK banking. Additionally, the trend towards securitisation has given additional impetus to the development of investment banking capabilities by the major UK banks.

NOTES

1. Commission of the European Communities (1977).
2. Drawing a distinction between recognised banks and LDTs. Recognised status is granted by the Bank to institutions of high repute and standing which can satisfy certain financial criteria laid down by the Bank. Other deposit-taking institutions must apply for licences and must satisfy various prudential and financial criteria set by the Bank in order to qualify for them.
3. *See* Bank of England (1986).
4. *See* Bank of England (1981).
5. *See* Bank of England (1980).
6. *See* Bank of England (1986).
7. *See* Commission of the European Communities (1983).
8. *See* Chapter 5.
9. *See* Chapter 4.
10. Which is part of the Eurobond market.
11. Perpetual FRNs, which are a cross between debt and equity, are counted as capital in some other European countries and are recognised as primary capital by the major US credit-rating agencies, even where no provision is made for conversion into equity. The Bank, however, proposed that the perpetual FRNs issued by Barclays and Natwest in 1984, which had no provision for conversion into equity, should not be regarded as primary capital. Such issues would, however, be counted as secondary or subordinated capital.
12. Which increased the tax liabilities on their leasing operations by announcing a phased reduction in capital allowances; *see* Chapter 2.
13. *See* Bank of England (1982a).
14. *See* Bank of England (1982).
15. Command Paper 9432 (1985).
16. Command Paper 9695 (1985).
17. *See* House of Commons Bill 95 (1985/6) and House of Commons Bill 238 (1985/6).
18. *See* Chapter 4.
19. House of Commons Bill 238 (1985/6).
20. *See* Bank of England (1971).
21. By the Stock Exchange following the agreement between the Chairman of the Stock Exchange Council and the Secretary of State for Trade and Industry, on 19 July 1983, that the practice of charging minimum commissions should be eliminated by the end of 1986.

3 Banking Supervision in the US

In October 1984 the Chairman of the FDIC[1] declared that a record 797 banks were on the problem list drawn up by the US bank supervisors. This was more than twice the 1976 peak, which followed the 1973–5 recession. By the end of the 1984–5 financial year seventy-nine commercial banks had failed. In 1983 there were forty-eight bank failures and there were forty-three and ten in 1982 and 1981 respectively. Since 1984 the situation has worsened. In 1985 the number of bank failures rose to 120 and the Chairman of the FDIC expected 150 banks to fail in 1986. Fifty-five banks had already failed by June 1986, the failure rate being roughly two a week. Additionally 1,400, or roughly one in ten of the US commercial banks, were being monitored. Most of the problem banks were situated in middle America where there are approximately 6,500 banks, almost half the nation's total, in an area which is known as the farm belt and which also contains the energy sector. Until the end of 1985–6 the farm banks[2] were the fastest growing group of banks on the problem list. The precipitous fall in oil prices in the first quarter of 1986 led the 563 energy banks[3] to become more of a problem than the farm banks, whose costs were reduced by the oil price fall. The US farm banks still had outstanding bank debt of $210bn in 1986, however, which is more than the combined debt of Latin America's two largest debtors, Mexico and Brazil, and around 5,000 of them still faced problems. Although the failures have mainly been amongst the small regional banks, a few of the top thirty US banks have also failed in recent years[4] and the failure of Continental Illinois (eighth largest), was only averted by a state rescue programme (see Appendix C). In addition there have been problems involving 'thrifts'[5] and the wider financial system.

Although the US banking system seems more prone to failures than most, the mid 1980s have been particularly bad, forcing comparisons with the failures that followed the Great Crash in 1929. That period saw the imposition of stringent regulations on banks, affecting the range of activities they could engage in, their freedom to set interest rates and the extent to which branching was permitted. Additionally, in 1933, the Federal Deposit Insurance Scheme was established and the law relating to the Federal Reserve System was refined.

It should be noted that the inclusion of a bank on the problem list does not necessarily imply that there is a risk of its imminent failure. Rather, it means that it is receiving special attention which may be due, for example, to the fact that it has not received payment of interest or principal on a loan. The US supervisors have been taking a tougher line on 'at risk' loans and monitor them closely in connection with their efforts to encourage banks to increase their loan loss provisions. Nevertheless, this heightened supervisory profile cannot account for the dramatic rise in the number of problem banks or for the number of failures.

A number of banks are still saddled with bad debts resulting from the problems faced by their clients during the US recession of the early 1980s. Although strong, the recovery was patchy, with marked regional and sectoral variations, and many banks are still nursing a number of problem commercial loans. Many sectors of manufacturing industry have suffered from import penetration and loss of export markets, owing to the overvalued dollar. There are also more specific problem areas. In the mid west and the west small farm banks have been suffering and even some of the large banks, such as First Chicago, have had to make large write-offs in connection with farming loans.

The farming sector has suffered from the widespread depression in commodity prices in the early 1980s and from general overproduction in the farming sectors of the US and the EEC. The Federal Farm Credit System (FFCS), to which the majority of farm banks belong, announced a first quarter loss of $20bn in 1986 and reported an increase in problem loans of $5.9bn. The farm banks lost $2.7bn in 1985 and were effectively bailed out by the government at the end of 1985. The farm banks' problems have been exacerbated because falling land and real estate prices have reduced the value of the collateral underlying their loans, and the more creditworthy borrowers have sought cheaper loans outside the system. The energy sector has suffered from falling petroleum prices, and many energy banks, such as those in Texas and Oklahoma, have been struggling as a result. Fifty-nine of the 563 energy banks hold the vast majority of the assets. Some fairly large regional banks are, therefore, involved and some of these banks also have exposures to Third World oil producers such as Mexico and Venezuela. Further, a relatively small proportion of the loans of the energy banks are to the major, and relatively safe, oil companies. Their problems are believed to be containable with an oil price around $15 per barrel but could become acute if the price stabilised nearer to or below $10 per barrel for a lengthy period. Oil prices rebounded from a floor near to $10 a barrel after the first quarter of 1986 but fell below $10 in July 1986 only to rebound again later in the month following a short term OPEC agreement to restrict output. Problems resulting from exposure to the energy sector have also hit larger banks. In July 1986, for example, Oklahoma's second largest bank, the First National Bank, was closed by US bank regulators because of difficulties with loans extended to the oil and gas industry. It was the second biggest bank failure in US history. Then in August 1986 BancOaklahoma, which had become the second largest bank in the state, was rescued by the FDIC. Four years earlier the regulators had closed another Oklahoma bank, Penn Square, which was a third of the size of First National and also suffered from large scale loan exposure. First National reopened shortly after its rescue as a newly chartered subsidiary of the Los Angeles based Interstate Bank operation. Since the Penn Square closure, Seafirst Corporation, another large bank, has been rescued after heavy losses in energy lending by Bank America. The largest failure in US history was that of the Franklin National Bank in 1974. This was due to heavy foreign currency exposure, however. Meanwhile the earnings of the large banks have been restricted by their exposure to Latin America,[6] which continues to cause them concern. The historically high real interest rates, which have resulted from an imbalance between fiscal and monetary policies[7] and have been a major cause of the dollar's overevaluation, continue to cause problems for borrowers in the troubled sectors. The fall in interest rates in the first half of 1986 should help both internal and Latin American debtors to service their debts, but further falls appear to be necessary to make a decisive impact, despite a further half per cent cut in July 1986.

The US has a highly fragmented banking system. This is largely a result of legislative restrictions on branching and types of business that can be undertaken. The largest banks,[8] although large by world standards, are not large in relation to the size and wealth of the population, and the banking industry in the US is nowhere near as concentrated as in the other OECD[9] countries.

Prudent banking requires the development of adequately diversified portfolios of risky assets through the avoidance of overconcentration, either geographically and/or by industry, in loan portfolios, and liabilities, on a large enough capital base and with sufficient liquidity to ensure the protection of depositors and investors and an adequate supply of funds to borrowers and profits to investors. Small localised banks cannot really avoid some concentration in their loan portfolios, because commercial loan opportunities are bound by regional location to a great extent. Further, large banks in states where branching is severely restricted will find it difficult to diversify adequately thier sources of funds or liabilities. In particular, they cannot rely on a cushion of retail deposits gathered through local branches.

There have also been problems in the wider financial system, and especially amongst the 'thrifts'. In August 1984 the Financial Corporation of America (FCA), which was the biggest real estate lender in the US, and therefore in the business of making normally safe, secured loans, suffered a massive loss of deposits—of similar scale to that experienced by Continental Illinois (Continental Illinois) (see Appendix C).

Savings and loan associations (SLAs) like FCA have their own deposit insurance scheme, run by the Federal Savings and Loan Insurance Corporation (FSLIC). FCA's assets were more than six times those of the FSLIC, whereas Continental Illinois's were approximately twice those of the FDIC. FCA had a low capitalisation, in common with most SLAs, but liquid assets.[10] Like most SLAs it was not heavily reliant on wholesale funds, and certainly less reliant on them than Continental Illinois. SLAs' performances had been weak as a result of the poor performance of the property market. FCA's problems stemmed from mismatching, that is, borrowing short-term to lend long-term and were compounded by the practice in the US of making fixed rate home loans at a time when borrowing was increasingly at variable rates.[11]

In July 1985 the Chairman of the Federal Home Loan Bank Board (FHLBB) claimed that a tenth of all SLAs were insolvent and that the funds of the FSLIC were inadequate. Direct investment in real estate was the biggest source of losses but a fall in interest rates would aid the weaker banks by helping their clients and reducing the cost of funding for the SLAs. In August 1984 Fannie Mai (Federal National Mortgage Association), the biggest supplier of housing finance in the US, announced tougher credit standards to stem the mounting losses on mortgages sold to it. This federally sponsored agency buys mortgages from SLAs and has been suffering from borrowers' inability to meet their loan commitments. In March 1984 it foreclosed on 3,000 properties and in June 1985 7,800. It consequently increased its loan loss provisions and raised the income level required to back mortgage loans.

May 1985 saw a savings bank crisis in Ohio. Seventy-one local savings banks were on the critical list and another 800 savings banks were on the nationwide problem list. A three-day 'banking holiday' was announced by the state governor, the first extended bank holiday since the 1930s, in order to stem a run on deposits, and there was serious concern that the banks would not reopen. The seventy-one banks involved contributed to a private, state-based insurance fund but this had been seriously depleted by the collapse of Home State, a SLA which had collapsed ten days earlier. Federal bank examiners descended to assess whether the banks should be given access to the federal scheme and all seventy-one were required to apply to the FSLIC for membership, prior to reopening. A few weeks later, following large withdrawals from the privately insured Maryland savings banks, the state governor limited withdrawals and put several institutions up for sale. Both Ohio and Maryland were forced to permit mergers to secure the savings banks and protect depositors.

The problems amongst the thrifts continued into 1986 when the FHLBB closed Mainland Savings of Houston. This SLA had been undermined by the collapse of the Texan real estate market, which had in turn resulted from the fall in oil prices. It was one of the largest US financial institutions ever allowed to fail. The regulators did not offer *de facto* insurance to large depositors in this case. They refused to honour large denomination certificates of deposit which had been used to finance the SLA's rapid growth, sticking to the rule that only deposits up to a maximum of $100,000 were insured. It was feared that this might cause large depositors in Texas and other SLAs to withdraw funds and thereby to precipitate further troubles. The cost of rescuing SLAs is, however, mounting and this decision can be seen as an attempt to restore market discipline. In 1986 1,200 SLAs were being monitored and the rate of failure seemed unlikely to fall. In June 1986 five Louisiana SLAs were closed and their combined assets were transferred to a newly created SLA, which had previously been set up to take over the assets of another failed SLA. This nearly doubled the number of SLAs closed in 1986 and underlined the serious financial strain on the FSLIC. The rescue cost $280m. Louisiana was one of the states hit hardest by the oil price fall. Additionally five struggling Californian SLAs were put up for sale towards the middle of 1986 and the regulators sought bids from banks and other thrifts.

Since the DIDMC Act[12] 'thrifts' have (1980) enjoyed deregulation of controls on interest rates and on types of business undertaken. This has brought them into direct competition with commercial banks and other financial institutions, and competition has become increasingly severe. In addition, high interest rates have made it difficult for borrowers to meet their obligations. The Maryland and Ohio banks were hit by fears over the adequacy of private state-based insurance. The vast majority of 'thrifts', however, have federal deposit insurance through the FSLIC, although the adequacy of this fund has now been questioned. FCA was kept afloat with federal aid and Home State was reopened in July. Deposits in this bank were, therefore, locked in for three months, causing great inconvenience. This implies that, even if there is little or no risk of loss for small depositors, deposits may be withdrawn to avoid them being temporarily frozen. Given the inadequate capitalisation of many 'thrifts' the commercial banks may eventually be called upon to help. This would bring nationwide branching still closer. The alternative would be a massive, and expensive, federal bailout.

As a result of regulators monitoring the SLAs more closely, back door reregulations may be taking place. Poor quality commercial loans, high risk investments and rapid and unplanned growth have resulted in liabilities being accumulated which are backed by unsound assets. The FHLBB approved new rules in early 1986 forcing SLAs to make cash provisions, of 20 per cent, 50 per cent and 100 per cent of the value of the loan, respectively, for 'substandard', 'doubtful' and 'loss' loans, and to bolster their capital positions. Provisions against real estate investments are also likely to be required following an FHLBB review of inflated real estate investment valuations. FHLBB research implies that since 1983 faulty or fraudulent appraisals have been a significant factor contributing to the near or actual insolvency of 322 'thrifts'. Questionable appraisals were discovered at 848 'thrifts'. About a quarter of these are insured by the FSLIC. Consequently, when the FSLIC rescues a thrift it finds that a significant part of the real estate portfolio is overvalued. The Chairman of the FHLBB expected the FSLIC to take over a further seventy troubled 'thrifts' at a cost of $115bn. This could entirely exhaust the FSLIC's funds. He consequently proposed that its funding should be increased by one or more of the following methods: the imposition of a supplementary levy on SLAs covered by the FSLIC, supplementary funding granted by Congress, and permitting the FSLIC to divest the real estate assets which it had acquired when rescuing SLAs.

He argued that something clearly needed to be done soon since the FSLIC's unobligated reserves were only $2bn compared with potential $15bn losses, from 'thrifts' already taken over, and futher losses from 300 'thrifts' which were still in business but technically insolvent. The sale of assets is necessarily a long term solution since they are unlikely to fetch a reasonable price if they are liquidated rapidly in the currently depressed real estate markets. Further, higher insurance premiums are likely to be resisted and would anyway hurt the troubled SLAs. In the short term, therefore, a US Treasury bailout at the expense of the US taxpayers may be inevitable.

The collapse of Home State was itself triggered by the collapse of ESM, a small treasury securities dealer, in March 1985. Thus problems are not confined to the widely defined banking system and there is significant interaction with the rest of the financial system, large sectors of which are unregulated, as is the case with government securities dealers such as ESM. Apart from triggering the Home State collapse, ESM's failure also led investors to demand to see the collateral of BBS, a bond-broking group, in April 1985 and this led to its demise. Savings bank clients of BBS suffered a $7bn outflow of deposits when the runs started.

Before outlining the US bank regulatory and supervisory system, some occurrences in the banking system of the USA's North American neighbour, Canada, should be noted. Canada suffered two regional bank failures in Autumn 1985—the first since 1923. The repercussions caused rumours about a sound wholesale bank necessitating the six largest of Canada's twelve remaining domestically controlled banks to stand behind it. Both failed banks had problem energy loans and the first failure led to the second because it was known to have heavy energy loan exposure. Full support for depositors was announced to contain the crisis, giving *de facto* insurance to nominally uninsured large depositors. The threatened wholesale bank had a fairly well-diversified portfolio but was ultimately forced to merge, as later was another bank, with a larger institution. Two of the remaining ten banks were still fighting to survive as independent entities in 1986. The question of whether there is still a place for regional banks, given that their dependence on small local economies virtually assures narrowly based portfolios, was raised. It was felt that if they were to survive they must have solid retail bases and diversified loan portfolios. The crisis amongst the small banks has diverted deposits towards the 'big six' banks which dominate Canadian banking, but these banks are facing increasing competition at home and abroad. The fall in oil prices has drawn attention to the exposure of the big banks to the Latin American energy-producing countries, the energy dependent economy of West Canada, and a number of large corporate debtors in the North American oil and gas industry.

A commission headed by Supreme Court justice Willard Estey was established to enquire into the autumn 1985 collapse of the Canadian Commercial Bank of Edmonton and the Calgary-based Northland Bank. The evidence submitted suggests that the report is likely to be critical of all parties: the regulators, the external auditors, and the banks' directors and management. Both of these Alberta banks were heavily exposed to the resource-based west Canadian economy and problems seem to have been exacerbated by weak management and inadequate supervision.

The collapse of these two banks caused an outflow of wholesale deposits from small institutions, straining their liquidity and causing a run on the Montreal-based, and eighth largest, bank, forcing it to merge with the larger National Bank in late 1985. It also led the Continental Bank of Canada and the Bank of British Columbia to seek liquidity support from the central bank, the Bank of Canada, and other sources. There have been calls for supervisory and regulatory reform and reform of the deposit insurance scheme and a banking industry surveillance committee has been proposed. This would be composed of senior retired bankers with powers to alert banks and regulators if problems are uncovered. It would introduce a self-regulatory element into the supervisory and regulatory structure. Some change in the regulatory apparatus is, therefore, expected soon in the light of these problems and the fact that the commercial banks have advanced 50 per cent of their combined equity to Mexico and also have a similar exposure to Brazil. The oil price fall in 1986 is a major threat. It has increased potential losses from their exposures to the west Canadian energy sector and Mexico. The oil-consuming economics of Ontario, Quebec and Brazil will, however, benefit and this may alleviate, and perhaps even offset, the problems they face.

These recent Canadian bank failures result from similar problems to those experienced by the US banking system, and help to indicate the causes of its instability and give a pointer to what needs to be done.

The structure of the supervisory system is rather complex in the US, partly because of the two tiers established by federal and state legislature.[13] The National Banking Act (1864) provided for national banks to be federally chartered and supervised by the Comptroller of Currency, whilst state authorities were to supervise state-chartered banks. In addition, state and national banks were to have 'competitive equality', which implied that interstate banking was virtually prohibited. Branching was also restricted by the McFadden Act (1927) and the Douglas Amendment to the Bank Holding Company Act (1956). These restricted the branching of national banks and bank holding companies (BHCs) and allowed states to set their own policies. This led to marked variations in state branching restrictions. Illinois was one of the strictest states and Continental Illinois and First Chicago had no branch networks. *De facto* branching has, however, been occurring apace owing to the exploitation of loopholes in the legislation. In June 1985 the US Congress approved a bill allowing nationwide interstate branching after five years. It also passed a separate measure to close the limited service bank loophole.[14] If the bill becomes law, after 1990 no barriers to interstate acquisitions will remain amongst states with reciprocal banking legislations. It will also apply to savings institutions and prohibit mergers among the top twenty-five banks and those leading to institutions controlling more than 1 per cent of the nation's deposits. The five-year lead period aims to allow regional banks time to establish interstate bank branch networks and systems.

In 1913 the Federal Reserve System (FRS) was established, following a major banking crisis, to regulate the flow of money and bank credit and to provide liquidity to banks in distress. In order to maintain decentralisation, twelve regional Federal Reserve Banks were established. These banks help monitor the progress of the money policy formulated by the FOMC, undertake supervisory functions delegated by the Federal Reserve Board (FRB) and provide various financial services primarily connected with the payments system. The FRB had a rather passive role until the bank failures of the 1930s, following which its control over interest rates was increased and it was empowered to impose interest rate ceilings. Membership of the FRS is compulsory for national banks and optional for state banks. The formation of the FRS led to its sharing supervisory duties with the Office of the Comptroller of Currency (OCC). These responsibilities were divided as follows: the OCC is primarily responsible for regulating national banks and the FRB concentrates on state banks which are members of the FRS, non-members being the responsibility of the state authorities. The Bank Holding Company Act (1956) gave the FRB responsibility for supervising BHCs and for monitoring mergers and takeovers concerning BHCs. The BHC Act defines a bank as an institution that dispenses currency, makes loans to commercial enterprises and takes deposits.

The experiences of the 1930s also led to the introduction of legislation, the Glass–Steagall Act (1933), which separated investment and commercial banking and led to the establishment of the FDIC to manage a fund to provide insurance of individual deposits up to a maximum limit. All members of the FRS were required to contribute to the fund and non-members were permitted to join provided that they were willing to accept the requirements laid down by the FDIC. Thus a third tier was added to the regulatory and supervisory structure. The vast majority of member and non-member (of the FRS) banks joined the FDIC fund scheme. Consequently, state banks are usually subject to both state and FDIC regulations and supervision if they are non-members of the FRS, and are subject to regulation and supervision by the FDIC and the FRB if they are members of the FRS, whilst national banks are subject to regulation and supervision by the OCC and the FDIC and BHCs are overseen by the FRB. Banks can and do switch between federal and state charters, according to perceived costs and benefits. Non-bank deposit-taking institutions, such as the 'thrifts', are subject to similar federal/state regulatory structure, and have their own deposit insurance schemes. Additionally, the SEC, set up in 1943, has the task of supervising the functioning of the securities market and imposes statutory controls for the protection of investors. This means that it can and does exercise a healthy interest in the capitalisation of banks and their activities in the securities market. Further, in April 1986, the FDIC supported the transfer of disclosure and reporting requirements for publicly held banks to the SEC, as recommended by the White House taskforce on banking supervision.

The taskforce, chaired by Vice-President George Bush, has examined proposals for rationalising the regulatory and supervisory system. These proposals included stripping the FRB of its supervisory responsibilities. They met with strong opposition from the FRB, which argued that its monetary-policy-setting responsibilities required it to have intimate knowledge of the banking system, which it could only gain by pursuing its supervisory responsibilities. Its lender of last resort responsibility, it argued, also required supervisory involvement to allow preventive action, and its responsibility for ensuring a sound and efficient payments system also required similar involvement. The Bush Committee's proposals, which have still to be acted upon, included the establishment of a new federal banking agency to take over the supervisory responsibilities of the OCC for national banks and smaller BHCs. Additionally it is proposed that the FRB should retain supervisory responsibility for the fifty largest BHCs and take over responsibility for state-chartered banks from the FDIC.

The traditional independence of regulators came under threat in 1986 when the Office of Management and Budget (OMB) suddenly asserted new, and the regulators believe unfounded, jurisdiction over the FDIC, the OCC and the FHLBB. This could restrict their flexibility in responding to deregulation, which has increased competition, reduced profit margins and increased the risks taken by banks.

Before discussing what can be done to reduce US banking instability, the implications of the Continental Illinois Crisis (see Appendix C) for the FDIS will be considered. It showed that large depositors with big banks enjoyed *de facto* insurance, even though the scheme only formally insured the individual deposits in banks contributing to the fund up to the value of $100,000. Large depositors with smaller banks do not seem to have the same cover and one would therefore expect that, if nothing is done to reform the scheme, large depositors will move to large banks. There has been little evidence of this so far but it could cause further instability if large scale transfers do occur. What is really required is a revision of the scheme that will encourage large depositors to break their deposits into smaller amounts and spread them around the banking system. This is after all one of the objectives of setting a maximum limit on insured deposit balances and it should also prevent a drainage of funds from the small- and medium-sized banks.

The method until recently favoured by the FDIC for dealing with failed banks, the 'purchase and assumption' transaction (PAT), gives uninsured deposits some *de facto* protection. Under such a transaction the FDIC replaces bad assets with cash, while deposits and non-subordinated loans are assumed by another bank. In such assisted mergers all depositors, insured and uninsured, are protected. The FDIC concluded in early 1984 that *de facto* insurance undermined discipline at a time when deregulation was allowing banks to undertake increasingly risky business. Also, because such transactions were used for larger bank failures it tended to provide larger depositors with greater protection. In an effort to impose market discipline, by encouraging depositors to influence management, it decided to introduce a modified payoff scheme (MPS) to replace the PAT scheme under which uninsured deposits would be protected only up to their expected value in receivership. Continental Illinois was the first serious test of the new approach and it was found wanting when the FDIC had to announce full protection of all deposits, with the Fed's backing, in order to prevent a run on the bank and possibly on other banks exposed to it. Further reforms of the FDIS deposit therefore seem to be required.

More generally, what can be learnt from the Continental Illinois affair? It is evident that problems can arise through overexposure, which may be unavoidable for small regional banks but for which there is little excuse in the case of larger banks where it is indicative of management failure. It is also clear the overreliance on the wholesale markets for funds and an insufficiently diversified deposit base can put the liquidity of a bank in doubt, especially once confidence is lost. The affair also raises a question mark over supervisory and auditing procedures and the adequacy of bank regulations.

The US banking system in general seems prone to overexposure. In the early 1980s small banks in the farm belt, the energy banks and the 'thrifts', whose business is traditionally concentrated in the real estate market, all suffered from overexposure to a particular type of business. In addition the large money centre banks developed large international loan portfolios, partly because geographic and other limitations on their domestic business encouraged them to be more outward looking. Because of their size and their presence in major money centres they were well placed to help in the recycling of the OPEC surpluses,[15] especially as Latin America developed a voracious appetite for loaned funds. Many of them consequently developed an exposure to Latin America that far exceeded their capital base. Because variable rate loans have become commonplace, in times of high interest rates struggling firms and even countries can find themselves unable to service their debts. Following the recession of the early 1980s, many banks had already opened intensive care units for their ailing corporate clients. The patchiness of the recovery, import penetration, loss of export markets, the LA debt crisis, and the problems in the farming, energy and property sectors have left many banks nursing bad and non-performing debts and ruing past portfolio development choices.

The root cause of US banking instability seems to be the branching restrictions, which have led to a proliferation of banks, many of which are regional in nature and therefore have limited opportunity to develop diversified loan portfolios. They have also forced some banks, such as Continental Illinois and First Chicago, to develop without a sound retail base, which can attract core deposits from diversified sources.

In addition, commercial banks have been losing custom. In 1950 they accounted for half of the financial services provided, whilst in 1980 their share had fallen to a third. This was largely due to restrictions on the array of services they could offer. As less risky business is lost to thrifts, securities houses and retail concerns, the risk in their portfolios has increased whilst management has searched for earnings. There has been a tendency to underprice or reduce the standard of credit quality in order to compete with less regulated institutions with different cost structures. They also raised leverage by allowing capital ratios to decline, thus reducing their cushion against risks. These factors combined with reduced liquidity and thinner margins, which are also subject to the risk of interest rate fluctions, have caused problems.

Strong economic growth in 1984 strengthened loan portfolios and banks used their improved earnings to build up loss provisions and restore capital ratios, under the guidance of the supervisors, and cut back on unprofitable activities. These changes may, however, prove insufficient to insure the system against future excesses because competition continues to intensify internally and internationally.

The structural defects must be addressed if the system is to be rendered more stable. The regulations on geographical consolidation are probably most burdensome. It would, therefore, help if the Congressional Bill on interstate branching and mergers was made law. The proliferation of limited-service banks is in fact adding to the number of banking institutions, since many of them are being opened by non-bank financial institutions. The loophole permitting their development should, therefore, be closed, as proposed in a separate Congressional Bill, and consolidation encouraged in order to help form banking groups which have diversified loan portfolios and sources of funds. This would also permit the pooling of capital and might allow banks to take advantage of economies of scale.[16] Henry Wallich has pointed out that product and geographic expansions compete for the use of a bank's resources.[17] He argues that branching should be given higher priority than movement into new product areas. The Treasury has proposed a Federal Institutions Deregulation Act to modify the Glass-Steagall Act, and in June 1985 the Treasury Secretary, James Baker, advocated that banks be permitted to diversity into new products and services to allow them to compete fairly for custom with less regulated institutions, through cross-selling of services.

Also under consideration are the proposals of the Bush Committee for the rationalisation of the supervisory structure. Other regulatory issues need attention as well. Some of the areas into which banks have diversified, or are likely to diversify into in the future, have little or no supervision, and other areas are supervised only at state level so that there is scope of legislation to ensure a wide and more consistent supervisory and regulatory net. As in the UK, any extension of investor protection will present a choice between a legislative and a self-regulatory approach. In April 1985, the then Vice-Chairman of the FRB, Preston Martin, advocated self-regulation of the banking system by a public oversight board. The general problem of regulating and supervising financial institutions which are part of conglomerates also needs attention.

We have noted that, in response to the increase in perceived risks, the banks have been required to raise their capital ratios and loan loss provisions. In September 1985, the Chairman of the Fed, Paul Volcker, argued that risk-related capital requirements should be imposed. In his view this would be preferable to introducing risk-related insurance premiums via a reform of the FDIS. We shall turn to proposals for a reform of the FDIS below. Whilst on the subject of capital adequacy, however, it should be noted that the Chairman of the Bank of America has argued that liquidity is viewed by many banks as being at least as important as, if not more important than, capital. He also notes that it is pointless to set capital ratios for the banking subsidiaries of BHCs, since BHCs can engage in window dressing by moving capital around their subsidiaries. More attention, therefore, needs to be paid to the capital adequacy of BHs and conglomerates.

An alternative to extending or reforming official regulation and supervision, and one more consistent with the US philosophy of encouraging market discipline, would be to shift some of the supervisory burden from regulators to depositors. But can the potentially descructive disciplinary mechanisms of the market place be harnessed to strengthen, rather than destabilise, the banking system?

Banks have four main characteristics. They have high financial gearing, which leaves them vulnerable to large withdrawals and increases the likelihood of such withdrawals in times of rumour. They hold unmarketable assets, such as loans, although there is a trend towards securitisation.[18] They lack transparency, making it difficult for markets to discriminate between banks leaving them subject to rumours. And they have withdrawable funds. Their interdependence through the interbank and Euromarkets and the development of cross-holdings of subordinated debt also adds to the risk of domino effects. The transparency problem also means that their financial condition can deteriorate without detection[19] and could be addressed by increasing disclosure requirements, which would also expose them more fully to market discipline. A residual uncertainty would probably remain, since the worry might persist that banks were hiding something. An expanded role for auditors, requiring them to publish more detailed independent reports and communicate directly with supervisors for example, might therefore also be required.

Another approach would be to remove *de facto* insurance for large depositors in big banks and extend partial coverage to them instead in order to keep them alert to the risks. It is not clear, however, that this is preferable to extending no formal cover at all, since whether the full or just some risk is to be borne, the incentive to withdraw remains and the cost of doing so is negligible. Alternatively, demand deposits could be given full insurance coverage whilst time deposits could be exposed to risks. This would focus, for disciplinary purposes, on the depositors who have the most incentive to monitor the credit status of banks and who are most responsive to the pricing systems.

The fundamental objection to reliance on market discipline is that uncertainty will always lead uninsured depositors to withdraw funds causing a crisis. They will not be responsive to a premium on interest rates to compensate for increased perceived risk. Further, even though the prospect of funding problems may deter excessive risk taking it is just as likely to encourage undue caution. It is after all a primary function of banks, and other financial intermediaries, to take on and pool risks and also to reduce them by holding diversified portfolios.

The risks they absorb on behalf of the community provide their main source of profit. If they took on board no risks then they would merely be fee-earning brokers occupying their market position by virtue of economies of scale. The financial system would be much less efficient in matching the contrasting needs of lenders and borrowers.

The dual deposit scheme,[20] has been proposed as one way of harnessing market forces to deter excessive risk taking whilst avoiding destabilising side effects. Banks would be required to hold two types of deposit: insured and uninsured. The uninsured deposits would be set at some proportion of the total which was low enough to prevent withdrawals from threatening insolvency but large enough to create a market for uninsured deposits. Uninsured deposits would attract a risk premium and could be used by the supervisory authorities to calculate appropriate risk-related insurance premiums[21] reflecting credit standing and portfolio risk, payable by banks to the FDIS. This scheme would ensure that risk taking by banks was penalised, that risk of large withdrawals was reduced, that lender of last resort facilities would not be open ended but confined to uninsured deposits and that knock-on effects would be reduced so that large banks could more easily be allowed to fail. Its disadvantages are that smaller banks would probably have to pay larger risk-related premiums, given their inability to pool risks to the same extent or to hold such diversified portfolios. They might also have to pay higher interest rates in order to compete for deposits with larger banks with greater advertising capacities. Also, the risk premium might not differentiate effectively between banks, so that more stringent disclosure requirements might need to be imposed. There would again be economies of scale in disseminating information, which would work against smaller banks. Finally the system would need policing.[22] The FDIC would clearly be the natural policing authority. Since a move towards a more concentrated industry would allow the banks to benefit from economies of scale and help to stabilise the US banking system, for reasons discussed above, these disadvantages are not particularly serious and increased policing by the FDIC or some other supervisory agency, paying more attention to portfolio and credit risks, is probably in itself desirable.

We have noted that structural reform is probably required to stabilise the US banking system. Branching restrictions, in particular, need attention and it is probably also desirable that banks be permitted to compete for business with other financial institutions on a fair basis. In mid 1986 these matters still awaited legislation, despite the various Congressional Bills under consideration, the passing of permissive legislation in a number of states[23] and the promptings of the bank regulators. The banking sector is still, however, viewed with suspicion by many Americans and state independence is jealously guarded. There are thus significant lobby groups making legislation politically sensitive and difficult to achieve.

There have, however, been a number of regulatory responses to the problems experienced amongst the banks and the 'thrifts'. In 1981 the US supervisory authorities[24] established a minimum 5 per cent primary capital ratio.[25] In 1984 the primary ratio was raised to 6 per cent and the total ratio to 9 per cent. Banks were also encouraged to reduce their dividend payments and build up their bad debt provisions. This made their equity issues less attractive and they were consequently encouraged to issue debt, which counts in total rather than primary capital. In February 1986 the FRB issue proposals concerning risk-based capital adequacy guidelines and invited comments. The proposed rules are similar to the Bank of England's risk asset ratio guidelines and are consistent with an international trend amongst bank supervisors towards risk-related assessment of capital adequacy. Risk-based ratios had in fact previously been applied, in the 1940s and 1950s, but had been abandoned in the 1960s in favour of more flexible controls. It is envisaged that the new guidelines will operate in tandem with existing total and primary capital ratios and that off balance sheet risks will be included in the assessment of capital adequacy for the first time. The latter development is also consistent with the evolving practice of bank supervisors abroad.[26]

Just prior to Easter 1986, the three main bank regulators announced an easing of capital requirements and accounting rules to help basically sound and well-managed banks through the current difficult period. These measures were aimed specifically at 'farm banks' but the regulators stated that they could be extended to 'energy banks' if the fall in oil prices made it necessary. This development caused unease amongst the antibanking lobby. The view of the regulators seems to be that the point is rapidly approaching where there are too many failures for the system to bear and that market discipline should be temporarily relaxed to ensure the viability of the industry. It is likely, however, that they have formed contingency lender of last resort plans to cope with the possibility that the antibanking lobby might succeed in reversing their initiative.

In March 1986 the FDIC announced plans to double the deposit insurance premium for troubled banks, to curb their ability to expand as fast as healthy banks and to contribute to its funding in the light of the rising demands being placed on the FDIS by the growing number of bank failures. The 1985 record number of bank failures had cost the FDIC dearly and forced it to reconsider its method of rescuing large banks. Current law prevented takeover of failing banks by out-of-state banks until it was too late. In 1986, the FDIC Chairman, with the backing of the other regulators, requested Congress to legislate to facilitate takeovers and allow the FDIC to initiate a rapid interim takeover of a failing bank's management whilst bids were assembled. This would obviate the need to nationalise, which was effectively the option forced upon the FDIC as a result of the Continental Illinois crisis. Currently the FDIC only takes over a bank after it has been closed by regulators. The July 1986 rescue of the First National Bank of Oklahoma was rushed through to take advantage of a federal law which permitted out-of-state buyers to purchase failing banks. This law expired later in July 1986 making new permissive legislation all the more urgent. In May 1986, the FRB proposed that restrictions preventing BHC from acquiring troubled 'thrifts' should be lifted, that Congress should pass legislation permitting easier out-of-state acquisitions of troubled banks, especially the 'energy' and 'farm' banks, and that the limitation on the size of bank that could be procured under the expiring law should be reduced.

The August 1986 rescue by the FDIC of BancOaklahoma followed the expiry of law permitting out of state acquisitions of failed banks. It was similar to the bailout of Continental

Illinois in some respects. The FDIC injected liquidity and assumed some of the bank's debts to keep it operating, and in return sought warrants to buy 55 per cent of its stock at a nominal price, ensuring that the shareholders contributed to the rescue programme. Additionally, the bank's Oaklahoma unit, where losses in the real estate sector had been the primary cause of the group's problems, was merged with the profitable Bank of Oaklahoma. Following merger and reorganisation BancOaklahoma's primary capital ratio was more than twice the minimum regulatory guideline of 6 per cent, other banks holding its term debt having agreed to convert a third of their lending to primary capital. The rescue was a departure from prevailing practices, possibly forced by expiry of the out-of-state aquisitions law. It may set a precedent for future rescues, at least until Congress passes permissive acquisitions legislation.

There still remains a significant lobby holding the view that more and larger banks should be allowed to fail. They argue that the longer a failure is delayed the more expensive is the eventual rescue. So far only relatively small banks have been allowed to fail but a large failure, they feel, is needed to provide a warning to the uninsured depositors who fund the aggressive banks. The problem is that the side effects on other banks of such a failure could be enormous, and to pursue such a policy the regulators would need to have immense confidence in their contingency lender of last resort plans.

There are a growing number of US banks that expect a restructuring of the US banking system, stimulated by technical change and the resultant opportunities for achieving economies of scale. Many regional banks have already formed themselves into sizeable groups in order to compete with the big money centre banks, and many analysts believe that another wave of intra- and even inter- (where reciprocal agreements exist) state mergers and associations is imminent.[27]

The problems facing the US banks and their debtors were eased by falling interest rates, which in July 1986 were $4\frac{1}{2}$ per cent below the heights reached in 1985. The FRB had come under increasing pressure to reduce interest rates as it became apparent that US growth was declining in the first half of 1986. In addition falling oil prices added to the problems faced by the energy banks and banks exposed to Mexico whilst the 'farm banks' and many SLAs continued to struggle. Despite reservations concerning the size of the US budget deficit and the risk of sending the dollar into a more rapid decline, the FRB was virtually forced to pursue an accommodative monetary policy.

The banking system does seem to have grown stronger since the 1984 Continental Illinois crisis. As well as the fall in interest rates there have been substantial increases in capital ratios, profits and loan loss provisions. The fall in oil and energy prices should also benefit some of the banks' energy consuming customers, including those in the farm sector.

The groups of problem banks remain, however, and some of the larger banks, including Bank America, continue to struggle. The 'thrifts' also faired better in 1985 and in fact made record profits. They have benefited from lower interest rates and the restructuring of their balance sheets using new mortgage loan instruments which better match their liability maturities. Many of the 4,000 or so savings banks have, therefore, been doing well, but a large number of institutions are still burdened with older fixed-rate loans and complete recovery is not imminent.

NOTES

1. Federal Deposit Insurance Corporation.
2. Farm and energy banks are banks with loans to the farm and energy sectors, respectively, that amount to 25 per cent or more of their capital.
3. *See* note 2.
4. e.g. First Pennsylvania in 1980 (twenty-third largest) and Seafirst in 1983 (twenty-ninth largest).
5. Savings and loan associations, savings banks and credit unions.
6. Which in many cases far exceeds their capital base; *see* Chapter 5 for further discussion.
7. The US budget deficit increased rapidly in the first half of the 1980s when the Federal Open Market Committee, which enjoys considerable independence from the White House and is answerable to Congress, was pursuing a fairly tight, anti-inflationary, monetary policy.
8. Including Citicorp and Bank America.
9. Organisation for European Cooperation and Development.

Banking Supervision in the US 49

10. Consisting of government securities and morrgages which are tradable in the US.
11. Because restrictions were lifted on interest rates payable on deposits by the Depository Institutions Deregulation and Monetary Control Act (1980).
12. Depository Institutions Deregulation and Monetary Control Act.
13. This had its origins in the anticentralisation sentiment in the country following the civil war.
14. Limited service or non-bank banks offer a restricted range of services. They commonly specialise only in commercial loans or deposit taking and related services. They are, therefore, not banks under the definition incorporated in the BHC Act, *see* below. They have been opened by banks, other financial institutions and retail concerns.
15. Which accrued to the members of OPEC following the massive oil price rise in 1973.
16. In the past, significant economies of scale have not been identified in the banking industry but the recent technological innovations are likely to have changed this picture. Further, recent comparisons between Canada, which permits nationwide branching, and the US do seem to indicate that consolidation could reduce costs; *see* Shipley (1985).
17. *See* Wallich (1984a).
18. Which effectively makes loans tradable.
19. As appears to be the case in the Johnson Matthey affair; *see* Appendix B.
20. *See* Dale (1984)
21. And perhaps capital requirements.
22. To avoid, for example, reciprocal deposits between banks designed to lower the costs of deposit insurance.
23. *See* Syron (1984) and Dunham and Syron (1984) for details of interstate banking experiments.
24. The FDIC, the OCC and the FRB.
25. Prior to 1981 no capital ratios were imposed, except on new banks. A practice had developed of comparing similar banks and encouraging the lowly capitalized banks in the group to raise their ratios.
26. *See* Chapter 4 for further discussion.
27. In September 1986, for example, California passed legislation opening the state to banks from the eleven western states with effect from July 1987 and to the remaining states from 1991. The legislation requires reciprocal access for Californian banks with each of the eleven states, however.

4 Supervision of the International Banking System

The international banking system grew initially as a result of the multinational branching of banks to serve colonial interests and the needs of multinational companies. The next stage involved the development of the London-based Eurocurrency market, which is an international multicurrency banking market in which the dollar dominates, and the proliferation of offshore banking centres.[1] Strictly international banking refers to the international operations of domestic banks and multinational banking refers to the conduct of banking business through offices in a number of countries. In this chapter the international banking system refers to all banks involved in international, as opposed to domestic, banking business and to the markets in which these banks interact.

In response to the threat to the stability of the international banking system from increasing risk, the supervisory authorities, especially in Europe, have adopted a cooperative response.[2] They recognised that the expansion of a bank beyond its national frontiers posed immediate supervisory problems due to the variation in the legal and supervisory regimes between countries. The supervisors in the bank's country of origin wanted to be assured that operations abroad were properly conducted and, therefore, wanted to satisfy themselves that the authorities in the overseas countries supervised the branches and subsidiaries of foreign banks situated in their territories adequately and fairly. The supervisory authorities also needed powers to regulate the branches and subsidiaries of foreign banks in their own country and wanted to know that their parents were adequately supervised. It became necessary to ensure that supervisory and regulatory responsibilities were fully and clearly allocated. This was the first major task of cooperation in the supervision of the international banking system. A closely related requirement was that of ensuring that the responsible authorities had access to relevant information.

Following the Herstatt collapse in 1974,[3] due to foreign currency exposures, the governors of the central banks of the Group of Ten,[4] plus Luxembourg and Switzerland, established a standing committee of banking supervisory authorities which has become known as the Basle or Cooke[5] committee. The understanding reached in 1975 on the division of supervisory responsibilities has become known as the first Basle Concordat. The Bank for International Settlements (BIS), the central bankers' bank situated in Basle, was used as the centre for these discussions. Supervision was deemed to be the joint responsibility of parent and host authorities, with both having the duty to ensure that surveillance of banks' foreign establishments was adequate. The supervision of liquidity was seen as the responsibility of the host authorities, in the first instance, since foreign establishments generally had to conform to local rules. The solvency of branches, which are an integral part of the parent bank, was viewed as primarily a matter for the parent authorities, whilst responsibility for subsidiaries lay with the host authorities. A later recommendation of the Basle Committee was that the supervision of banks' international business should be carried out on the basis of consolidated data in order to provide a global picture of each bank's activities. This tended to shift the burden of monitoring and supervising foreign subsidiaries to the parent authorities. The importance of supervision using consolidated data was illustrated dramatically by the collapse of the SMH bank, a highly regarded private German bank, in late 1983. SMH had developed an overly exposed position by lending extensively to a building machinery manufacturer. This was not identified by the supervisory authorities because the bulk of the lending was channelled through the bank's Luxembourg subsidiary. The Bundesbank's case for requiring German banks to present consolidated accounts was emphatically strengthened and German banking law was changed accordingly in 1984.

The collapse of the Italian Banco Ambrosiano's (BA) Luxembourg subsidiary in 1982 illustrated the weaknesses of the 1975 Basle Concordat. The supervisory authorities in Luxembourg and Italy disclaimed responsibility for supervising or providing lender of last resort cover because BA's Luxembourg subsidiary was technically a holding company rather than a bank. This prompted a reappraisal of the Concordat and as a result a revised Concordat was published in June 1983. Under the new recommendations, the Italian authorities would be responsible for ensuring that an intermediate holding company, such as BA's Luxembourg subsidiary, was covered by adequate supervision or else that the parent bank was prohibited from operating such a subsidiary.

Apart from closing such supervisory gaps, the new Concordat contained two innovations. Firstly, it embodied the principle of consolidated supervision. This would have uncovered BA's Luxembourg subsidiary's problems. Secondly, it addressed the question of adequacy of supervision. If a host authority considers the supervision of the parent institution of a foreign bank operating in its territory to be inadequate then it should either prohibit or discourage continued operation, or impose specific conditions on its conduct of business. Additionally, where the parent authority considers the host authority's supervision to be inadequate it should either extend its supervision to a degree that is practical, or discourage the parent from continuing to operate the establishment in question. The aim was to reduce the tendency for banks to gravitate toward the least supervised centres, which were usually the offshore banking centres. Consolidated accounting should strengthen overall supervision by ensuring that parent authorities supervise risks on the basis of global operations. Concerning solvency, under the 1975 Concordat responsibility lay with host authorities, but under the 1983 Concordat it has become the joint responsibility of the parent and host authorities. The general aim is to ensure that subsidiaries are separate legal entities with adequate capitalisation. Concerning liquidity, primary responsibility for both foreign branches and subsidiaries remains with the host authorities on the grounds that they are more familiar with the operation of local money markets.

The major weakness of the 1983 Concordat is its failure to spell out clearly the responsibility of parent banks for foreign offshoots. The problem is that responsibility is in fact more of a moral than a legal nature. The Bank of England, for example, seeks 'letters of comfort'[6] from the parent institutions. Legislation in the Concordat signatory countries may be required to remove this weakness.

The present supervisory arrangements were worked out by the major industrialised countries but they were becoming increasingly accepted around the world. It is to be noted that the arrangements relate to supervisory responsibilities and not to lender of last resort responsibilities. The possible need for a world lender of last resort will be discussed in Chapter 8. The 1983 Concordat states categorically that it does not address the provision of lender of last resort services. It is feared that a clearly defined statement concerning the allocation of lender of last resort responsibilities might lead to excessive risk taking,[7] and the related problem that if 'soft' supervisory banking centres[8] could rely on, for example, the FRB to bail out subsidiaries of US banks then there would be little need for their authorities to regulate and supervise and little risk to US banks from operating in a 'soft' centre. The FRB has, however, argued that, given the principle of parental responsibility, branches and subsidiaries should look to parent banks if they find themselves in liquidity problems and the parents may then need, in turn, to look to their central bank.

Another important area of cooperation has involved exchange of information. In many countries this has been restricted by law so that legislation such as the UK Banking Act (1979) has been required to temper banking secrecy constraints on information flows. The OECD has been trying to establish an agreement between its member countries to achieve a relaxation of bank secrecy to help counter tax evasion. Switzerland, together with Austria and Luxembourg, which also have relatively tight banking secrecy regulations, rejected an OECD committee's proposals in July 1985, however. Switzerland has been under pressure for some time, from the US especially, to relax its bank secrecy rules. It held a national ballot on the issue in 1984 which supported the retention of the secrecy regulations. There is, therefore, some way to go before free exchange of information becomes a reality. Further, the first EC banking directive (1977)[9] has encouraged the harmonisation of banking law and supervisory practices in the EEC, which should make supervision, at least in Europe, easier. As we have noted before, the 1979 UK Banking Act conformed to the principles of this directive.[10]

Despite the progress made, it has been argued[11] that the present *ad hoc* coordination of national support arrangements might not be sufficient to contain the threat of a collapse of a major multinational bank or keep pace with change and innovation. It is argued that the Basle Concordat is inadequate because it does not enable 'hard' financial centres to force 'soft' centres out of business even though, through consolidated accounting, it is making it harder for banks to channel questionable business through foreign subsidiaries in 'soft' centres. To eliminate 'regulatory arbitrage', the practice of channelling business through branches in the most leniently regulated centres, regulatory arrangements may need to be improved and backed by a formal legal framework.[12] Such measures might conceivably be complemented by: the extension of deposit insurance on an international scale, regulation and supervision of the interbank markets and Euromarkets, and the extension of insurance to assets and in particular loans, as mooted in connection with the Latin America debt crisis (to be discussed in the next chapter).

Apart from the Basle Committee there is the EC Banking Advisory Committee which aims to coordinate the supervisory systems of the member countries of the European Communities. It was created in 1977 to assist the European Commission in ensuring the proper implementation of the first EC banking directive and the European Council directive (1973);[13] on the abolition of restrictions on freedom to provide banking and financial services within the EC. The Advisory Committee was given a number of specific tasks such as deciding on the appropriate content of the numerators and denominators of capital ratios. Where appropriate, it was to reach its decisions following consultations with the relevant supervisory authorities on technical issues. It was also required to prepare new proposals, for consideration by the European Council, concerning further coordination in the supervision of credit institutions, confining itself to matters of policy rather than concrete problems involving specific institutions.

The Advisory Committee has three representatives from each member state and from the Commission. Commercial banks are not represented. The UK representatives are selected from the Treasury, the Bank of England and the Registry of Friendly Societies. The Committee's inaugural meeting was in June 1979 and meetings have been held six-monthly subsequently. It works in close collaboration with the 'Contact Committee', an informal group of representatives from the supervisory authorities of member states. Advisory Committee discussions are seen as the main route through which further coordination of regulation and supervision of banking systems can be achieved within the EC. It has hitherto been mainly concerned with the achievement of consistency in capital and liquidity requirements and has championed consolidated supervision. Its proposals in these areas have been entirely consistent with those of the Cooke Committee. More recently it has also concerned itself with the elmination of discriminatory practices preventing cross-border branching within the EC.

The main impetus for international supervisory coordination has come from the Basle Committee, which to some extent liaises with the Advisory and Contact Committees. It has, therefore, come from within Europe but it has begun to exert a major global influence. The US banking supervisory authorities, particularly the FRB, are not represented directly at the BIS but nevertheless have participated in its work and have been responsive to the proposals of the Basle Committee. This has become particularly apparent in recent work on and off balance sheet risks, as we shall see below. Further afield, the Offshore Group of Banking Supervisors first met in Basle in October 1980. It was founded by representatives from sixteen countries which operate offshore banking centres. Its principle aim is to establish an identity of purpose; both within the group and with other supervisory authorities. The Committee has been particularly concerned with the question of allocating supervisory responsibility between parent and host authorities, exchanges of information, reporting requirements and licensing.

Other supervisory groups include one covering the Latin American and Caribbean countries. Its first meeting was in 1981 and a statute was agreed in 1982. Twenty-one Latin American and Caribbean countries participated. The Nordic Supervisory Group is probably the oldest. It was established in 1920 and holds annual meetings concerning supervisory harmonisation, the exchange of information and other matters.

An issue that has recently caused concern amongst supervisors is the need to achieve a regulatory balance, in the sense of avoiding over- or under-regulation. Underregulation encourages both bad practices and fraud and may give a financial centre a bad name and eventually lose it business. Overregulation pushes business towards less regulated centres. The UK supervisors have become acutely aware of this need to achieve balance in order to maintain London's prominence as a financial centre. Given the growing incidence and public awareness, in the mid 1980s, of fraud in the City it has been deemed necessary to tighten regulation. The proposals contained in the Financial Services Bill,[14] which will involve the establishment of a number of self-regulatory organisations overseen by a securities and investment board with some statutory backing, are designed not only to achieve the protection of small investors from fraud and bad practices but also to eliminate bad practices from markets in which professionals primarily deal. A degree of regulation will, for example, be introduced into the Eurobond market for the first time. It is, however, feared that overstrict regulation might drive away business, such as that taking place in the largely London-based Euromarkets. The self-regulatory approach has, therefore, probably been chosen to maximise flexibility. It also ensures that the participants contribute significantly to the costs of establishing and running the regulatory system.

An encouraging development has been that offshore centres, Hong Kong being the prime example, have also found it necessary to reregulate. In Hong Kong the regulatory and supervisory system was tightened significantly in 1986 following a series of bank failures, a number of which had involved bad practices and mismanagement, and a review of the regulatory and supervisory arrangements by a representative from the Bank of England. The risk that this tightening might force business to less regulated or 'softer' offshore centres was presumably judged to be less than the loss of business likely to result from not taking action to restore confidence in the system. Anyway, it may be no bad thing to drive out bad business if at least some good business is attracted in its place.

Two issues have moved to the top of the international supervisors agenda as 'deregulation' and globalisation have gathered pace during the first half of the 1980s. 'Deregulation' has involved: financial innovation, an increase, where permitted, of banks' involvement in the capital markets, and the opening of access by some countries which had previously barred them to foreign banks for certain types of business. As regards financial innovations, banks have been developing new financial instruments, such as note issuance facilities (Nifs), which have contributed to a process of securitisation. This effectively involves issuing and dealing in securities rather than making traditional loans. From this business banks accrue fee income and often offer credit lines and underwriting facilities. They thus incur contingent liabilities but, because they are not formal loans, they do not appear on the balance sheet. The supervisors have consequently felt it necessary to ensure that such off balance sheet risks are provided for and that banks active in the capital markets are adequately supervised. This not only requires the coordination of supervisory practices and exchanges of information amongst bank supervisors but also similar coordination amongst capital and equity market supervisors, the latter becoming necessary because of the gradual process of globalisation in share trading that has been occurring. UK banks are able to deal in the Stock Exchange, through their newly developed investment banking subsidiaries, following the reform of the Stock Exchange, the Big Bang, which came into effect in October 1986. Foreign banks, commercial or investment, are also able to participate. UK and other foreign banks have also been gaining access to the stock and securities markets in Japan, the US and elsewhere. Round-the-clock trading in the equity markets is fast becoming a realistic prospect. The second issue, which is clearly related to the first, involves ensuring that banks from various countries compete fairly, on a so-called level playing field, and that there is reciprocity of access in the sense that if one country allows banks from another country to operate in its markets then it would expect its banks to have similar opportunities in the other's markets.

In its quarterly report, in October 1985, the BIS warned that changes in the international capital markets might contain the seeds of future problems for the banking system. Rapid changes in the international financial markets had occurred since 1982, when there was a marked slowdown in international bank lending following the onset of the Latin American debt crisis, which is discussed in the next chapter. Banks became increasingly involved instead in the Eurobond market and there was a rapid development of new instruments. Four areas of concern were highlighted. Firstly, banks were left doing business with higher risk borrowers who were unable to raise funds on the capital markets. Secondly, the growth of off balance sheet business involved underwriting and contingent liabilities at thin margins. Thirdly, the sharp increase in bond market participation had led banks to accumulate marketable securities which might appear to have increased their liquidity but could lead to problems in the case of a general tightening of credit conditions. Finally, it was difficult for bank supervisors to assess, and to assure adequate provision for, risks associated with these developments because past experience gave little guidance.

As a result of further study the Basle Committee issued a set of guidelines,[15] in March 1986, for bank supervisors. Three main types of risk were identified. Firstly, funds might not be available to meet commitments incurred. Secondly, swap agreements might introduce interest or exchange rate risk. Finally, banks might unwittingly accumulate large credit risks. The report provided no firm prescriptions for the capital backing necessary to cover these risks, leaving decisions on this to the descretion of the supervisory authorities. The Committee expressed its concern at the lack of information on the extent to which banks had become involved in financial innovation and judged information provided by banks to be insufficient to give shareholders and depositors a reasonable impression of these developments. It therefore advocated a greater disclosure of information. In April 1986 the BIS published a substantial report,[16] by a study group established by the central banks of the G10,[17] on recent innovations in international banking. It argued that financial innovation had opened a Pandora's box and that although it may have increased financial efficiency it had also made the financial system more vulnerable to stocks and less easy to understand. The two main developments had been securitisation, which had blurred the distinction between banks and other financial institutions, and the limitations placed upon independent monetary policy by increased capital mobility. We shall consider the latter further in Chapter 7. It also noted that these innovations had raised questions concerning the allocation of lender of last resort responsibilities and that the blurring of distinctions between banks and non-banks made the process of regulation more difficult. There were risks of prudential oversight and central banks, therefore, had either to extend their supervisory jurisdictions to cover non-banks or to ensure effective allocation of supervisory responsibilities with other non-bank supervisors. The report concluded that regulators and supervisors will find it difficult to keep up with market developments and that the world banking system has grown to a position where it is beyond the power of national authorities to control. Further, risk is increasing as good credit risks are increasingly borrowing directly on the bond markets, reducing the quality of remaining assets. Given this trend banks may be less able to deal with sudden liquidity shocks, especially as the innovations have been mainly introduced by large institutions leading to a concentration of risks. The off balance sheet intiative marked the first attempt by the Basle Committee to coordinate regulation at the supranational level. Previously it had aimed to allocate supervisory responsibilities amongst national authorities and at finding common definitions of banking concepts like 'capital'. It did not establish universal capital standards for off balance sheet risks but did the next best thing by identifying the problems and proposing remedies. It marked the beginning of the globalisation of supervision to parallel the evolution of global markets.

Following the Basle Committee report, the Bank of England published a discussion paper in March 1986 which followed its proposals closely. In May 1985 it had imposed capital requirement on Nifs of half that applied to loans, and this requirement will be reviewed in the light of the comments invited on the discussion paper. The US and Japanese supervisors published proposals in 1986 that will require capital backing for Nifs equivalent to 30 per cent of the value of loans. In 1986 the German supervisory authorities followed the more cautious UK line. Thus although there has already been considerable reaction to the Basle Committee report the capital requirements imposed have not been uniform, a matter to which we will return below.

The financial world has become one in which services that cannot be provided onshore are provided offshore, those that cannot be provided on the balance sheet are provided off the balance sheet, and those that cannot be provided with existing instruments are provided with new ones. International banks are transforming themselves from traditional intermediaries, between depositors and borrowers, into financial engineers in the capital markets, intermediating between investors and capital users. They are becoming deal makers rather than loan makers in order to continue to service the needs of their large corporate and government clients. The supervisors have shown that they are aware of the need to keep up, but can they? They are also aware of the need to ensure coordination in securities regulation and supervision. In June 1986 the Governor of the Bank of England argued that the increasing international dealing in stocks and shares made it imperative that regulators in various countries worked together more closely. This reflected concern that US commercial banks, which are barred from share dealing in the US and supervised as banks, will be dealing in shares in the City after the Big Bang and will need to have their equities business adequately supervised. More generally, because banking and capital markets were becoming closer, with borrowers moving between them, it was felt that banking and securities regulators needed to work together more closely. Additionally, as mentioned above, the growing globally traded share market needs supervision.

A forum discussing coordination in the supervision of securities markets already exists in the form of the

International Association of Securities Commissions (IASC). It has hitherto been dominated by regulatory bodies from North and South America and has developed the reputation of being a rather ineffectual organisation. In July 1986, however, the IASC held its annual meeting in Paris, its first outside the American continent, and the delegates agreed to a fundamental reform of the organisation aimed at converting it to a genuine international securities watchdog. It is to set up a permanent secretariat in Quebec and will establish a series of regional committees in addition to the already existing American Committee. It also agreed to allow more European countries to join. The IASC has been dominated by the US SEC and has admitted non-American members[18] only since 1983. The impetus for bolstering the IASC has come primarily from the SEC which seems in response to foreign opposition to have abandoned its previous attempts to extend the SEC's jurisdiction overseas in favour of a more cooperative approach.

Also in July 1986 it became evident that bilateral negotiations between US, French, Japanese and UK stock exchange regulatory bodies were likely to come to fruition in September 1986 when a series of bilateral agreements were expected to be signed.[19] These agreements aim to crack down on international securities fraud and insider dealing and to provide for exchanges of information. It is hoped that other European countries will also participate. The Chairman of the SEC has been a driving force behind these negotiations in order to ensure that the SEC and the US Justice Department have the necessary international collaboration to follow up investigations into securities infringements committed in the US, and that overseas supervisory bodies can count on similar cooperation from US authorities. He singled out banking secrecy laws as a major obstacle inhibiting investigations into stock exchange infringements because they often made it impossible to trace funds. At the IASC meeting the Chairman of the London Stock Exchange, Sir Nicholas Goodison, acknowledged that securities market supervisors were lagging behind banking supervisors in cooperating to police international markets and that, with the increased worldwide convergence of hitherto separate financial markets, close cooperation between banking and securities supervisory authorities was required.

Goodison's comments can be seen in the light of the fact that, in the run up to the Big Bang in October 1986, London became the adventure playground of the world financial system. It provided a particular attraction to US and Japanese commercial banks, which are barred from investment banking business in their own countries, and also new opportunities for the major investment banks and securities houses of those countries. The interest shown by US and Japanese foreign banks has caused particular problems for the UK supervisors, who wish to ensure that both investment and commercial banking business are adequately supervised. In particular the Bank of England sought assurance that Japanese securities houses seeking banking licences in the UK, which will permit them to enter into commercial banking business from which they are barred at home, are adequately supervised at the Japanese end in line with the Basle Concordat. This led to a reciprocity dispute with the Japanese Ministry of Finance, which has separate banking and broking supervisory divisions. The latter and not the former are responsible for regulating and supervising the Japanese securities houses—hence the problem. The dispute was complicated by the fact that UK merchant and commercial banks were at the time seeking securities trading licences in Japan. Talks between the UK Treasury and the Bank of England and the Japanese Ministry of Finance and the Bank of Japan seemed to have largely overcome these problems in the first quarter of 1986. The position was made easier when the German Deutsche Bank devised a new way into the Tokyo securities business at the end of 1985. It obtained a licence for a Hong Kong subsidiary in which it had sold a half share to other non-bank investors. Since then other European banks, including National Westminster's County Bank, have followed a similar route. Some US commercial banks are attempting to gain entry into the Japanese securities market by purchasing UK broking concerns that have already secured licences or by applying for licences through their newly acquired UK subsidiaries. These developments are increasing the pressure on the Ministry of Finance, also coming from within the Japanese banking community, to revise the rules separating investment and commercial banking.

The opening of access to business previously reserved for domestic financial institutions, the removal of withholding taxes,[20] the lifting of exchange controls and other deregulatory acts have generated an expectation amongst the initiators that their domestically incorporated financial institutions should receive reciprocal treatment elsewhere. The UK Financial Services Bill,[21] which became law in November 1986, includes a reciprocity clause (151), which was brought forward to take effect before the end of 1986 in order to exert further pressure on the Japanese authorities concerning the granting of securities licences to UK firms. Clause 151 empowers the DTI to disqualify or restrict companies from countries that do not offer reciprocal opportunities. In Germany, the Bundesbank has made it clear that its deregulatory measures, offering opportunities to foreign banks, only applied to banks emanating from countries providing reciprocal access. When it permitted foreign banks, in June 1986, to participate in the consortium of banks, which place federal government, post and railway bonds, it took the opportunity to emphasise the importance it placed on reciprocity. In 1985 the Bundesbank permitted foreign banks to lead manage Deutsch Mark Eurobond issues. Japanese banks were, however, excluded until Tokyo offered similar freedom to German banks.

The reciprocity issue relates to the desire to see the creation of a level playing field, where regulatory, supervisory, tax, reporting and other requirements on banks are consistent and banks from particular countries are not handicapped or advantaged. Many banks, and to some extent their supervisors, feel that the system is far from fair at the moment and claim that the Japanese institutions enjoy a particular advantage that accounts for their rise up the league tables which measure bank size and profitability. In May 1986 the Chairman of Barclays Bank went so far as to accuse Japanese financial institutions of 'dumping' financial services. In 1985 the Japanese banks overtook the US banks as the largest holders of foreign banking assets. In particular, Barclay's Chairman argued that they were able to undercut other banks because they faced less stringent capital requirements at home.

In response to the pending UK reciprocity legislation, the Bundesbank's stance and views such as those expressed by the Barclay's Chairman, the Deputy Governor of the Bank of Japan warned in June 1986 that further expansion of Japanese financial operations abroad might be curbed. It might depend on foreign banks being accorded more freedom and *de facto* equality in Japan, since Japan's success abroad had been due largely to opening up of overseas markets and the tolerance of those concerned. He argued that the time had come to reciprocate by opening, liberalising and internationalising Japanese financial markets. Some steps had already been taken in the early 1980s in response to US pressure aimed largely at increasing the attractiveness of the yen as an international currency. Action was still, however, needed to lift interest controls on small deposits of less than Y100m, and to eliminate the segmentation of banking and securities business and of ordinary and specialised banks. He noted, however, that both these proposals face strong domestic opposition, due to sectoral interests. Further, he observed that international yen business was moving out of Japan to avoid restrictions and regulations and that the return of this business would allow more efficient supervision and direct lender of last resort cover.

Meanwhile the Ministry of Finance (MOF) has proved anxious to comply with the Basle Committee's views on adequate capitalisation and in May 1986 announced new regulations requiring all banks to achieve equity to asset ratios of 4 per cent within five years, the commercial banks being required to comply by 1987. It also required banks to report on a consolidated basis, including overseas business. At the time the equity requirement stood at 3.3. per cent. Banks were to be allowed to use 70 per cent of their hidden reserves to bolster their capital ratios. The general belief of the MOF was that Japanese banks were adequately capitalised by virtue of their large hidden reserves. It was, however, keen to conform with the Basle Committee guidelines and is also planning to introduce a risk asset ratio in line with a report by the Financial System Council, which is an advisory body within the MOF.

The Bank of England is keen to promote a level playing field in the UK and has warned foreign banks that they must abide by the same rules as domestic banks or risk being reported to their own regulatory authorities. The aim is to iron out inequalities whilst ensuring prudential business conduct in London. Whilst welcoming the Bank's initiative on off balance sheet risks as a step towards efficient regulation the Chairman of the British Bankers Association, in June 1986, warned that the proposed framework was discriminatory. He drew attention to the variation in the capital backing requirements for off balance sheet risks imposed by national supervisory authorities. In particular, the Bank, along with the Bundesbank, is operating and proposing more stringent requirements than those being considered by the US and Japanese authorities. This question of equal treatment of banks by their national regulatory and supervisory authorities has thus become a contentious one, especially in the area of off balance sheet risks, which involves highly competitive business undertaken at fine margins. It is perhaps not surprising that it has arisen in an area that has already left bank supervisors struggling to find a suitable response. The perhaps surprisingly pessimistic view was expressed, in 1986 by Mr W. P. Cooke,[22] that a level playing field was virtually impossible to deliver internationally because it would require a level of supervisory coordination far in excess of anything so far envisaged. An even more pessimistic view of the prospects for official regulation of the securities markets was expressed by Michael Hewitt, the Bank of England's head of financial supervision, at a legal conference in Singapore in September 1986. He felt that official international supervision was unlikely to reach the level of coordination achieved in banking supervision through the Basle Concordat. Instead he believed that associations of practitioners[23] might be better suited to creating a regulatory system for the market.

NOTES

1. On offshore banking centres *see* McCarthy (1979).
2. On the internationalization of the banking system *see* OECD (1983) and for a detailed analysis of supervisory responses *see* Dale (1984).

3. See Channon (1977) or Dale (1984) for accounts of the Herstatt Bank's collapse and its implications and also the collapse of the US Franklin National Bank, which also had international implications.
4. The ten major industrial countries—Belgium, Canada, France, Germany, Holland, Italy, Japan, Sweden, the UK and the US—which established the IMF's General Agreement to Borrow (GAB) in October 1962.
5. After the Chairman of the Committee on Bank Regulations and Supervisory Procedures, Mr W. P. Cooke, formerly Head of Banking Supervision at the Bank of England and currently head of the International Supervisory Coordination Division.
6. In which the parents state their financial obligations concerning their subsidiaries and offshoots.
7. As banks take the implied insurance of their loans for granted and undertake more risky, and potentially more profitable, business.
8. Such as offshore banking centres.
9. Commission of the European Communities (1977); see Cooper (1984) for discussion of this directive.
10. See Cooper (1984) for further discussion.
11. By Dale (1984) for example.
12. See Dale (1981).
13. European Council 73/183/EEC.
14. House of Commons Bill 238, (1985/6).
15. Committee on Banking Regulations and Supervisory Practices, March 1986.
16. See Bank for International Settlements (1986a).
17. The Group of Ten countries who had participated in the GAB; see Chapter 7.
18. These include Australia, France, Hong Kong and the UK.
19. The impending agreement between the UK's DTI and the US SEC on exchange of information was expected to be followed by a more formal set of treaties and to speed up negotiations over other bilateral agreements involving other countries.
20. These are special taxes on the interest earned by foreigners in domestic markets. They were removed in 1985 by West Germany following a previous move by the US and have subsequently been removed and reduced elsewhere.
21. House of Commons HC238 (1985/6).
22. See note 5.
23. Such as the Association of International Bond Dealers.

5 The Latin American Debt Problem[1]

The growth in the indebtedness of the Third World less developed countries (LDCs),[2] following the 1973 oil price rise (OPEC I),[3] generated concern about the adequacy of the supervisory arrangements for the international banking system and the lender of last resort cover for that system. Some of the implications for regulation and supervision have been discussed in previous chapters and the need for a world lender of last resort will be considered further in Chapter 8. In this chapter the origins and history of the Latin American debt problem will be briefly reviewed and then proposals for its resolution will be considered.

5.1 THE ORIGINS OF THE PROBLEM

The imbalance of trade between OPEC and the rest of the world that developed following OPEC I created a need for the massive OPEC surplus to be recycled. The large international commercial banks received massive desposits from OPEC countries and proved willing to undertake the recycling through the medium of the Eurocurrency markets. They were, in many cases, actively encouraged to do so by their governments and the IMF.[4] The LDCs were avaricious borrowers because of their need for development funding and their suspicion of private investment from overseas and dislike of tied aid. The commercial banks rapidly expanded their lending—to the LDC deficit country governments and public enterprises in the main, although there was some lending to the private sector. It transpired that because of the 'fungibility'[5] of money, the loans were not always used to their best effect. In particular they were not generally used to fund well-appraised and planned projects. Instead they were often used to fund military programmes and even invested abroad.[6] The net result was that by the late 1970s the debts of many of the non-OPEC LDCs had accumulated. Latin American countries, particularly the larger ones, had been the biggest borrowers and, with no pressing need to undertake structural adjustment because of the continuing availablity of short term funds, short term debt continued to grow.

The second oil price increase, the OPEC II shock, occurred in 1979. The ensuing recession in the major Western economies, which resulted in part from their imposition of restrictive monetary and fiscal policies, drove up interest rates and restricted demand for imports. This in turn contributed to a fall in many commodity prices. Most Latin American countries rely on one or more commodities as a source of foreign currency revenue. These events led to a worsening of the trade balances of the non-OPEC LDCs, a slowing of their growth rates, and an increase in the costs of servicing their international debt. The latter resulted because of the practice of making loans on a variable interest rate basis, which had become increasingly widespread since the mid 1970s. Further, the high US interest rates in the early 1980s led to an appreciation of the dollar relative to the domestic currencies of the LDCs and, because most of their debt was denominated in dollars, it became potentially harder for them to meet the capital and interest payments on their accumulating debt. They consequently needed to boost exports, especially to the US, in order to earn dollars. To the extent that they were oil importers, again because oil prices are set in terms of dollars, the cost of these imports as well as other dollar denominated imports rose. The result was a rise in short term external debt as a proportion of national product, export revenue and foreign currency reserves.

Some of the most prolific borrowers were oil-producing LDCs such as Venezuela, an OPEC member, and Mexico, who effectively used their projected oil revenues as collateral. When oil prices started to fall in 1981, because the world recession and energy conservation efforts reduced demand for oil whilst non-OPEC production and hence aggregate supply was increasing,[7] their oil export revenue projections proved overoptimistic.

5.2 THE MEXICAN CRISIS

In late 1982, Mexico had to declare a moratorium on the interest payments due on its debts. In order to protect the international banking system, the US Treasury and the FRB stepped in as lenders of last resort.[8] It was necessary to contain the crisis because, apart from governments, a large number of commercial banks around the world had exposure to Mexico. The large US banks were particularly heavily exposed to Mexico, and to Latin America in general.[9] Thus once the Mexican crisis broke, the additional exposure of US banks to other Latin American countries was likely to cause concern to the depositors in and shareholders of those banks. The stability of the US banking system was thus under threat and so too was that of the international banking system.

The US Treasury provided a $1bn loan in return for $1.3bn worth of oil, to be supplied over a fifteen-month period. Meanwhile the FRB arranged a meeting with other central banks at the BIS. A $1.85bn loan was arranged. The FRB supplied half and the balance was supplied by the other participating central banks. This provided breathing space whilst the IMF entered into protracted negotiations with the commercial banks to assemble a rescue package. The IMF offered to provide a $1.3bn loan conditional on agreement with Mexico over a 'letter of intent'[10] which would lead to the instigation of policies designed to reduce Mexico's trade deficit and boost its foreign currency reserves. Mexico needed $2.55bn to repay the BIS and FRB loan, $1.5bn to boost its reserves, and faced a balance of trade deficit of $4.25bn. It therefore needed to borrow $8.3bn. A loan of $2bn was promised by the US and other governments. The banks were, therefore, expected to put up $5bn and were warned that if the money was not forthcoming the managing director of the IMF would not recommend the acceptance of the Mexican programme, to be outlined in the forthcoming 'letter of intent', to the IMF's board of directors. Mexico would then have to default on capital as well as interest payments. The banks were given a month to raise the money and agreed to extend their existing exposure to Mexico by 7 per cent, which required the FRB to waive regulatory impediments in the US. The agreed rescue package was, therefore, put together as a result of central banks leaning on the big banks, who in turn leant on the smaller regional and local US banks. Ninety per cent of the private bank money was raised on time, the full $5bn being raised soon after, and so was the $2bn contribution by the major governments.

5.3 THE AFTERMATH

Since the Mexican crisis broke other large Latin American debtor countries, including Brazil, Venezuela and Argentina, had to reschedule their debts and a number of African and Asian LDCs have also had to apply to the IMF for help. The problems of the debtors were usually compounded by 'capital flight'.

Because capital is often invested overseas covertly, to bypass exchange controls, it is impossible to gauge exactly the extent to which residents of the Latin American countries have invested abroad. Estimates[11] suggested that the debts Mexico and Argentina accumulated in the last ten years were matched by capital flight and that most of the new money lent to Latin America in 1982–5 was offset by capital flight. Capital flight is both a symptom and a source of the problem and must be stemmed if a meaningful solution is to be found. It is probably caused by high and variable inflation rates, which in turn generate uncertain returns relative to those available in the US and Europe where positive real interest has been available on investments throughout the 1980s. If this diagnosis is correct, then to stem capital flight the Latin American countries must stabilise and perhaps even reduce their inflation rates. Further, in order to earn sufficient foreign currency to service their debts, and especially dollars, in which their debt is largely denominated, they must run a balance of trade surplus especially with the US. In order to ensure the sound performance of their loans, commercial bank syndicates normally refuse to release negotiated loan funds until the country concerned has agreed an economic programme with the IMF, designed to stem capital flight and assure ability to service the loan. Because the loans to the Latin American countries were so large, and in order to prevent over-concentration of exposure to individual borrowers, the practice of forming loan syndicates developed in the 1970s.[12] It should be noted that because flight capital often finds its way back into the banking system, which lent the money in the first place, it has a higher redeposit ratio than normal, especially for international loans. To the extent that banks can relend the 'flight capital', profits earnt on loans to Latin American countries can implicitly be increased. We shall return to this point below.

In order to stem capital flight Latin American debtors are being encouraged to liberalise and reform their financial systems to stimulate domestic saving, but this is a long term solution. In the short term they have been forced to raise interest rates. The problem then arises that high interest rates increase the cost of servicing national debt and make it virtually impossible to hit the targets on fiscal deficit agreed with the IMF.

Not surprisingly, following the Mexican crisis the commercial banks tried to reduce their exposure to country risks and after 1982 new lending to the LDCs first levelled off and then declined.[13] The banks became increasingly interested in their domestic business, extending the range of financial services they offer, securitisation[14] and lending to less risky, developed countries such as France and Sweden. The central banks of the major Western nations cautioned the larger commercial banks about the impropriety of withdrawing funds too quickly, since this would exacerbate the problem. The large commercial banks in turn put pressure on smaller banks to discourage them from leaving the loan syndicates involved in the reschedulings. In addition to the perceived increase in the riskiness of lending to LDCs the profitability of the business also declined. This was because prior to the crisis there was great competition between banks to join the syndicates, which caused margins to be reduced. The competition was significantly increased by the influx of interest from smaller, especially US, banks and it is therefore not surprising that the larger banks were unhappy about their attempts to pull out as soon as the going got tough. An informal agreement, requiring new loans involved in rescheduling to be proportionate to existing exposure, seems to have been reached amongst banks. The rescheduling of debts that followed the crisis often involved lower interest rate margins, which were agreed in order to help the debtors to afford the repayments. This further reduced the banks' profit margins, although, to the extent that flight capital is redeposited with lending banks and is relent, they received some compensation.

In 1984 US interest rates began to rise again in response to the conflict between the FRB's relatively tight monetary policy, which was being pursued to contain the inflationary effects of a booming US economy, and the growing US budget deficit. The rapid economic growth and the high interest rates proved an irresistible attraction to foreign, especially Japanese, funds, which helped to supplement US savings and offset both the budget and the current account deficits. The result was a rapid appreciation of the dollar. With both the dollar and the interest rates rising there was a growing risk that the problem could reach crisis proportions again. In response, the Latin American countries met in the Columbian city of Cartagena, causing concern that a debtors' cartel would be formed which might default on the debt. In the event the Cartagena Agreement put forward a number of proposals, to be considered by their creditors and the IMF, including: the establishment of a special IMF facility to alleviate the impact of high interest rates, the revision of IMF conditions, making them less stringent, the introduction of a mechanism to allow the postponement of interest payments, the limiting of interest payments to a certain proportion of export earnings and a reduction in interest rates.

The possibility of a debt boycott generated discussion about the costs and benefits of defaulting. This involved an attempt to evaluate the effectiveness of the sanctions that could be imposed on the defaulters. Default can, as a substitute for borrowing, be a method of financing.[15] By defaulting the debtor forfeits access to new funding but it is possible that the savings from non-payment of interest might exceed the projected need for new funding. Default would, however, lead to a rapid withdrawal of export credits and the defaulter would need to have built up substantial foreign currency reserves against this eventuality.[16] It would also postpone further the time when normal borrowing on the money and capital markets could resume.

As regards sanctions, attempts by governments to seize physical assets, such as ships, would in most cases contravene international law.[17] This is because it would mainly be private companies' assets that would be impounded, rather than the governments', and the governments taking such action would be acting not on their own debts but on those of their domestic banks. There is also a risk of retaliatory action. The physical investments of foreign companies established in Third World countries could be taken over. The major usable sanction would probably be the freezing or confiscation of financial assets held by the defaulting governments abroad. Since these assets are increasingly being deposited in safe havens, such as the BIS or Swiss banks, these sanctions are unlikely to be prohibitive. The defaulting governments would also need to consider the effects of their actions on the commercial opportunities of their private sector companies abroad. Finally, the debtors' need for export revenues to earn foreign exchange to buy the imports required for exapansion, especially when some of their existing foreign currency reserves might be frozen, would leave them open to retaliatory trade restrictions and embargoes imposed by the governments of creditor banks.

5.4 1985: THE TURNING POINT?

The dollar continued to appreciate in the first quarter of 1985, although US interest rates had begun to fall towards the end of 1984, following an easing of monetary policy in the US in response to continued worries about the US financial system in the wake of the Continental Illinois[18] crisis and in the light of the problems being experienced by banks exposed to the farming and oil sectors and the 'thrifts'.[19] Apart from these prudential influences on interest rate policy, it became apparent in 1985 that the growth in the US economy was slowing down significantly. The FRB could therefore afford to take a more relaxed attitude about monetary policy because inflationary pressures were subsiding. The decline in the US growth rate and the effects of the growing US trade deficit became a major cause for concern. The key to the improvement in a country's debt problem is the achievement of a rise in export revenue relative to debt servicing costs. The most significant contribution to the alleviation of the 1982 crisis conditions had come from the growth in export earnings by the debtor nations. The Latin American debtors in general, and Mexico and Brazil in particular, benefited from the growing US economy and the appreciating dollar, since they combined to raise the dollar value of their export earnings and protect them from the effects of generally falling commodity prices. A declining US growth rate meant that demand for imports by the US economy, and exports from the LDCs to the US, would decline. Additionally, in the face of a deteriorating US trade deficit, there were increasingly vociferous calls for action to reduce import penetration from within the US. The risk arose that protectionist measures would further reduce the LDC's potential for export earnings. The World Bank warned,[20] that any reduction in the world growth rate would lead to a re-emergence of the crisis, because the prospects for export-led growth in the debtor nations would deteriorate significantly. These nations need a fairly high level of growth in order to maintain the standard of living of their growing populations. Their standard of living deteriorated appreciably over the post crisis, low or negative growth, period and it was feared that further deterioration would add to the risk of political instability in Latin America, which is notoriously unstable and which is nurturing new democracies.[21] With the US growth rate declining, the world growth rate would also decline unless the rate of growth picked up in other industrial countries. The US was growing steadily, if slowly, in 1985 and there were signs of growth elsewhere in Europe, although the growth rate in Japan was declining. The worry was that unless non-US growth accelerated the decline in the US growth rate would not be compensated for. The IMF, the World Bank, and the US government guardedly urged West Germany and Japan to relax their tight fiscal policies.[22] Another worrying factor was the effect of the continuing US budget deficit. This had grown steadily during the 1980s and had been financed to a great extent by capital inflows, especially from Japan. It became apparent that the US had for the first time in postwar history become a major debtor nation and that there were substantial net outflows of money from the Latin American debtors.[23] The US has traditionally been a net capital exporter and a major source of investment funds for the Third World. It was forecast that the US would become the largest debtor country in the world by the end of 1985 and that it was absorbing approximately half of the world's savings. Something was clearly amiss when an economically strong country like the US was competing on the international money and capital markets for funds urgently needed by the LDCs to maintain the interest and capital payments to their creditors, which included the US government and US commercial banks and US industry.

In 1985 the suspicion grew that the standard IMF conditional programme was not the required medicine and that a more gradual and long term treatment was indicated. A lot depended on the credibility of the IMF package and the extent to which it was politically acceptable to the creditor and debtor countries involved. Many Third World countries have expressed reservations about the package[24] but most have acquiesced when necessary. Negotiations with the IMF have not been without their problems[25] and brinkmanship has been used to wring concessions out of the commercial banks concerning rescheduling terms. The US banks have found themselves under particular pressure because they are required to declare loans as non-performing[26] if no interest payments are received over a ninety-day period. This in turn means that anticipated interest payments cannot be counted and announced profits are consequently reduced. The US monetary authorities averted this problem in 1984 by arranging an emergency loan package for Argentina, with the help of other South American debtor nations, which was not made conditional on an agreement with the IMF.[27] The problem, however, re-emerged in 1985 and another bridging loan was required.[28] The fear was stimulated that further difficulties could arise if the other South American states, perhaps coordinated through the Group of American States or the Cartagena group, adopted the Argentinian approach in dealing with the IMF and the commercial banks. The extent to which they are constrained from doing so depends on the credibility of the possible sanctions against them, as we have mentioned above.

The standard IMF package required monetary and credit restraint, a reduction in the public sector borrowing requirement, the abandonment of complex exchange controls, wage constraint and the removal of 100 per cent wage indexation, removal of at least some price controls, and devaluation. Some economists argued that it was too draconian and that it aimed to provide a short term solution to balance of trade difficulties, rather than a long term solution to the fundamental balance of trade problem of the particular country.[29] There were also specific criticisms concerning the inflationary effects of the large devaluations usually required, the removal of price controls, and of high interest rates required to hit fiscal and monetary targets. The credibility of the programme was enhanced by the successful and rapid response to it by Mexico, which appeared to be out of the woods in 1984. Critics argue that the Mexican success merely illustrated their point. They claimed that Mexico's problem was not a structural one. Instead it resulted from economic mismanagement which was highlighted by the oil price decline. By contrast, they observed, Brazil was generally agreed to be doing everything right, by borrowing to finance the rapid growth it experienced in the 1970s. The world slump had brought with it significant balance of trade problems for Brazil and structural adjustment seemed to be required. The IMF programme, they concluded, was unlikely to solve Brazil's problems. There was also the question of its political acceptability in Brazil where there had already been strikes in response to the deindexation of wages. Additionally, although Brazil had always signed, howbeit after lengthy negotiations, the requisite letter of intent to the IMF, it had repeatedly experienced difficulties in fulfilling the declared intentions.[30] The political acceptability of the programme in Argentina was also questionable. Argentina was judged to be in a strong bargaining position since it had a strong potential for earning export revenues,[31] fairly substantial foreign currency reserves, and a fairly low propensity to import. It should be noted, however, that any concessions wrung out of the commercial banks reduce further the profitability of their lending and gives them even greater incentive to reduce their country risk exposure.

In the event 1985 saw a significant worsening of Mexico's position; falling oil prices continued to reduce its export revenue and it suffered from a slowdown in the US growth rate. The extent of its fall from grace was evidenced by the fact that it was about to be censured by the IMF for its failure to meet agreed public expenditure and budget deficit targets when the September 1985 earthquake disaster struck. Mexico's problem lies largely in its heavy dependency on oil which, in 1985, contributed 70 per cent of its export earnings and 45 per cent of Treasury receipts. Its problem was compounded by capital flight, although its extent was disputed.[32] Whilst Mexico's affairs were deteriorating, Argentina surprisingly introduced an austerity package, called the Austral Plan, in mid 1985. It involved a wage and price freeze and currency reform.[33] Shortly afterwards Argentina came to an agreement with the IMF and the banks which eventually led to the conclusion of a multi-year rescheduling agreement (MYRA).[34] Venezuela also concluded a MYRA agreement with the banks in early 1985. Brazil, however, dragged its heels in negotiations with the IMF, preferring to push through a social programme promoted by its newly elected administration. Its strong export performance allowed it to service its debts reasonably comfortably. In February 1986 it activated the Cruzado Plan, also known as the Plan Tropical, which was similar to the Austral Plan and involved currency reform,[35] deindexation and the introduction of wage and price freezes. The policy proved surprisingly popular and was designed to tackle inflation directly and to stem capital flight. Following the further large falls in oil prices in early 1986,[36] Brazil's trade surplus in the first half of 1986 hit record levels and consequently there was no pressing need to conclude an agreement with the IMF. Without an agreement with the IMF there was little prospect of negotiating a MYRA with the commercial banks, although it continued negotiations with the Paris Club[37] and the commercial banks concerning the restructuring of the current debt.[38] Another significant development in 1985 was the decision by Peru to restrict payments due on its foreign debt to 10 per cent of export revenue. This immediately complicated its negotiations with the IMF and the commercial banks.

The prevailing approach to the debt problem had been formulated at the 1984 economic summit attended by the seven most powerful industrial nations and confirmed in the 1985 summit and the spring 1985 meetings by the IMF and IBRD Advisory Committees.[39] This involved treating the debt problem of each nation on a case by case basis and ensuring economic adjustment, to reduce inflation and eliminate the balance of trade deficit, by requiring adherence to an IMF adjustment programme. Once agreement with the IMF was reached the commercial banks were urged to agree to supply the necessary supplementary finance prior to disbursements of IMF funds. Where countries had been cooperative and had responded and adhered to the IMF adjustment programme they were to be rewarded by a restructuring of their debts involving both rescheduling over a long period, rather than on a one or two yearly basis, and refinancing where necessary on more favourable terms. These were designed to reduce the debtor's immediate financial needs, thereby bringing nearer their return to normal commercial borrowing and the end of forced lending by the commercial banks. As we noted above two major MYRAs were concluded in early 1985, with Mexico and Venezuela. These MYRAs both involved repayment periods of over ten years, more favourable interest rate terms, new loans and provision for non-US banks to switch a proportion of their exposure into their domestic currencies over a period of years. They also included provisions for the IMF to extend its surveillance beyond the period in which it was providing financial support. Venezuela did not expect to have to borrow from the IMF during the period of the MYRA, and Mexico's borrowing from the IMF was due to expire before the end of the MYRA. The 1985 economic summit and World Bank and IMF Advisory Committee meetings endorsed the principal of extended surveillance by the IMF. Following the 1984 summit it was expected that governments would lead by example and instigate MYRAs for Mexico and Venezuela, perhaps through Paris Club negotiations. In the event it was not until 1985 that they started to contemplate MYRAs in connection with Brazil's debt restructuring. An agreement with Brazil is unlikely to be concluded, however, until it comes to some agreement with the IMF.

The 1985 economic summit and spring World Bank and IMF Advisory Committee meetings also concluded that the debtor countries needed to grow out of their debt. Export growth was viewed as particularly important and in this connection it was observed that tendencies towards increased protectionism should be stemmed and that world growth needed to be maintained. In particular the 'growth gap' left by the slowdown in US growth needed to be filled. Regarding protectionism, a new round of GATT[40] negotiations was proposed. It seemed to be accepted that the European and Japanese economies should compensate for the declining US growth rate but no agreement was reached about how this should be done.

The IMF has consistently argued that its programme is essential for the establishment of long term growth in debtor countries and that it is not unduly restrictive in the short run. As mentioned above, there have been numerous criticisms of the appropriateness of the IMF package, arguing broadly that it reduces domestic growth, makes short term containment of inflation more difficult and concentrates on short term measures to improve the trade balance. The 1985 Inter-American Development Bank (IADB) report produced evidence to show that the Latin American countries had suffered falling living standards in the three years prior to 1985 and that they had fallen by 3 per cent in 1984, bringing them back to 1977 levels. Real poverty was being experienced and endemic diseases, which had been eradicated ten years previously, were returning. The IMF in turn countered that, due to the debt problems, growth was already faltering prior to the introduction of IMF programmes. In the light of these developments and the potential risk of a re-emergence of crisis conditions, at the IMF/IBRD annual meeting in spring 1985 the Group of Twenty-Four[41] stressed the need to consider long term solutions to the debt problem involving: more symmetry of adjustment between creditor and debtor nations, expanded IMF and IBRD financing special IMF facilities to alleviate the burden of high interest rates, increased capital funding through international agencies, an easing of IMF conditionality and a reduction in protectionism. As we noted in the previous section, the Cartagena group of Latin American debtors have made similar proposals, and they called in 1985 for a political dialogue with the creditor nations to discuss permanent and durable solutions and the need for new trade and international monetary arrangements.

The case by case, short leash approach involving IMF conditionality, MYRAs and extended IMF surveillance seemed to be working, but there were growing risks that crisis conditions could re-emerge if the debtors export revenues fell relative to the costs of debt servicing in the face of falling world economic growth and commodity prices and rising protectionism. There was also an increasing risk that political tensions within the debtor countries could become explosive if growth could not be maintained at a rate exceeding that of population growth. In order to achieve growth, however, import restrictions in the debtor countries would have to be relaxed. Given pressures from both the export and import sides, balance of trade problems could re-emerge[42] and with interest rates still high and commercial bank lending being cut back there was not much room for optimism. The object of this approach to the Latin American debt problem was to avert a crisis in the international banking system by reducing the bank's short term exposure through the introduction of MYRAs. In the mean time it was hoped that the banks and the debtor countries would grow out of the debt problem so that there could be a return to normal commercial borrowing and capital flows into the debtor nations could resume. The onus of adjustment was, therefore, on the debtor nations and it was hoped that the banks could grow around their loans to these countries so that they would diminish in relative importance. The major cost of the debt problem to the banks has been the rising capital requirements and bad debt provisions urged on them by their supervisors. Capital ratios had probably become unduly low anyway, prior to the crisis, given the increased risks involved in engaging in the growing international banking business. The bad debt provisions could, however, have been put to profitable use. Additionally the locking of a proportion of their funds into lending to debtor nations for a considerable period ahead had reduced their ability to respond to new opportunities. Shareholders in the banks also suffered but whether this will hold in the longer term is debatable. UK bank share prices, for example, initially fell as a result of the crisis but subsequently rebounded as the situation seemed to have been contained. The taxpayers in the creditor countries have so far suffered little. Given government complicity in the recycling process and accepting the principle that the burdens of adjustment should be shared, they might yet be required to contribute to a long term solution. The burden of adjustment has, however, so far rested on the debtor nations and particularly on their poor.[43]

5.5 THE PLAZA AGREEMENT, THE BAKER PLAN, OPEC III AND GATT

Between the 1985 spring and autumn meetings of the IMF and the IBRD there seemed to have been a major re-evaluation of the prospects for the short leash solution to the debt problem.

The growing US trade deficit contrasted with the large trade surpluses being recorded in Japan and West Germany, as well as Brazil and some of the major Latin American countries. The US manufacturing and farm sector lobbies pressed Congress for protectionist legislation. To head off these pressures, which might have sparked a trade war,[44] the finance ministers and central bank governors of the G5[45] met in New York's Plaza Hotel in September 1985 and agreed to undertake coordinated intervention through their central banks to reduce the overvalued dollar. The latter had been slowly drifting downwards since the first quarter of 1985. It was also hoped that as the currencies of other countries appreciated their monetary authorities would be able to reduce their interest rates, permitting some reduction in the US rate as well. The drop in US interest rates and the fall in the dollar would make it easier for Latin American countries to service their debts and might also stimulate the US economy, the growth rate of which was declining.[46] Combined with the maintenance of free trade, this would help Latin American countries to continue to earn the dollars they needed. The downside risks were that the US budget deficit would continue to grow and, with the money supply growing rapidly and the dollar depreciation likely to have an inflationary impact, the FRB would feel unable to reduce interest rates, that US growth would continue to slow and that the dollar's depreciation would not reduce the trade deficit fast enough to satisfy the protectionist lobbies.

In October 1985, at the annual IMF—IBRD meeting, the Baker Plan was launched. It was named after the US Treasury Secretary James Baker III and more formally called the Programme for Sustained Growth. It incorporated three essential and mutually reinforcing elements: firstly, and most importantly, the adoption by principal debtor countries of comprehensive macroeconomic and structural policies supported by international institutions to promote growth and balance of payments adjustment and reduce inflation; secondly, a continued central role for the IMF in conjunction with increased and more effective structural adjustment lending by the multilateral development banks (MDBs), in support of the adoption by principal debtors of market-oriented policies for growth; thirdly, increased lending by the private banks in support of comprehensive adjustment programmes. It was emphasised that the case by case approach was to remain and it was later reaffirmed that, although the plan placed emphasis on growing out of debt, economic adjustment remained essential. The difference was that medium to long term programmes for adjustment agreed with the IMF and the IBRD were to be put in motion in place of the short to medium term adjustments previously negotiated with the IMF alone.

Baker suggested that the success of the plan would require $40bn worth of financial support over the three-year 1986–8 period. The MDBs were expected to provide an additional

$20bn and the commercial banks would have to increase their exposure by a matching amount. He argued that this was not a large amount in real terms, when spread over three years. The relevant MDBs, in the case of the Latin American countries covered by the plan, were the IADB and the IBRD. Baker declared that the US administration was willing to sanction their increased funding if they could make more rapid disbursments, and find more efficient uses for them, than they had achieved in the previous year. The fifteen countries covered by the plan included ten Latin American debtors[47] and five others.[48] They were the world's major, non-Eastern bloc, debtors. The plan also discussed the possibility of creating a superbank to handle commercial bank loans. Commercial banks were finding it increasingly difficult to syndicate loans for balance of payments adjustment and showing a preference for project lending, which was declining. The hope was that the superbank would establish a formal machinery for loan formation, and thereby accelerate disbursements, in place of the increasingly problematic informal syndication procedure. No action had been taken by mid 1986 but, in the light of the Mexican loan proposals discussed below, it may yet be necessary. At the time many believed that the plan had underestimated the finance required to resolve the problem.

The Baker Plan's theme was growth-oriented adjustment. Later Baker stressed not only that it was necessary for the debtors to grow, following the period of austerity and falling living standards, but that growth in the creditor countries, to maintain export-earning opportunities for the debtors, was also essential. It was particularly important that the 'growth gap' left by the slowdown in the US economy, which would possibly increase with the fiscal contraction necessary to reduce the budget deficit,[49] should be filled and that protectionist measures should not proliferate. The Baker Plan was heralded as the second phase, following on from the IMF's short leash initiative, in the resolution of the debt problem.

The OPEC III oil price shock in the first quarter of 1986 appeared to be a bonus for the growth-oriented solution. In December 1985 Saudi Arabia had successfully, though not without dissent,[50] persuaded OPEC to adopt a policy of regaining its market share. Saudi Arabia expanded its production towards its previously agreed quota and ceased to act as the swing producer within OPEC. The consequence was a rapid price fall, which was temporarily halted and partially reversed by fears of a Middle Eastern conflict[51] and the Chernobyl nuclear disaster in the spring of 1986, which raised doubts about the nuclear energy option. The price fall resumed as the traditional summer trough in oil demand transpired but this latter fall was reversed by a surprise OPEC agreement to restrict supply over a three-month period in August 1986.

The fall in real oil prices more than wiped out the 1979 OPEC II shock and might possibly, if resumed, return prices to their pre-OPEC I levels. Consequently, it forced a major re-evaluation of the debt problem. Of the Baker fifteen, eight are oil importers and seven are oil exporters.[52] The importers clearly stood to gain but the exporters relied heavily on oil for their export revenues. The five Latin American exporters accounted for $150bn of the region's $360bn debt. Of these five Venezuela, an OPEC member, and Mexico were the major debtors and the largest oil producers. The largest debtor, Brazil, and Argentina were major beneficiaries. Mexico emerged as the major problem debtor, Venezuela having already requested a renegotiation of the MYRA agreement concluded in 1985. Venezuela's problem may, however, prove to have been underestimated since the renewed fall in the oil price, in the summer of 1986, further damaged its trade balance prospects. In June 1986 complications had arisen because interest payments by autonomous public sector enterprises were delayed. Such problems had beset previous bank dealings with Venezuela. Then, in July 1986, the Venezuelan Congress passed legislation requiring private sector companies to repay their foreign obligations, in local currency, to a new Exchange Compensation Fund, which would issue fixed-rate government-guaranteed bonds to international creditors. The plan covered the $7bn private sector debt and received a hostile reception from banks which were considering Venezuela's request to adjust its $21bn public sector debt-rescheduling agreement to achieve a less onerous repayment's schedule. The banks complained that the conditions on the bonds, which have a fifteen-year maturity and a 5 per cent coupon, ensure that they would immediately trade at a huge discount.

More indirectly, it was felt that the fall in oil prices might have the immediate effect of stimulating world growth and thereby easing the debt problem. This was because falling energy prices would reduce inflation and thereby raise real income and permit the easing of anti-inflationary monetary policies and reduced interest rates. The central banks of the major G5 countries engineered coordinated interest rate reductions in the first half of 1986, seemingly as a follow-up to the Plaza Agreement, but in the second half the coordinated reduction met resistance.[53] The US interest rate reductions, however, approached the 3 per cent which War on Want (1985) estimated would reduce the Latin American debt burden by $40bn, equivalent to the increase in finance suggested by the Baker Plan. Additionally, it appeared that the oil price fall was having a J-shaped effect on the world's economy. Growth in the major economies actually slowed down in the first quarter of 1986. This was attributed to the fact that the fall in energy prices had not been fully passed on to consumers who seemed to be taking advantage of any price reductions to increase savings anyway. This in turn may have been a response to the fall in inflation rates induced by falling oil and other commodity prices. Meanwhile oil-producing countries, particularly the OPEC ones, reduced their expenditures rapidly and so too did the oil-producing sectors in the UK and the US. The initial impact of OPEC III on world growth, therefore, appeared to be negative but most countries forecast a rebound in growth in the latter half of 1986 and positive long run effects. A small rebound did occur but the effects have taken longer to unravel than expected. A positive stimulus was expected in 1987 but its impact will depend on underlying economic trends, which remain uncertain in the major industrial countries, the US, Japan and Germany, following the 1986 exchange rate realignments. Following the OPEC III shocks world growth forecasts by institutions such as the IMF, the IBRD and the OECD were all revised upwards, but only to levels that had been forecast a year earlier. At best, therefore, OPEC III was only expected to compensate for the decline in growth likely to result from the slowdown in US growth, which it was supposed to partially offset. The general slowdown in growth in the major economies recorded in the first quarter of 1986 made these projections decidedly doubtful.

Japan for example is a major beneficiary of the oil price fall. It is a country with a high propensity to save and in 1985 it had a net capital outflow of $50bn. It replaced OPEC, which was actually withdrawing money from the international credit system, as the major supplier of funds and presented the world with a new recycling problem. Japan, however, has a well-developed financial system and has been doing its own investing, which accounts for the recent rapid growth of Japanese financial institutions. There is little sign that Japan will recycle funds towards countries worst hit by the oil price shock. The US has so far been the major beneficiary and has been happy to be so, since it would otherwise have found it immensely difficult to fund its budget deficit in a non-inflationary manner. Even Japan's growth has faltered, however, partly due to the problem, which Germany also faces, of adjusting to the revaluation of its currency, especially relative to the dollar. This is having a major impact on its export sector, the engine of its growth hitherto.[54]

The world economic recovery, which appeared to be faltering in the first quarter of 1986, had been from the deepest recession since the 1930s and, although prolonged by postwar standards, it was the only cyclical recovery on record in which terms of trade had actually improved for the OECD countries at the expense of the commodity producers. In mid 1986 the prospects for future growth were extremely uncertain and so too were the prospects for further significant interest rate reductions.[55] Further, trade prospects were not rosy in the light of growing protectionism and disagreements between the US and its major trading partners,[56] despite the forthcoming new round of GATT negotiations. The latter negotiations were launched in September 1986 in Uruguay. They are to cover trade in services and agricultural goods for the first-time. Past successes in reducing tariffs on manufactured goods and commodities have been increasingly offset by the introduction of non-tariff barriers such as voluntary export quotas. The chances of making progress in the GATT negotiations and preventing a further retreat towards protectionsim are dependent upon the strength of world growth and progress on the major trading imbalances, especially that between the US and Japan. The latter imbalance was also showing a J-shaped response to the yen's massive appreciation[57] and the Japanese trade surplus hit record levels in the second quarter of 1986 whilst the US deficit resumed its growth. This was severely trying the patience of the US Congress. It tabled a protectionist trade bill in mid 1986, which the President was hard pressed to block in the absence of success in persuading Japan and Germany to take up the growth torch. The autumn 1986 mid-term elections installed a Democratic Party majority in the US Senate. Consequently the White House's ability to block future protectionist legislation emanating from Congress has probably been seriously curtailed.[58]

The managing director of the IMF and the Chairman of the FRB have continued to stress the need for coresponsibility[59] and enhanced collaboration, between the IMF and the IBRD, in resolving the debt problem and dealing with the re-emergence of the Mexican crisis via the Baker Plan. In May 1986 Equador, which had been hit by the fall in oil prices, had its attempts at economic adjustment rewarded under the Baker Plan. The US government extended a credit facility and Banque Paribas arranged a new loan facility. By June, however, the President of Equador was finding it increasingly difficult to impose further austerity measures, due to electoral discontent. Meanwhile additional evidence that governments and commercial banks are willing to commit funds on the level envisaged in the Baker Plan is meagre. In mid 1986, for example, the plan was nearly nine months old and Mexico had received no new funding for eighteen months, a period in which oil prices had been falling. The banks seemed to feel that they were strong enough to withstand a major default[60] and seemed more intent on reducing than increasing their exposure. They also felt that governments should do more: through their export credit agencies, through Paris Club reschedulings, by easing regulatory restraints, and by increasing IMF, IBRD and IADB funding. In March 1986, through the Institute for International Finance,[61] the banks called on the IMF and the IBRD to strengthen their efforts to find a long term solution and urged more government involvement.

The Baker Plan initially seemed to provide for smaller banks to drop out in order to speed up loan syndication. Larger banks, especially in Europe, only endorsed the plan on the understanding that forced lending practices remained intact. These required creditors to contribute to new loans in line with their exposure. The complexity of loan syndication negotiations was, however, contributing to the banks' 'debt fatigue'. In May 1986, the US Treasury clarified the issue. It wanted smaller banks to stay in but urged the banks to speed up loan preparations and resolve their differences. Twenty per cent of the banks hold 80 per cent of the debt and syndication can involve literally hundreds of banks. Apart from differences between large and small banks there are also those between the US and the European banks.[62] The latter are more disposed to capitalisation whilst the US regulators are against this, preferring banks to put up new loans.

The Baker initiative seemed to have reached an impasse in the first half of 1986, with neither the banks nor the governments wanting to show themselves too willing to lend for fear that they would reduce the obligations of the other parties. Increased funding for the MDBs, and the IBRD and IADB in particular as far as Latin America is concerned, had yet to be negotiated. The US Congress had yet to sanction increased funding and was trying to make a capital increase for the IADB conditional on the bank agreeing to a change in its voting rules to give the US power of veto. This was strongly opposed by the Latin American members. Baker continued to pressure Congress for increased funding, however, pointing out the MDBs were more cost effective than aid, from a budgetary perspective, because contributions were likely to be matched by other countries and would increase the MDBs' borrowing power. He estimated that a $1 increase in budgetary authority by Congress would translate into a $60 increase in lending authority.

Thus, in the first half of 1986, the case by case approach in its new growth-oriented form was still intact but crisis conditions had returned in Mexico, which a year or so earlier had been held up as an example of the success of the short leash approach. Since August 1982 it had proved willing to take the medicine but it had received no new finance since the beginning of 1985, when it had concluded its MYRA. During that period oil prices had been falling, at first slowly, but then precipitously in the first quarter of 1986. In 1985, oil accounted for 70 per cent of Mexico's export earnings and 45 per cent of its Treasury receipts. With a debt of $96bn to service the oil price fall, which at $10 a barrel would approximately halve its receipts, was clearly too much to bear.

It was not clear whether Mexico's case would be treated as a special one or whether it would be covered by the Baker Plan. Its substantial financial needs would absorb a large proportion of the sums envisaged in the plan. This money might be better used to help the countries amongst the Baker fifteen which faced less acute problems. The US refused to bail Mexico out but exerted pressure on Mexico and the IMF to come to a compromise agreement. The BIS also stated that it was unwilling to provide bridging finance, as it had in August 1982, because the banks were not unduly threatened and the matter was in the hands of the IMF and the IBRD.

In June 1986 Mexico's reserves were almost depleted. The sticking point in negotiations with the IMF was the inability to agree on a budget target. It had become clear in the second half of 1985 that Mexico had little chance of hitting previously agreed budgetry targets and it was about to be censured by the IMF when the September earthquakes struck. Mexico was finding it difficult to hit the targets not only because of falling oil revenue but also because rising interest rates had increased the cost of servicing the national debt. The high interest rates were required to stem capital flight and generate domestic savings. There was, however, also some evidence that the government had tried to stimulate growth ahead of the July 1986 elections. In mid 1986 the budget deficit was approaching 13 per cent of GNP against a proposed IMF target of 5 per cent. Mexico offered to try to reduce it to around 6.5 per cent by the end of 1986.

The negotiations between Mexico, the US government, the FRB and the IMF were complicated by a change in the finance minister, which seems to have been a political move in the run up to the elections. Finance minister Herzog was replaced by Gustavo Petricioli, following repeated criticisms in the press that Herzog had been overcompliant with the wishes of the creditors. The government faced a real risk of losing the elections and there were riots and demonstrations, during the World Cup in June 1986, that showed the strength of popular discontent. Mexico City has, by some estimates, the largest population of all the world's cities and it grows daily as people move from the countryside into the shanty towns. There was a growing feeling of nationalist defiance against the 520 'gringo' creditor banks, most of which were US based. The new finance minister drew attention to the choice between debt financing at current levels and development, stressing that the latter must be given a higher priority. Many millions of people are starving in Mexico, following the years of IMF-imposed austerity, and unless growth resumes at a level significantly higher than population growth the government might well find it difficult to keep control. The US clearly has an interest in avoiding political instability at its borders and, despite previous criticisms of the government of President Miguel de la Madrid and allegations of ballot rigging in the July 1986 elections, was willing to negotiate with it to achieve a resolution of its debt crisis.

Mexico was seeking a rescheduling of $15bn dollars of its debt, new money, and repayments linked to the principle that it should pay what it could afford, which in turn largely depended on oil revenues. The IMF's position was not based on short term prudential considerations alone, it was also concerned that Mexico's budget deficit was in danger of growing to the point of being unmanageable. Some compromise on the debt issue was clearly required to resolve the crisis and the US seemed to be pressing Mexico and the IMF to reach one.

In July 1986 Mexico and the IMF reached agreement on a new package of economic reforms which was expected to pave the way for a new $10bn financing package, including $1.5bn in IMF loans, $1.9bn in IBRD loans and between $5bn and $7bn in commercial bank loans. Both sides appeared to have adopted a more flexible approach, with the IMF proving willing to agree to economic targets that would reflect the adverse impact of the oil price fall on government revenue and, therefore, on the budget deficit. It was also agreed that if the oil price fell below $9 a barrel, further multilateral funds would be released, whilst if it rose above $14 per barrel agreed funding would be reduced. The IMF also took account of the adverse impact that high domestic interest rates were having on Mexico's budget deficit, as it had done previously with Argentina and Brazil. Conclusion of the financing package had, however, to await a commitment from the commercial banks. They had expected to be asked to contribute $2.5bn; rather than the $5 to $7bn envisaged by the IMF, in the eighteen months to the end of 1987, as part of a growth-oriented economic reform programme consistent with the Baker Plan. Not only was the sum larger than the banks had expected but their commitment was to be a longer term one and they were required to contribute to the oil price contingent finance facility. Their obligations were also to be made contingent upon the growth rate achieved by Mexico, with lending expanding to meet any growth shortfalls. Many commentators viewed the expanded flexibility and growth orientation that the IMF had built into the programme as a new departure and one much more consistent with the Baker Plan than previous IMF programmes.

If the IMF proves willing to negotiate similar programmes with other debtors, rather than to argue that Mexico was a special case, then the Mexico agreement could mark a significant revision of the Third World debt strategy. In this case at least, the IMF does seem to have been responsive to the political reality of the situation in Mexico and its role will be able to be presented, by the Mexican government to its people, as a constructive one. A more cynical view is that the IMF had merely proved responsive to political pressure from the US. If the financial package is to come into effect the banks must cooperate. Whilst the FRB, which has been closely involved in the negotiations, can exert some pressure on US banks, their cooperation is far from assured. Some reappraisal of the banks' relationship with the IMF seems certain following this agreement, especially if it marks a change in the IMF's treatment of debtors in general. Given the sums involved, it will provide a major test of the loan syndication procedure, and the initiative discussed in the Baker Plan of forming a superbank to speed up loan formation may yet have to be taken.

The banker's immediate response was to express concern that they might, in the future, be expected to participate in similar deals with a whole range of countries that had suffered from the impact of falling commodity prices. It seemed likely that, in order to get the loan syndication rolling, the banks would want to see the extent to which governments were willing to share in the burden of financial support. A greater emphasis on cofinancing schemes with the IMF might also be helpful. Whilst the package was being assembled, bridging finance was required. The US sought contributions to a $1.6bn bridging loan from some of the industrial countries' central banks, Latin American governments and commercial banks. Even the assembly of the bridging loan proved to be a difficult task—the Bundesbank, for example, proving reluctant to contribute and the leading commercial banks making disbursements of the banks' $500bn contribution conditional on progress in the assembly of the longer term package which was part of the IMF agreement.

Meanwhile Argentina and Brazil waited in the wings. Argentina urgently needed finance following the fall in grain prices. Grain and beef accounted for 70 per cent of Argentina's exports and the area under grain production had been falling. Negotiations with Argentina had been postponed whilst the IMF dealt with the Mexico crisis. Brazil's financial needs did not appear to be so pressing because its trade surplus had reached a record level in the first half of 1986, and it had successfully negotiated substantial loans from the IBRD. Toward the end of 1986, however, its trade surplus was declining at an alarming rate and the Cuzado Plan was becoming increasingly unpopular. Both countries were hoping to benefit from the IMF's seemingly more flexible approach, which might well mark the first significant step in enacting the Baker Plan. The plan will ultimately fail unless the banks and the governments in the industrial countries increase their financial commitments. In July 1986, speaking at the annual meeting of the UN Economic and Social Council, the managing director of the IMF again drew their attention to their coresponsibility in the resolution of the debt problem. He also drew the attention to the consequences of the problem for human welfare in the debtor countries and urged urgent action.

5.6 ALTERNATIVE SOLUTIONS

The Institute for International Economics (IIE) published a report in 1985 which assessed the merits of twenty-four proposals aimed at helping to resolve the Latin American debt problem.[63] Many of these suggestions stopped short of proposing a global solution but might usefully supplement the Baker Plan. The various proposals can be formed into three groups: those that aim to reduce problems caused by fluctuating interest and exchange rates, those that aim to maintain or increase the current flows of finance to the LDCs, and those that aim to reduce the need for current finance by lengthening the repayment period and transforming the debt into a tradable form.

In the first category there have been a number of proposals aimed at reducing the dependence of the debt on the dollar exchange rate. For example, the exposure of debtor countries to problems resulting from the fluctuating value of the dollar may be partially alleviated in the future if agreements akin to the 1985 Mexican rescheduling proliferate which allow creditor banks to convert the debts to their own currencies. This should help to reduce the dependence of debts on the dollar. Further moves along these lines would appear to be possible. The debt's value would have been more stable if it had been denominated in terms of special drawing rights (SDRs) or European currency units (ECUs). Such proposals would also have the advantages of spreading lender of last resort responsibilities amongst central banks and thereby reducing reliance on the FRB, and possibly reducing interest rates payable by the LDCs, since they are lower in a number of the creditor countries than in the US. Concerning interest rates, a number of commentators have suggested that a special IMF loan facility should be established. The IMF already provides such facilities to help countries suffering from the effects of sharp falls in commodity prices and rises in oil prices. The precipitous fall in oil prices in early 1986 has consequently provoked proposals for the former to be extended to include oil prices or the latter to be used to help Mexico and other oil-producing debtors. A similar facility could be established to cover for sharp rises in interest rates so that countries undertaking IMF programmes could receive compensation for rises in interest rates. The funds could be raised by the IMF in the normal manner[64] but more imaginative funding could be explored, such as SDR issues. The FRB and a number of regional US banks have suggested 'rate capping' as an alternative. The US Treasury did not back the proposal and it was rejected at the 1984 economic summit meeting. 'Rate capping' involves the setting of a ceiling on the interest a debtor is expected to pay in any one year. Payments would be deferred if they exceeded the ceiling. Such proposals contain the seeds of a longer term solution of the type contained in the third group of proposals, to be discussed below. The World Bank adopted a version of rate capping in its cofinancing loan to Paraguay in 1984, which fixed in advance the size of the debt service payments Paraguay was liable to pay each year. In the event of a rise in interest rates the principal payments would be reduced and deferred with the possible effect of lengthening the period of the loan. The banks involved in the cofinancing were given first call on any principal payments. The IADB has argued that debt service payments should not exceed 25 per cent of export earnings, and that MYRAs should incorporate the principle of capacity to pay.[65] In this connection interest and other charges should be reduced, repayment periods lengthened, and the effects of interest rate fluctuation should be eliminated. This view has, as we have noted, been adopted by the Cartagena Group and the Group of Twenty-Four.

Regarding the second group of proposals, there is a potential conflict between the maintenance of commercial bank lending near to, or above, the level prevailing in 1985 and increasing government bank lending, directly or indirectly, through export credit agencies or international agencies. The ultimate aim is to reduce the LDC's reliance on short term debt finance from banks by substituting capital flows. In the short term, however, it has been necessary to attempt to maintain or increase bank lending whilst the debtor countries adjust their economies so that they can attract overseas investment. In order to ensure that banks continue to participate, governments had, at least until the Baker Plan was announced, proved reluctant to provide the necessary funding to allow the international agencies to increase their lending significantly. The US Congress, in particular, had only grudgingly agreed to requests from the IBRD and IADB for fairly meagre increases in their funding. Other governments have developed the practice of providing their supplementary contributions to the IBRD only after the US has agreed to its contribution. Nevertheless, there is a limit to the amount of pressure that the IMF and the central banks can put on the commercial banks to maintain or increase their present 'forced' lending levels. As the crisis reverted to problem status after 1982, the commercial banks, especially the smaller regional US banks, tried with some success to reduce their exposure to LDC debtors.[66] To counter this tendency there have been various proposals aimed at encouraging, rather than 'forcing', commercial bank lending at levels near to or above those in the mid 1980s. Cofinancing arrangements involving the IBRD and the development banks have already been mentioned and these are widely favoured. For them to make a significant impact, however, the IBRD will require additional funding. The Baker Plan acknowledged the need for extra funding for the IBRD and the development banks, particularly the IADB in the case of Latin America. It also required a complementary increase in commercial bank lending. By mid 1986 there had, however, been no firm commitments from either the banks or the governments. The US Congress still seemed reticent and the banks remained unwilling to increase their lending without firm evidence that governments would also cooperate. The Baker Plan, therefore, lay in the balance. it was clear that increased lending, especially to Mexico, would be required to resolve the debt problem but neither the banks nor the governments were willing to increase their contributions without assurance that they would be matched by the other parties. The governments, particularly the US Congress, felt that if they permitted a significant increase in lending by international agencies then the banks would be let off the hook at the expense of the taxpayers. The banks in turn were concerned that if they proved willing to increase their exposure the governments would be relieved of their responsibilities concerning the debt problem. Further, many governments probably felt that since the major debt problem was Mexico's and because the US had a vested interest in resolving Mexico's problems, to protect its banks and maintain political stability on its borders, they could take a back seat. It does appear, however, that if the debt problem is to be satisfactorily resolved governments will eventually have to increase their lending, directly or indirectly, and perhaps their aid provisions at the expense of their taxpayers.

One measure that has been widely considered because of its potential for restoring the banks' willingness to lend to LDCs is the establishment of an insurance facility. Lord Lever (1983) has suggested that governments should extend the role of existing export credit guaranteeing agencies so that they can insure loans and exports of capital as well as exports of goods. The major export credit agencies would establish a central agency to pool information and consult with the IMF and the IBRD. As a result LDCs would receive sufficient funding to ensure that the banks' current debts cease to be non-performing and the banks would not need to carry large bad debt provisions. Johannes Witteveen (1983) argued that it would be better for the IMF to set up its own insurance facility so that the provision of insurance could be backed by IMF conditionality in the case of the more risky loans to countries in need of IMF assistance. The introduction of such a scheme by the IMF would require a change in its statutes since it is currently not permitted to provide insurance cover. Such an arrangement would free central banks from the need to urge the commercial banks to maintain their lending to LDCs whilst also requiring them to raise capital and bad debt provisions and allow them to concentrate on their supervisory tasks. Henry Wallich (1984) considered Witteveen's and other proposals for loan insurance. He noted that the banks are currently making their own insurance provisions in the form of bad debt provisions and that it would be more efficient for them to pool their reserves in an insurance fund. If, however, as many believe to be the case, some countries' banks have not set aside enough in the way of provisions, for in some countries[67] reserves can be hidden, then the pooled reserves may also prove insufficient and outside sources of funds may also be required. The size of the fund required depends on what is to be insured. If the object was purely to encourage new lending then the case can be put for excluding rescheduled loans, for example. The outside funding could take the form of a permanent donation or a loan. The latter would be preferable if the governments wished to avoid subsidising banks. The loan could come from central banks, perhaps through the BIS, the IBRD, from governments via export credit agencies or from the IMF, following a change in its statutes. Another possibility is reinsurance provided by the private sector insurance industry. Such insurance schemes could be national or international. Given that the banks have not established insurance funds voluntarily some public sector initiative would appear to be required. A larger international fund would probably be more efficient, because the individual contributions by banks could be smaller, and it could be managed by the IMF, the IBRD or the BIS. Citicorp[68] arranged a private insurance deal in 1984 with the US Cigna insurance company to cover it against loss on some of its loans to LDCs, which was abandoned in 1985. It is believed that the US insurance industry regulators were unhappy with the arrangement. This does not auger well for future involvement of private sector insurance companies. The major problem with the insurance proposals is the risk of moral hazard. If participation in the schemes were to be voluntary the big banks might prefer to go it alone, reducing the size of the fund significantly, and to rely on *de facto* insurance from their central banks through their lender of last resort responsibilities. Further, the schemes might encourage increased risk taking by banks. This suggests that the insurance sheme should be combined with increased regulation and supervision of the international financial system by the international agency managing the fund and that premiums and contributions should vary in accordance with the soundness of the bank and the business in which it is engaging.

Other suggestions for increasing banks' voluntary lending

include refinancing. The IMF or the IBRD or the BIS could provide debtor countries with the necessary funds to pay back their loans to the banks or take over the loans from the banks by establishing a new agency to buy debt at discount. Such suggestions suffer from the weakness that they might encourage debtor countries to pursue more reckless policies. They would therefore have to be offered in conjunction with IMF loan conditionality. This would mean that only loans to the most risky countries would be eligible and then only to the end of the period of IMF conditionality. Extended surveillance by the IMF combined with the threat that the refinancing facility could be withdrawn, which would also lead voluntary bank lending to dry up, could, however, deter abuse. The major disadvantage, when compared with insurance schemes, is that the banks would not be expected to put their bad debt provisions to use in helping to resolve the debt problem.

Additionally, the Group of Thirty, an influential group of academic economists and central and other bankers, has suggested that the IMF should be able to borrow on the Eurobond and Eurocurrency markets in order to increase its lending power and to soak up funds which were previously lent by the commercial banks to the LDCs but which were now being diverted to other sources through these markets. The IMF would then move nearer to being able to adopt the role of world lender of last resort, given the high credit rating it would enjoy. The IMF would also be able to boost its own reserves through SDR issues. The conservative 1:1 gearing ratio[69] of the IBRD could also be relaxed and it could thereby be allowed to borrow more. Opponents of such a relaxation, from both within and outside the IBRD, argue that it would lead to a reduction in the IBRD's credit rating. This would increase the costs of its fund and force it to charge higher interest rates at the expense of the developing countries. They consequently feel that more government funding is necessary.

There have also been a number of suggestions for improving capital flows to LDCs, which are viewed as essential to resolve the problem by reducing the LDC's reliance on debt. It should be noted that actions taken to restore the financial position and reduce inflation in the debtor countries should also, hopefully, lead to a repatriation of 'flight capital'. The IADB has proposed the establishment of an Inter-American Development Cooperation (IADC) to encourage direct investment in Latin America. This proposal has received support from the Latin American countries but the IADB's funding is under threat from the US Treasury, which wants it to tighten up its lending policies. The IBRD could also contribute in this area through cofinancing of investments, but this again would probably require increased funding, which seems to be constrained by US policies.

The International Finance Corporation (IFC), which is an IBRD affiliate, suggested a debt for equity swap facility in 1984. This facility would allow private sector foreign debt to be converted into equity. The first stage would be the establishment of an investment company to take over private sector loans from the creditor banks. The company would then try to help debtor countries to restructure their finances by turning loans into equity. It was argued that this might relieve some of the pressure and provide an opportunity for institutional investors to make funds available for speculative and lucrative investments in Latin America, perhaps involving some cofinancing arrangement with the IBRD. Finally the IBRD has created a billion dollar insurance agency designed to encourage companies to invest in poorer countries. The Multilateral Investment Guarantee Agency (MIGA) was formally launched in 1986 and will promote investment, offer advice, and attempt to overcome LDC governments' suspicion of external investment. It is to be funded by the major Western governments and, most importantly, the US has already agreed to support its funding. This will complement the work of the IFC, which is independently funded and aims to promote development through the private sector. Since 1974 it has been involved in over 150 joint ventures between foreign and domestic private investors. In the mid 1980s it offered a new advisory service, drawing on its past experience, to encourage foreign direct investment in developing countries. The role of the IFC and the prospects for increasing the flow of risk capital to the LDCs are discussed in Ryrie (1986).

The third group of solutions essentially involve much longer terms and more fundamental restructurings of debts. They aim both to reduce the debt overhang and to reverse the negative transfer of income from the debtors to the developed countries. Old and, in the short term, essentially unpayable debts could, for example, be replaced by new low interest long maturing debts subject to the debtor countries continuing with infrastructural projects and structural adjustment. The commercial banks would be allowed to rediscount their existing loans with the central banks or perhaps an international agency such as the IMF or the IBRD in a phased way. Alternatively part of the interest due could be capitalised by the provision of long term loans. As banks continued to grow through their other business the importance of their exposure would be progressively reduced. Inflation would also reduce the value of their outstanding debt. As the problem was resolving itself loan loss reserves would be reduced and released for lending. It has been argued that the debt repayments really need to be spread over decades rather than years. The problem is that because the banks cannot raise matching long term, say thirty-year, deposits some innovation involving the concept of deferred marketability is required. The banks could, for example, agree to a thirty-year rescheduling. The first ten-year period could involve a conventional rescheduling except that part of the interest might be 'capitalised' or added to the rescheduled debt. After ten years the debt would be converted into twenty-year FRNs,[70] which the banks could sell if they wanted. If the debtor was by then on the road to recovery the FRNs could be sold at little or no discount. If not, then the discount would be potentially large but this would be covered by the provisions that the banks had had ten years to build up. Such solutions need to consider how banks can be induced to cooperate. The problem of the debt overhang still needs attention, and lending in the short term must somehow be increased.

We have mentioned that the IIE has assessed twenty-four proposals which aim to help to resolve the Latin American debt problem by changing the nature of commercial bank lending to LDCs.[71] It favoured MYRAs linked to performance, expanded insurance and guarantees of bank lending to LDCs, expanded cofinancing of bank loans by multilateral development banks, some form of interest rate capping and the creation of a compensatory finance facility at the IMF for interest rate fluctuations. It stopped short of recommending the sort of long term solution discussed above.

The package of measures favoured by the IIE might usefully be supplemented by a special facility to help oil exporters cope with the difficulties caused by the fall in their export revenues following the rapid fall in oil prices in 1986.[72] Additionally, or alternatively, future reschedulings should be more flexible, allowing interest payments to vary with ability to pay. This could be achieved by agreeing that repayments should not exceed some percentage of export revenue, for example. The introduction of export revenue sensitive interest payments requirements would largely eliminate the need for a special fund facility to cover for interest and commodity price fluctuations and make interest rate capping unnecessary.

The alternative to new initiatives such as those discussed is to stick with the short leash, case by case, approach and let the market sort it out. Advocates of this solution hope that somehow the debtors will grow out of their problems and that the growth in banks' other assets will reduce the problem of the Latin American debt overhang. Debtors' growth would increase their ability to service current debts and increase banks' willingness to refinance and reschedule on reasonable terms. The banks' growth would reduce the importance of Latin American debt in their balance sheets. As banks grew stronger they could accelerate the repackaging of the debts into a securitised form and trade them, accepting the necessary discounts. There has been some repackaging of this sort but a well-developed market in securitised Latin American debt does not yet exist. This is probably because wide knowledge of the discounts at which the debt is trading could well shock equity holders and depositors until capital and provisions are further strengthened. As the debt declines in relative importance, however, banks may feel able to increase trading. For the US banks, the practice of actively trading debt at a discount would lead their auditors to instruct them to write down the value of non-traded Latin American debt and their supervisors to require them to increase their provisions. The best rated Latin American debt has been changing hands at only 80 per cent of its face value and a large quantity has been trading in the 30 to 40 per cent discount range. Trading so far has been amongst banks trying to improve the spread of their country exposures. The size of the discount, which would probably be larger if a greater volume of debt was traded, shows, however, why banks have proved reluctant to increase their exposures and have indeed tried to reduce them.

With the renewed onset of the Mexican crisis following the oil price fall in June 1986, a series of new long term debt solutions emerged. Mr J. Makin (1986), Director of Fiscal Studies at the American Enterprise Institute, suggested that the Mexican crisis could be defused by acknowledging Mexico's inability to pay and writing down the value of the loans. This would risk both a liquidity crisis amongst banks, especially those in the US, and encouraging similar requests from other debtors. A solution, therefore, had to be found which would not damage bank liquidity and would encourage Mexico to pay. New money was not the answer and was unlikely to be forthcoming, he argued. Instead a conditional writedown was required and this would enhance the value of existing loans because it would reduce the expectation of new loans. With Mexican debt trading at around 60 per cent of its book value, an equivalent writedown would reduce the earnings of a typical US money centre bank by 11 per cent, he estimated, and they would additionally be required to increase their loan loss provisions. He suggested that the banks should be allowed to write down their loans in phases over ten years. The effect would be to give the banks an interest free loan at the expense of the taxpayers. Mexico would not be relieved of its obligations because written-down loans could be reissued as long term liabilities of Mexico to the treasuries of the major creditor nations and if the new instruments were held by banks then there would be little or no effect on their liquidity. The interest on outstanding loans could also be capitalised for five years and Mexico's performance monitored by the IMF and the IBRD. An interest rate incentive could be built in to encourage and reward good performance. Makin calls this conditional capitalisation. Improved performance would allow Mexico to repurchase written-down debt and loans could be written up again as prospects improved. Conditional capitalisation would stabilise the values of existing loans at realistic levels and enhance the value of loans to some of the other Latin American debtors, especially Brazil and perhaps also Argentina, and provide the time necessary for the Baker Plan to work, Makin concludes.

W. R. Cline (1986), Senior Fellow at the IIE, notes that the large US banks have more than half their capital in loans outstanding to Mexico. He estimates that capital flight from Mexico has been exaggerated and that the real fiscal deficit is only 1 per cent of GNP, compared with 4 per cent in the US, when the inflationary component of interest payments is removed. The prevailing IMF requirement that Mexico should aim for a deficit of 5 per cent of GNP,[73] therefore, implied that Mexico should achieve a fiscal surplus and was inappropriate. Cline suggested that Mexico should instead instigate a package, involving a wage–price freeze and monetary reform, akin to the Austral and Cruzado Plans adopted by Argentina and Brazil respectively. The prevailing fiscal stance of Mexico, which implied a small real fiscal deficit or surplus, meant that the foundations were in place for the success of such a plan. In addition he argued that the authorities should persevere with their policy of devaluing the peso in order to encourage non-oil exports and import substitution. The IMF should use its compensatory finance facility to support Mexico in view of lower oil prices and the IBRD should disperse a number of loans rapidly. Banks should provide the $2.5bn worth of new money envisaged in late 1985 and lend a further $1.5bn in 1986, in the form of five- to seven-year notes that would be redeemable when oil prices had recovered, to say $20 a barrel, for a specified period. Cline felt that all the measures were politically feasible with the exception perhaps of the wage–price freeze. Even the latter might be sold internally, however, if it permitted a domestic interest rate cut.

US Senator Bill Bradley, a contender for Democratic nomination for the next US Presidential election, proposed a relief plan for the most heavily indebted countries in late June 1986.[74] He suggested that the US should convene an annual summit on debt management during each of the first three years of the coming round of GATT negotiations. This would provide an incentive to Third World countries to drop their resistance to discussing services and other issues in the new round of GATT and would accommodate their demands for an intergovernmental political dialogue on the debt issue. Senator Bradley argued that the Baker Plan would prolong the policies that had created the crisis by emphasising new loans, instead of interest and debt relief, thereby creating more debt and increasing bank exposure to risk of default. Under the Bradley Plan creditors could negotiate annual relief with eligible debtor countries at summits chaired by the IBRD president. Large and small banks, as well as governments, would participate in a package which might include: a 3 per cent reduction in interest rates for one year on loans, a 3 per cent writedown of principal on outstanding loans, and $3bn new lending a year by international agencies to assist project lending and structural adjustment. To qualify for relief LDCs would have to agree to liberalise trade, take measures to reverse capital flight and encourage internal investment, and pursue domestic growth policies with broad domestic political support. Senator Bradley estimated that trade–relief packages could eliminate up to two-thirds of the annual debt burden. The plan has the advantage that it formally links trade, debt, and aid, as advocated by the Group of Twenty-Four and UNCTAD.

The measure apparently in vogue in 1986 for solving the debt problem, which had received endorsement from the US Treasury, was debt for equity swapping. These swaps involve the exchange of outstanding loans for equity interests in the debtor nations. Chile had been running a fairly successful programme since 1985. It was devised by its central bank to encourage domestic investors to purchase the country's foreign debt notes. The scheme had led to the retirement of a small, though significant, part of Chile's $20bn foreign debt. In the last six months of 1985 it was estimated to have reduced Chile's debt by 8 per cent. The notes were sold by foreign banks at a discount. The Chilean central bank offered to purchase the notes, at their face value, for pesos. The pesos received then had to be used immediately to pay domestic peso debts, to acquire new peso assets, or, in the case of foreigners or Chilean residents abroad, for investment in Chile. The central bank did not use its own foreign currency reserves so that the notes had to be bought with the purchaser's own dollar balances. This encouraged the return of flight capital or else the purchase of dollars. The scheme tried to direct to Chile's benefit some of the losses creditors were willing to take. The programme was revised, when necessary, to respond to changing market conditions by adjusting discounts to induce sales of debt whilst not unsettling exchange markets.

The idea of debt–equity swapping grew in acceptance, even amongst previously hard line banks, in the wake of the renewed Mexican crisis and the realisation that the debt problem would be a long drawn out affair. It is consistent with the Baker Plan in that it provides a market-oriented solution to the problem. It reduces the overhang of debt on which interest had to be paid. Equity only provides a return related to performance, ensuring that resources only flow out of a country when it is doing well and has sufficient resources. Holders of equity also have the prospect of capital gains as a country's position improves. Because of numerous practical problems, it is unlikely that debt-equity swapping will play more than a minor role in resolving the problem. It might, however, have a lasting psychological impact by mobilising investment inflows, reversing capital flight and improving LDCs' attitudes towards foreign investment.

There are basically two ways of converting debt to equity. A bank can agree to do this and substitute equity for other assets. This provides banks with opportunities to buy into financial institutions in the LDCs. More commonly, the lending bank sells debt at a discount to an industrial or commercial company planning investment in the country concerned. The company may be able to have the debt redeemed, in local currency and at full face value as in the case of Chile. The proceeds can then be used to finance investment at low cost.

A major obstacle to developing debt–equity swap agreements is the strict barriers to inward foreign investment erected by many LDCs. In Mexico, for example, it is impossible to buy into banks which are state owned. Opportunities could abound if the countries concerned prove willing to accept substantial foreign equity holdings because Mexico, Argentina, Brazil and Chile are all adopting privatisation programmes, which are consistent with the Baker Plan's emphasis on improving the market efficiency of economies in order to induce growth. But lenders also need to consider carefully the effects of selling debt at a discount in swap agreements because of the its effect on the assessment of the value of the remaining portfolio of Latin American debts. We have noted that this consideration has already damped interest in the development of a market for securitised Latin American debts. For securitisation or debt–equity swapping to make a more marked impact some easing of capital, provisioning and reporting requirements by the supervisors, especially in the US, would appear to be required. The banks have of course drawn their supervisors' attention to this fact.

On the face of it the scope for equity finance is large compared with past levels of direct investment, even in the mid 1970s. Its resurgence depends both on confidence and on the debtors' willingness to accommodate larger flows. Debtors may also feel that increased investment flows should supplement rather than replace lending.

Although the crisis seemed to have passed in the mid 1980s, with the exception of Mexico and possibly Venezuela and some of the smaller Latin American oil producers, the Latin American debt problem is likely to require attention until beyond the end of the century. It will probably be supplemented, and perhaps even surpassed, by the problems arising in other LDC countries, especially those in sub-Saharan Africa where debt problems are rapidly approaching crisis proportions. Nigeria, for example, is another major debtor which has been severely effected by the oil price fall. Only Nigeria and the Ivory Coast are covered by the Baker Plan. For every dollar flowing into Africa in 1986, two dollars were flowing out in interest payments. Data published by the OECD in 1986 showed that the net flow of resources from the LDCs to the OECD countries,[75] OPEC members and the Eastern bloc had fallen for the fourth successive year and was 40 per cent below its 1981 peak. Aid, export credits and banking flows had all declined. In 1986, the IMF and the IBRD revealed that they had become net absorbers of funds from the Third World, because interest and principal payments on past lending exceeded new lending. In response the UN committee for development planning argued that the flow of international finance to LDCs needed to be doubled by 1996 if they were to achieve minimum politically acceptable growth rates of 5 per cent.

Unless such finance is forthcoming, countries other than Mexico will be put into the position of having to evaluate seriously the benefits and costs of defaulting. The commercial banks are judged by many, including the OECD, to be able to withstand the shock of a major default. Whether or not they could withstand coordinated action by groups of debtors is another matter. The incentive to renege on debts is likely to increase as long as countries like Mexico are not being rewarded with new funds for their efforts to achieve adjustment through the imposition of programmes agreed with the IMF and the IBRD. In the absence of a marked increase in the commercial banks' willingness to lend, which seems unlikely to transpire, the onus to act is on the governments and the international agencies and development banks, which in turn depend on governments for an increase in their financing capabilities.

It would be extremely ironic if some governments imposed trade sanctions on South Africa, provoking it to declare a moratium on its debt payments and encouraging other debtor countries to follow suit, resulting in the same governments also imposing trade sanctions on them. In many cases aid would be more appropriate than further government financing, direct or indirect. It is no longer sufficient to view the problem as one of dealing with a potential international financial crisis. Many millions of people are involved. It is the poorest people in most of the countries under the IMF's wing that have suffered as a result of the austerity so far imposed. The more privileged classes, with vested interests, have tended to work against reform and protected themselves by contributing to capital flight. Bank profits, are, therefore, being protected largely at the expense of the poor and creditor governments, who share the blame, should act, in spite of the potential electoral consequences. In most cases they could of course blame the situation on previous administrations. If they do not act then the political stability of many countries and the plight of millions lie in the balance. The net outflow of funds from many LDCs must be reversed by more lenient financing and aid. If the UN's special session on Africa, in June 1986, is anything to go by then aid is not likely to be forthcoming on a sufficient scale. The UN General Assembly endorsed a five-year recovery plan drawn up by the African states but there was no matching commitment to meet its external financing requirements. A debt initiative is clearly required for Africa. The irony is that the US is absorbing a large proportion of the world's savings and that Japan's trade surplus has been largely channelled into the funding of the US budget deficit. If the US could reduce its budget deficit then the Japanese funds would be released for other purposes. A doubling of Japan's aid assistance, which was 0.3 per cent of its GNP, would have a massive impact and yet cost only three weeks' worth of its current account surplus in June 1986.

The Baker Plan, with its emphasis on growth-oriented adjustment matched with finance, needs expanding in coverage and the banks should be induced to participate. The plan could usefully be complemented with elements of the Bradley Plan in order to tie together debt and trade negotiations. It is essential that a trade war be averted. One could, however, be sparked by Congressional legislation unless the Reagan administration can continue to veto it successfully. The new round of GATT negotiations, initiated in September 1986, is crucial and so is action to ensure that OECD growth is maintained in the light of the slowdown of the US economy. Without freedom of access to growing export markets the LDCs cannot hope to achieve the export earnings necessary to service their debts. Additionally, faster disbursements by and additional funding for the IBRD are urgently required and the IMF should ease up on its short leash austerity requirements. It appeared to have done so in its dealings with Mexico in July 1986, but this should be confirmed. The IMF and the IBRD should develop a longer term view of adjustment and continue to increase the coordination of their policies. For their part, the LDCs are likely to have to accept, as a matter of course, the long term monitoring and surveillance of their economies. It is essential, however, that their cooperation is suitably rewarded.

Unless policy coordination amongst OECD countries, discussed in Chapter 7, is further enhanced and cooperation between OECD and LDC countries is developed and combined with a longer term view of the debt problem, then the possibility of a future crisis remains. In order to cover for this latter contingency, arrangements concerning the sharing of lender of last resort responsibilities need to be made by the OECD central banks, the BIS, and international agencies such as the IMF and the IBRD. We shall discuss this matter further in Chapter 8.

NOTES

1. *See* Cohen (1981) for a detailed account of the origins of the problem and Lever and Huhne (1985), Nunnenkamp (1986) and Lomax (1986) for accounts of the origins and history of the problem.
2. For simplicity we shall not distinguish between LDCs and newly industrialised countries (NICs), even though some of the major Latin American debtors fall into the latter category.
3. OPEC is the Organisation of Petroleum Exporting Countries; *see* Danielson (1982) for an account of its evolution.
4. *See* Lever and Huhne (1985).
5. i.e. the ability of money made available for one purpose to free other money for other uses.
6. *See* Lever and Huhne (1985).
7. North Sea oil production, for example, increased rapidly in the early 1980s.
8. *See* Kraft (1984) for a detailed account of the Mexican rescue.
9. Although European banks had two-thirds of the Latin American exposure, *see* Lever and Huhne (1985) for details.
10. 'Letters of intent' make detailed policy proposals and set targets for key economic indicators.
11. By Morgan Guaranty in particular; *see* War on Want (1985) and Lever and Huhne (1985) for details. These have subsequently been disputed by Mexico's Central bank and by Dr W. Cline of the Institute for International Economics who argue that they are gross overestimates; *see* Cline (1986).
12. *See* Lever and Huhne (1985) for further discussion.
13. *See* the Bank for International Settlements Annual and Quarterly reports in 1985 and 1986 for details.
14. *See* Chapter 14.
15. *See* Crawford (1985), Cohen (1985) and Lever and Huhne (1985).
16. *See* Lever and Huhne (1985).
17. *See* Lever and Huhne (1985).
18. *See* Appendix C.
19. *See* Chapter 3.
20. In its *World Development Report*, July 1985.
21. Civilian government returned to Argentina in late 1983 and to Brazil in early 1985.
22. Statements to this effect were careful not to stimulate inflationary

expectations and usually advocated a reduction of market rigidities, especially in the labour market.

23. *See* Lever and Huhne (1985).
24. For example in the Press Communique of the thirty-first annual meeting of the Intergovernmental Group of Twenty-Four on IMF Affairs; *see IMF Survey* 29 April 1985 for details.
25. Argentina and Brazil have engaged the IMF in lengthy negotiations, for example.
26. The status of sovereign loans is reviewed twice yearly by the US Inter-Agency Country Review Committee, which includes representatives of the Federal Reserve, the Federal Deposit Insurance Corporation, and the Comptroller of Currency. Loans may be downgraded to a 'substandard' or 'value-impaired' status without being formally declared as 'non-performing', in which case they would have to be removed from the balance sheet, causing a marked reduction in profits. Under the International Banking Act (1985), when loans are declared 'substandard' banks are not required to set aside reserves but are warned that reserve provisions will be mandatorily required if interest and principal payments are not returned to a regular basis. In the case of 'value-impaired' loans, reserves must be set aside to cover potential losses and the banks must write down the value of their loans and hence profits are reduced.
27. The package, agreed in April 1984, involved a $500bn bridging loan consisting of $200bn from the US and $300bn from the four Latin American countries, including Mexico and Brazil, which was guaranteed by the US. The IMF was believed to have given the package implicit backing. As a result Argentina was able to resume interest payments in April.
28. The time it amounted to $483bn and involved the US and eleven other countries including Japan, France, Canada, Mexico, Brazil, Venezuela and a number of smaller industrialised countries. The UK, West Germany and Switzerland refused to take part in the loan, which was made in June 1985. Argentina's overdue interest was paid in late June 1985, thus preventing Argentinian loans being downgraded to a 'value-impaired' status; *see* note 26.
29. *See* Spraos (1984).
30. Especially concerning monetary, government spending and inflation targets.
31. Prospects for grain exports were good in 1984, owing to a good harvest and a Russian shortage. Beef prices were also good and beef and grain together account for about 70 per cent of Argentina's exports.
32. *See* note 11.
33. i.e. devaluation and the introduction of a new currency, the Austral.
34. *See* below.
35. i.e. devaluation and the introduction of a new currency, the cruzado.
36. Dubbed the OPEC III oil shock; *see* Section 3.
37. The Paris Club is the forum within which countries negotiate the restructuring of public sector debt owed to the seventeen governments

of the Development Assistance Committee (DAC) of the OECD. Debts restructured by the Paris Club consist of loans from the creditor governments and private export credits which are guaranteed or insured by export credit agencies in the creditor countries. The Club has no written rules but abides by a set of procedures developed since it came into being in 1956. It does not normally negotiate with countries to which export credit guarantees are suspended.

38. These negotiations were complicated by the failure, in 1985, of three Brazilian private sector banks which the government had refused to support. The banks owed money to many of the 700 creditor banks involved in the restructuring. The creditor banks argued that they had been encouraged to make loans to the failed banks by the Brazilian authorities. No state guarantees had been given, however; the question was one of moral responsibility. Much of the foreign lending had passed through Brazil's banking system, under government resolution sixty-three. Until the dispute is resolved the creditor banks are likely to be unwilling to continue to lend through the private banks, especially at a time when the Brazilian financial system is under strain as a result of the deindexing introduced by the Plan Tropical. The Brazilian banks had, for example, made lucrative returns on index-linked government bonds.
39. See *IMF Survey* 29 April 1985 for details.
40. The General Agreement on Trade and Tariffs.
41. Which represents the Third World countries at the IMF and the IBRD; see Chapter 7.
42. See Solomon (1985) for further discussion.
43. See War on Want (1985).
44. Given simmering trade disputes between the US and a number of its major trading partners and between the EEC and Japan.
45. G5 is the Group of Five major industrial countries; see Chapter 7.
46. Growth fell from 8.5 per cent in 1984 to 3 per cent in 1985.
47. Brazil (OI), Argentina (OI), Bolivia (OE), Columbia (OE), Equador (OE), Mexico (OE), Peru (OE), Venezuela (OE), Chile (OI) and Uruguay (OI). (OE = oil exporter, OI = oil importer.)
48. Nigeria (OE), Ivory Coast (OI), Yugoslavia (OI), Morocco (OI) and the Philippines (OI). (OE = oil exporter, OI = oil importer.)
49. In line with the Gramm–Rudeman–Hollings Act (1986).
50. From the triple alliance of Libya, Iran and Algeria.
51. Following the US air strike on Libya and as a result of the increasing tension between Syria and Israel and an intensification of the Iran–Iraq war.
52. See notes 47 and 48.
53. Especially from Germany and Japan; see Chapter 7 for further discussion.
54. See Chapter 7 for further discussion.
55. See Chapter 7 for further discussion.
56. Concerning farming, services and manufacturing trade.
57. Which had, in July 1986, exceeded 40 per cent against the dollar since the lows of the first quarter of 1985.

58. *See* Chapter 7 for further discussion.
59. Between the debtors, the large medium and small commercial banks, the industrial country governments and the IMF and the IBRD.
60. This view was shared by the accounting firm Peat Marwick, which published a report in June 1986 surveying allowances for sovereign risks. It discovered an overall improvement in banks' ability to withstand defaults. Reserve provisioning, however, varied between countries according to the IBCA, a London-based banking analysis company. It published a report in November 1985 which estimated that large US banks had made provisions amounting to 10 per cent of their outstanding debt. A similar figure was estimated for the UK, whereas the French and German banks were estimated to have made provisions of about 20 per cent, with the Swiss banks' provisions exceeding this and the Japanese banks having provisions of 5 per cent. Exact figures were not available due to the existence of hidden reserves and differing accounting conventions. The IBCA noted that this variability was likely to cause problems in negotiations concerning the Latin American debt, the banks with larger provisions being more willing to take a loss. The IBCA recommended that all banks should raise provisions to at least 20 per cent of their exposure, to cover the discount at which loans were being traded.
61. *See* Chapter 7.
62. Which, together with the Japanese banks, hold two-thirds of the debt.
63. Institute for International Economics (1985).
64. *See* Chandavarkar (1984) for details of IMF funding.
65. *See* Cohen (1985).
66. *See* Bank for International Settlements annual reports 1985 and 1986.
67. Such as West Germany, Switzerland and Japan.
68. The large US banking group.
69. *See* Chapter 7.
70. Floating Rate Notes, *See* Chapter 4.
71. Institute for International Economics (1985).
72. The IMF already has a compensatory finance facility (CFF) to help the producers of some commodities, and it introduced a special oil facility to help LDCs cope with oil price increases. It established a special facility in 1986 to help Mexico cope with the oil price fall and this could be widened so that other oil-producing LDCs could qualify. Given the generalised fall in commodity prices in the first half of the 1980s the CFF could usefully be expanded and the major beneficiaries of the price fall, the industrial countries, would be natural contributors to its funding.
73. At a time when it was approaching 13 per cent.
74. At a privately sponsored international monetary conference which met in Zurich on 28–30 June.
75. *See* Chapter 7.

6 European Monetary Integration

6.1 THE PRESENT ARRANGEMENTS[1]

Monetary integration is an integral part of the overall process of economic and political integration within the European Communities (EC). The European Monetary System (EMS) represents a step on the road towards European Monetary Union (EMU) and the formation of a European Monetary Fund (EMF). The EMS has two major components: the European Monetary Cooperation Fund (EMCF), which is essentially a foreign currency reserve swapping agreement, and an Exchange Rate Mechanism (ERM), through which the participants attempt to maintain exchange rate relationships within a 2¼ per cent band with the currencies of other member states. The UK and Greece are members of the EMS but do not participate in the ERM. The new members, Spain and Portgal,[2] face a programme of adjustment to full membership and do not yet participate in the EMS.

The European Currency Unit, which is based on a basket of currencies, is the numeraire used for fixing exchange rates within the ERM. The basket includes the currencies of all EMS member states weighted in accordance with each country's share of output and trade. Changes in the ECU's components were envisaged when the EMS was established in March 1979. The first revision of the weights occurred in September 1984 in order to take account of the new EC membership of Greece and the inclusion of the drachma in the EMS and the ECU and further changes will clearly be required when Spain and Portugal participate in the EMS. The currency realignments that occurred in the first four years of the EMS had altered the relationships between the currencies making up the ECU and there had also been some change in the relative output of and trade flows between the member countries. The revised weights aimed to take account of these factors. Significantly, there was a reduction in the weighting on the Deutschmark, from 37 per cent to 32 per cent of each ECU, and the Dutch guilder, which have been the strongest currencies. There were fears that this might reduce the attractiveness of ECU-dominated bonds, bank accounts and bank loans, but there has been little evidence of this.

The initial agreement by the Council of Ministers in March 1979 setting up the EMS envisaged that consideration would be given to progressing to a second stage of monetary integration in March 1981. It would have involved the establishment of a pool of reserves in a European Monetary Fund, which was seen as an embryonic European central bank. This second phase, which has not been entered into, would involve a major step towards political union; requiring the transfer of some responsibilities from national central banks to a potential European central bank. This in turn entails the possible loss of control, by member state governments, over monetary and exchange rate policy. The Bundesbank, which has constitutional responsibility for the Deutschmark and monetary policy in the Federal Republic of Germany, opposed moving to the second stage on the grounds that there had been insufficient monetary policy convergence. A major obstacle preventing the establishment of an EMF or a European central bank is that it would be a supranational organisation. Many regard the EC as a potential federation of countries, so that European central banking responsibility should lie with something more akin to the FRS of the USA. In this case the central banks of the member countries of the EC would remain intact but their actions would be co-ordinated by a central board or committee on which they would have voting rights.

The Banking Federation of the EC (1980) outlined the roles of the ECU in the first stage of the EMS. These were: to act as numeraire for fixing exchange rates within the ERM, to perform the function of unit of account within the EC, and to serve as a reserve asset with limited usage for transactions between central banks. In the second stage of integration the EMF would replace the EMCF and the ECU would become a more widely used means of payment with its reserve asset role substantially extended. Preconditions for wider use of the ECU were judged to be the following: the elimination of legal obstacles in member states so that ECU accounts and ECU-denominated securities could be held by the private sector, the provision of lender of last resort facilities, in connection with private sector ECU accounts to commercial banks by their central banks or the EMF, the introduction of short term assets in ECUs to enable the commercial banks to hold ECU reserves assets and the central banks to discount them in performing their lender of last resort functions, and the development of an ECU capital market, which is connected to the desire to develop a European capital market with freedom of capital flows within the EEC, in line with the Treaty of Rome.

There has already been some progress towards the development of an ECU-denominated capital market. The BIS[3] has reported[4] on the growing number and value of ECU-denominated Eurobond and FRN issues and on the growing private market in ECU-denominated bank accounts and loans.[5] Since the ECU does not yet exist as a currency, cash withdrawals from such accounts have to be made in the constituent currencies but other transactions can be made in ECU units. A group of eighteen commercial banks set up a clearing house for ECUs in 1983 but following the rapid adoption of ECUs for private transactions they approached the BIS, which has experience of clearing official ECUs for central banks but is not an EC institution and does not normally undertake such business for commercial banks. In February 1986 the BIS agreed to act as the central clearing agent in an international clearing system for bank deposits denominated in ECUs.[6] In so doing it made it clear that it was not willing to extend lender of last resort cover for private ECU deposits and only undertook the business once it had assured itself that it would not assume such a role *de facto* and that it would not undermine efforts by individual EC countries to control their own money supplies. Also, in March 1985, the central banks and finance ministers of the member countries gave their blessing to a package designed to encourage the use of the ECU as an official reserve asset. In future, non-EC central banks will be permitted to hold official ECUs in their reserves and remuneration on these reserves will be raised from the weighted average of the discount rates on the component currencies to a level closer to market rates. In addition the ECU would be used more extensively, relative to the dollar, for currency interventions within the ERM. The package stopped short of introducing measures to encourage greater private use of the ECU, partly out of deference to opposition from the Bundesbank.

The EMS had its sixth anniversary in March 1985. Under the ERM, exchange rate fluctuations between the participants appear to have been considerably reduced. In addition inflation rates and monetary policies have converged, though perhaps less than the German authorities had hoped. There were seven realignments of currencies within the ERM between March 1979 and March 1983. There then followed a period of stability which was broken in July 1985 when the Italian lira came under pressure. Italy had been experiencing both high inflation and strong growth relative to most of the other EMS members, especially Germany. This had caused a deterioration in the balance of payments, owing to rising imports, and pressure on the exchange rate. The crisis was sparked by the purchase of a substantial amount of dollars by the state energy group (ENI) to make a debt repayment. The Bank of Italy chose not to intervene to protect the lira and a political controversy resulted. On Black Friday, 19 July, following the ENI exchange rate dealings the lira depreciated rapidly against both the dollar and the Deutschmark and the Italian Treasury suspended dealings in the lira. Over the weekend European monetary officials arranged a realignment of EMS exchange rates. The lira was devalued by 6 per cent and the other currencies were revalued by 2 per cent. The realignment was not as complex as most of the previous ones, which had involved adjustment of the exchange rates between various countries rather than a simple devaluation of one currency relative to the others. The previous realignment, in March 1983, was caused by the weakness of the French franc relative to the Deutschmark. It was part of a package deal in which the French government agreed to toughen its austerity measures to deal with the country's balance of trade and inflation problems in return for German acquiescence on the realignment. The result of this policy convergence was the period of stability that ended with the lira's devaluation. The July 1985 realignment was accompanied by the announcement of austerity measures by the Italian government, designed essentially to reduce the government deficit. Thus recent realignments have been agreed subject to measures being imposed to increase policy coordination in the hope that this will reduce the need for further realignments. The lira returned to normal trading on the following Monday and made some gains against the dollar. Pressure for a further realignment in the latter half of 1985 was expected because of the strength of the Deutschmark relative to the Belgian and French francs, which in part reflected the lower inflation and stronger export performance of Germany and the decline in the attractiveness of the dollar. The French and German governments successfully intervened to prevent any realignment prior to the March 1986 general election in France. Following the election, which installed a conservative government in place of the socialists, a realignment was agreed in April 1986. This basically involved a 5.8 per cent devaluation of the franc against the Deutschmark. There was no crisis, the realignment following a weekend of negotiations between EMS country finance ministers. The franc was devalued by approximately 3 per cent and the Deutschmark was revalued by approximately 3 per cent. Other changes included a revaluation of the Dutch guilder by 3 per cent and a 1 per cent revaluation of the Danish krone and the Belgian franc.

The European Commission appointed a new President in 1985, M. Jacques Delors. He adopted the portfolio on monetary affairs and made it clear that he aimed to make progress in the area of European monetary integration. In October 1985 he unveiled proposals for developing the EMS and enshrining it, along with the procedure for establishing the EMF as an embryonic central bank, in the articles of the Treaty of Rome. The plan viewed the ECU as the foundation of the system and envisaged the EMCF being given the autonomy necessary to perform its task and eventually being converted to an EMF. The writing of the EMS into the Treaty would permit the European Commission to make proposals for the further development of the EMS, which previously could only be tabled by the Council of Ministers. Delors's proposals also provided for the European Commission to be represented on the EMCF board, places on which had previously been confined to central bank representatives.

Despite a cool reception by the Bundesbank and opposition from UK and German Ministers to the implied future loss of autonomy by their central banks, Delors strongly defended the proposals, which were being considered along with a wider package. In December 1985 a compromise agreement was reached by the ministers concerning the reform package that included monetary affairs in the Treaty. This could prove a double-edged sword for proponents of further integration. Future development of the EMS now requires unanimous intergovernmental conference and ratification by national Parliaments, instead of unanimity in the Council of Ministers. Eventual participation in the EMS and the ERM is now, however, seemingly required of all EC members, including the UK, by the Treaty. Further, the EC has succeeded in gaining a say in the development of the EMS but the procedure for its reform now appears to be more difficult. The prospects for further monetary integration will be discussed in the next section.

6.2 FUTURE PROSPECTS

The major European central banks already cooperate externally through their membership of the BIS. The BIS collects and disseminates information and provides central banking services to its members.[7] Through it they also pool funds and make loans to member banks and to non-member countries. Hence the BIS, alongside the EMCF, performs some central banking functions in Europe. Any further development towards a European central bank, and European monetary integration in general, would require cooperation between the member countries and their central banks involving the coordination of monetary, and probably fiscal, policies and some loss of autonomy.

The Bundesbank is constitutionally constrained to protect the value of the Deutschmark and is independent of the government. Any progress towards the establishment of a

European central bank with control over the supply of ECUs, and other currencies, that implied a reduction in the Bundesbank's control over the Deutschmark would therefore require constitutional amendment. The Bundesbank and the German government are unlikely to sanction such developments until they are satisfied that there has been sufficient convergence of policies and performances within the EC. The Bundesbank believes that steps towards a European currency are conceivable only if the institutional preconditions for a uniform European monetary policy have been created beforehand and agreement on a common European central bank system has been reached. Further progress on integration and the expansion of the private role of the ECU should await greater convergence in monetary, and perhaps fiscal, policy and inflation than so far achieved and the elimination of the current weaknesses in the EMS. It has argued that greater freedom of capital movements, which would impose market discipline and encourage convergence, are a prerequisite for further integration initiatives, and so are UK membership of the ERM and the adherence by Italy to the 2¼ per cent band, rather than the 6 six per cent transitional margin, on the lira.

In 1985, the Bundesbank argued that lack of convergence had caused Italy and France, among others, to maintain restrictions on capital mobility which were anachronistic six years after the formation of the EMS. Unlike Germany, both countries recognised the ECU as foreign exchange, but both subjected it to exchange controls. For French citizens this amounted to a *de facto* ban on holding ECU accounts and also prevented them from acquiring ECU claims[8] in unlimited amounts, as their German neighbours could do. In the light of these arguments the Bundesbank has not supported the extension of private use of the ECU. This is because it is not a currency, and cannot become one until the central banking machinery is established to control its supply, and also because its private use reflects not the strengths but the weaknesses of the EMS. To the extent that its popularity derives from the protection it gives against the exchange rate risk involved in intracommunity capital transactions, which the EMS is supposed to eliminate, as well as the interest rate differentials that contribute to the flows that cause them, the private use of the ECU reflects the shortcomings rather than the strength of the EMS.

Nevertheless, in June 1985 a slight softening of the Bundesbank's stance on the private use of the ECU was detected. The Bundesbank announced that it was not going to drop its ban on residents holding private ECU bank accounts in Germany but would become less dogmatic on the issue in future, especially if other EC countries removed obstacles on the use of the ECU in their territories. The Bundesbank claimed that ECU accounts had not been permitted so far because they might set a precedent for other forms of indexation in West Germany and that it was not hostile to the ECU as such. Section 3 of West German currency law forbids indexed liabilities in the form of debts whose value depends on other currencies but which are payable in Deutschmarks. The introduction of ECU-denominated private accounts into West Germany would, therefore, require an amendment to this law. There is a further risk that an uncontrolled increase in the use of private ECUs might undermine the Bundesbank's monetary control policies. Initial interest in ECU accounts and loans has come from the weak-currency countries[9] so that, as long as the Deutschmark remains strong, interest in Germany and hence impact on monetary policy is likely to be small. There is, however, some evidence that German citizens hold sizeable ECU accounts in the Luxembourg subsidiaries of German banks.

From the Bundesbank's comments it is clear that it would not object to the development of an ECU-based currency once sufficient policy and performance convergence had been achieved, provided that its supply was controlled by some form of European central bank which was independently constituted and so given freedom from European governmental pressures, in the manner of the Bundesbank's relationship with the West German government. As far as permitting the opening of private ECU accounts in Germany is concerned, it appeared that Germany might consider a deal involving, in return, action to reduce restrictions on capital flows, especially in Italy and France, membership of the ERM by the UK, adherence to the $2\frac{1}{4}$ per cent, rather than the current 6 per cent, margin by the lira, and greater efforts by other EC countries to reduce their inflation rates. The package agreed by the Bundesbank with the other EC central banks to promote the official use of the ECU at least showed some willingness to support further European monetary integration.

Statements made by the President of the Bundesbank, Mr Karl Otto Poehl, in April and May 1986 appeared to indicate a warming of the Bundesbank toward prospects of further monetary integration. The Bundesbank had previously been keener to stress the obstacles than to commit itself to the ultimate goal. Poehl expressed satisfaction with the fiscal and monetary convergence being achieved and with the falling inflation rates and close cooperation between the EC member country central banks. The Bundesbank was also encouraged by the March election of a French government whose policies were more in accord with its own than the previous socialist one. It was particularly pleased by the commitment being shown by France and Italy to the removal of exchange and capital controls. It issued a strong plea for the UK to join the ERM, stating that consolidation and evolution of the EMS could make a major contribution to political and economic integration in Europe but UK membership was a prerequisite. It even stated that the final aim should be a European currency issued and controlled by a European central bank but warned that this development was a long way off. Poehl accepted that UK membership would give the system a different quality but rejected the view that it would reduce stability, despite its petrocurrency status. He stated that the other prerequisite for consolidating the EMS was full integration of money and capital markets achieved through the removal of controls and restrictions. The UK is viewed as a major ally in pursuit of this goal.

Since the inception of the EMS in March 1979, there has been an intermittent debate within the UK concerning the merits of UK membership of the ERM. Initially the Treasury view, as voiced by Chancellor Geoffrey Howe, was that the time was not ripe to join. The pound was entering a period of uncertainty due to its assumption of a petrocurrency status, because sterling oil revenue had begun to flow, oil exports were increasing and the OPEC II oil price increase was beginning to bite. Additionally, the pound was overvalued, partly as a result of the oil factor. With the re-election of the Thatcher government and the appointment of a new Chancellor, Nigel Lawson, in June 1983, the debate concerning the merits of UK membership resurfaced. Oil prices had fallen somewhat by 1983 and the pound had depreciated. In addition the government appeared to have adopted a policy of keeping sterling exchange rates within unpublished bands against the dollar and the trade-weighted index. Some commentators therefore asked why the government did not choose to join the ERM and thereby formally announce exchange rate targets and enjoy the help of other ERM member central banks, through the EMCF and related credit mechanisms, to keep sterling within its band.[10]

In January 1985 the pound depreciated considerably against the dollar, the Deutschmark, and the trade-weighted index as a result of weakness in the oil market and a suspicion of laxity in the government's pursuit of monetary targets. The UK monetary authorities responded by engineering a $4\frac{1}{2}$ per cent interest rate rise whilst interest rates in the ERM-participating countries were raised by a much smaller amount, to prevent their depreciation against the dollar. In Germany, for example, they were raised by $\frac{1}{2}$ per cent. The March 1985 UK budget statement announced that the exchange rate would figure more prominently in the medium term financial strategy (MTFS).[11] Many commentators argued that the drastic rise in interest rates could have been avoided if the UK had been participating in the ERM and there were renewed calls, by the Confederation of British Industries (CBI) and the Alliance parties for example, for the UK to join. In the summer of 1985, however, the pound appreciated against the Deutschmark and many supporters of membership felt that the optimum time for entry had passed. They felt that entry should occur at exchange rates, especially against the Deutschmark, that would give the UK a 'fair' competitive position and that such rates prevailed in early 1985 but no longer held in the summer of that year.

The exchange rate at which sterling would enter the ERM is of course one that would be set following negotiations with the other participating countries, whose concept of a 'fair' exchange rate might differ from that of the UK government. It is, however, probably true that conceptions of 'fairness' will be influenced by the prevailing exchange rates, but trade balances will also need to be taken into account. Therefore, undue emphasis on the current exchange as an indicator of the appropriateness of time of entry has probably been given.

In the latter half of 1985, especially following the September Plaza Agreement,[12] the dollar depreciated against all the major currencies and the pound depreciated against the Deutschmark. Following the change in OPEC policy,[13] announced in December 1985, the oil price slumped in January 1986 and the pound began to depreciate rapidly, partly due to its petrocurrency status but also due to renewed worries about laxity in monetary policy. Having fallen in a number of stages since January 1985, interest rates were again raised in January 1986, this time by 2 per cent. The authorities responded to concerns about its monetary policy by effectively demoting money and promoting the exchange rate as an indicator of monetary policy in the March 1986 Budget statement. This had been heralded in the Chancellor's October 1985 Mansion House speech. The Chancellor also went to some length to point out in his Budget statement that the UK economy was not heavily dependent on oil, which accounts for only 5 per cent of GNP, nor was its trade balance. Since then the pound proved less responsive to oil price fluctuations and arguments against UK membership based on sterling's petrocurrency status seemed to have lost some weight. In the three months following the March Budget statement oil prices were fairly stable and even rose above the lows hit in April. There was renewed pressure on sterling in July 1986, however, following a fall in oil prices to below their April nadir. The extent to which this was attributable to the oil price fall was difficult to determine, however, since the dollar had staged a minor and short-lived recovery at the same time and there were political considerations generating uncertainty about the future prospects of the Thatcher government. The pound again stabilised following the surprise OPEC production-limiting agreement in August 1986 and the ending of the Parliamentary session. By then the pound had depreciated approximately 20 per cent against the Deutschmark since January 1986.

The UK Treasury has opposed UK membership of the ERM for a number of reasons.[14] The ones stressed most recently have been the impropriety of joining until the dollar and oil prices have stabilised. This view is also strongly advocated by Loehnis (1985) of the Bank of England. Because of the petrocurrency effect and the dollar effect, he argues that it will prove impossible for the pound to participate in the ERM without frequent realignments. The pound could of course be allowed a wider band, like Italy, until the influences of these effects died down. The petrocurrency effect results from the fact that the UK is a large net oil exporter whilst Germany and the other ERM members are large oil importers. Changes in oil prices and the dollar, in which oil prices are denominated, effect the balance of trade of the UK and the other members in opposite directions and will, therefore, have a destabilising effect. This argument may, however, have been overplayed since the non-oil sector of the UK economy also stands to gain from falling oil prices. The fall in the dollar has, however, added to the strains on currencies within the ERM since the Deutschmark is a major reserve currency and an alternative to the dollar, whose attractiveness has declined. A falling dollar, therefore, forces the Deutschmark up relative to other ERM members, because of its increased attractiveness. The pound too is a reserve currency which benefits from a fall in the dollar, although its status as a major international currency continues to decline, especially with the increased interest in the ECU and the yen.

During 1985 and 1986 the pound fluctuated by over 20 per cent against the Deutschmark. Such fluctuations are aided and abetted by the fact that neither the UK nor Germany operates exchange controls restricting capital flows. It is not clear that membership of the ERM would have inhibited capital flows between Frankfurt and London or the relative flows to these financial centres from New York and elsewhere. The dollar, however, appeared to be approaching levels consistent with the balancing of trade flows in mid 1986, although some argued that a further 10 to 15 per cent depreciation might be required.[15] Future massive swings in the dollar exchange rates cannot of course be ruled out unless the international monetary system is reformed, an issue to which we will return in Chapter 7. In the short term, however, it would appear that the dollar effect resulting from the inclusion of two reserve currencies, or bipolarity, may be less important and the sterling/Deutschmark exchange rate will depend more on economic fundamentals. In mid 1986 these included an inflation differential of nearly 4 per cent in Germany's favour and a much more rapid rise in unit labour costs in the UK.

The Treasury and the Bank are also concerned that ERM membership would result in a loss of autonomy concerning monetary and exchange rate policy. It is after all true that an objective of the system is to force convergence in monetary and perhaps fiscal or budget policy and, as a corollary, inflation rates. Given that the dominant currency in the ERM would remain the Deutschmark and that the Bundesbank has a tighter monetary and the German government a tighter budgetary policy than that prevailing in the UK, there seems little to fear on this score for a government whose objectives really are sound financial management and inflation control. The Thatcher government's policies, as laid down in the MTFS, after all profess to accord with these goals. The Bundesbank is, however, not only insulated from UK influence but also from that of the German government. It is not accountable to any electorate, and it would be calling the tune.

A related concern is that membership would require the government to sanction larger and more frequent interest rate changes and additionally or alternatively to intervene more frequently on the foreign exchange markets, committing larger amounts of reserves than previously. This argument is a bit weak in the light of the experiences in the Januarys of 1985 and 1986 which had left the UK with an interest rate differential of up to 5 per cent against ERM member countries. Further, alternative methods of monetary control such as base control, which is believed to have been seriously considered by the Treasury though opposed by the Bank of England, would also require large interest rate fluctuations.

In October 1984, the Treasury was urged, by the Bank and the Foreign Office, to reconsider its position on ERM membership and Whitehall undertook a study of the costs and benefits of UK participation. Also, as a result of pressure for entry, a House of Commons Treasury and Civil Service Committee was set up to assess the merits of membership. It reported in November 1985 and published two volumes of evidence.[16] The committee voted five to four against membership in the short term though it did not rule out future participation. It therefore reaffirmed the government's position that the time for membership was not yet ripe. The opponents of entry were divided into two groups. One argued that the pound was still overvalued against the Deutschmark, a view subsequently supported by the Public Policy Centre (PPC), a think-tank with links to the Social Democratic Party, in March 1986. The PPC did not, however, concur that this ruled out immediate entry since, if sterling entered with a wider margin of ± 6 per cent like Italy around their estimate of the appropriate rate, the prevailing overvalued rate could have been accommodated. The Deutschmark would simply trade at near the bottom of its band with sterling initially. By August 1986 the pound had depreciated by a further 10 per cent or so and was close to the appropriate rate calculated by the PPC. The other group, comprising of the Labour Party members of the committee, opposed membership for more fundamental reasons. They were concerned about the loss of policy independence and were unwilling to commit a future Labour government. More generally, they felt that the EMS imparted a deflationary bias due to the policies of the Bundesbank. The select committee did, however, acknowledge that membership would be likely to confer the benefits of more stable exchange rates, facilitating financial planning by industry in connection with their investment and export strategies, and a counter-inflationary influence, especially on wage bargaining. There was thus some support for the CBI view that membership would benefit its members by reducing exchange rate volatility. There was also indirect support for the CBI view that membership would afford protection to sterling and allow a substantial reduction in the UK's interest rate differential with the participating countries, thereby reducing industry's costs.

In 1985 the government seems to have reverted to the policy, which had proved successful in the early 1980s, of using high exchange rates as an anti-inflationary weapon. It has the direct effect of reducing import prices but it was also hoped that it would exert pressure on industry to reduce wage costs in order to maintain competitiveness in foreign markets. It was thus being used in place of an incomes policy. To the extent that joining the ERM at a higher rate of exchange with the Deutschmark than the CBI would like would keep up this pressure but allow a reduction in interest rates, and consequently industry's costs, membership would not be inconsistent with this policy. Further, it might encourage the de-indexation of wages, as it had in other ERM member countries, and thereby exert a downward pressure on real wages. Economists and analysts at major US investment banks, such as Chase Manhattan Securities and Goldman Sachs, observed that the UK monetary authorities had seemingly adopted a 'punk' ERM policy of shadowing the participating currencies through interest rate changes whilst maintaining exchange rates at levels designed to force the manufacturing sector to control wage costs. The CBI seemed to accord with this view and its President and General Secretary both appealed to its membership to control wage costs at their 1985 annual conference.

More fundamental reservations about entry were expressed by Goodhart (1986) and Walters (1986). Sir Alan Walters is a former economic adviser to the Prime Minister, Margaret Thatcher, and was still believed to be influential. He concluded that it would be difficult for a small country like the UK, with no exchange or credit controls to pursue fixed exchange rates because capital movements on a potentially large scale would make monetary policy perverse. Things might be different if the EMS were to develop into a currency board system akin to that in Hong Kong, where the monetary system responds quasiautomatically, with reserve and currency changes, to any pressure on the foreign exchanges. Otherwise successful entry would require some reimposition of capital controls and probably domestic credit rationing. Budd (1986) considers Walters's argument that free capital flows will tend to equalise nominal interest rates and, given differing inflation rates, cause differential real interest rates, making them higher in Germany, for example, than Italy. This in turn would cause a divergence in monetary policies. Budd concludes that the capital flows would also alter reserve positions and that trade flows would tend to equalise inflation rates. The resulting pressure on reserves would force countries with high inflation to cut their budget deficits, forcing convergence. In other words policy, and eventually inflation and real interest rate, convergence would be assured by the free market flows that Walters had argued would have perverse effects.

Goodhart (1986) noted that growing dissatisfaction with domestic policies had caused a shift in attitude towards favouring UK membership of the ERM. The performance of the sterling M3 money aggregate had weakened confidence in monetary targeting and high wage inflation continued alongside very high swings in interest and exchange rates, adding to uncertainty. He argued that the volatility of interest rates is likely to increase within the ERM, because exchange controls are being progressively lifted in Italy and France[17] and will eventually be removed by the new members. This would lead to larger capital flows within Europe and particularly between its two major financial centres, London and Frankfurt, in the bipolar system that would result from UK entry. These flows would be large relative to the reserves that the authorities could use without putting them at risk by borrowing or operating on forward markets. UK entry into a system with increasingly free capital flows would lead to stability only if the government was willing to give up its national policy-making autonomy, he argued. Goodhart favoured reduced autonomy and the development of a Euro central bank along with a Euro fiscal authority, but acknowledged that this was futuristic. In the short term the choice lay between free markets and floating exchange rates with autonomy, as in the UK, or ERM membership with autonomy and exchange controls, as Italy and France had previously chosen. Thus he concurs with Walters that exchange controls would need to be reimposed to preserve autonomy following UK entry. He concludes that an optimal currency area can be formed only when the political institutions are sufficiently developed. Poehl has, however, made it clear that these cannot be put into place without UK participation in the ERM and action to achieve free capital and monetary flows, which the UK is expected to support. Since the present UK government is extremely unlikely to reimpose exchange controls, and the Labour opposition[18] also pronounced against them in 1986, entry would indeed appear to imply a loss of autonomy.

Samuel Brittan[19] has pointed out that the choice between depreciation and/or reserve commitment is one that exists within or outside the ERM. He argues that pressures on sterling may well be more severe outside the ERM. Joining it would not affect market forces but might influence the market's concept of the level of the likely sterling/Deutschmark rate to which a number of central banks, and not just the Bank of England in isolation, would be committed. He also argues that the bipolarity and dollar effect arguments have been overplayed and that, given that exchange rate targeting has already been adopted, the UK should enter.

Why then did the government continue to defer entry when ERM membership would reinforce its anti-inflationary strategy and support its efforts to pursue exchange rate targets? In April 1986 speeches by the current Chancellor, Nigel Lawson, and the previous Chancellor and current Foreign Secretary, Sir Geoffrey Howe, urged ERM entry, when the time was right. Lawson went so far as to say that he saw no role for exchange rate policy outside the ERM. Other Cabinet Ministers also pronounced in favour of entry. Prime Minister Thatcher, however, made her opposition to entry clear. She stated in the House of Commons that she wished to retain the option of letting sterling take the strain in times of speculation against the pound, rather than be forced to use large amounts of reserves or to raise interest rates further. This in turn raised the questions of why she would expect a run on sterling and whether the reserve position was particularly weak.

The UK had in fact increased its foreign currency reserves substantially in September 1985 by borrowing $2.5bn through FRN[20] issues. This had sparked speculation at the time about an imminent ERM entry. Previously the reserves had been judged inadequate, by the Bundesbank amongst others. After September 1985 there was little significant intervention, except that against the dollar involving purchases rather than sales, and reserves increased until August 1986 when there was renewed pressure on the pound requiring significant supportive intervention. The government further bolstered its reserves in September 1986 with a $4bn FRN issue. With the added support of other central banks, through the EMCF, the

UK's reserve position would probably now be adequate. The UK experience of reserve loss when it had to protect sterling in the 'snake'[21] in 1972, however, still weighs heavily in Treasury and perhaps Mrs Thatcher's considerations.

Mrs Thatcher's opposition seemingly derives more from arguments akin to Walters (1986), which imply that membership would result in a loss of policy-making autonomy, especially in the face of a sterling crisis. But why was a sterling crisis expected in the near future? Oil prices seemed unlikely to fall much further and their renewed fall in June and July 1986, which was subsequently reversed, had only caused a hiccup for sterling. Sterling did in fact depreciate further against the Deutschmark in the autumn of 1986, forcing the Chancellor to raise interest rates by a percentage point. This was regarded as a belated adjustment to the fall in oil prices, which had by then rebounded following the temporary OPEC output agreement and in response to the prospect of rising oil demand in the autumn and winter months. By December 1986 the Chancellor and the Bank of England judged sterling's adjustment to be complete. It had been achieved relatively smoothly, without a major crisis, although at some cost to the UK's foreign currency reserves. There was renewed speculation about sterling's imminent entry into the ERM, but this was again discounted by the Prime Minister. Another causal factor could be a renewed loss of confidence in the government's anti-inflation policy, but this could be dealt with by UK entry and following the course set by the good ship Bundesbank, which is unlikely to do anything rash. The balance of trade prospects were, however, a bit gloomy in the medium term, because of the decline in the oil surplus, rising unit labour costs and high consumption levels, which were sucking in imports. Some feared that there was a risk of jitters following the Big Bang[22] in October 1986, especially if it caused a few early casualties, resulting in an outflow of funds from the City. Commonly, however, a sterling crisis occurs in the run up to an election in which a change in government, and more particularly the return of a Labour government, is likely. The depreciation of the pound in autumn 1986 was in fact attributed in part, by some commentators to speculation about an early election at a time when Labour held a lead in the opinion polls. Thatcher's current opposition, combined with her longer term commitment, to joining the ERM could therefore be interpreted as an indication that a general election would be called prior to the end of the government's term in 1988. It was expected that the depreciation in the exchange rate and the rise in interest rates, in the autumn of 1986, would lead to a small rise in inflation in 1987, but the policy of combining high interest rates with relatively, in terms of competitiveness, high exchange rates would be unlikely to lead to sufficient growth to make an impact on unemployment. The government's prospects over the forthcoming year were consequently likely to be better, with inflation rising only slightly, than they would be thereafter, when inflation was expected to rise more rapidly due to pressures from continued wage inflation and high liquidity. It was this high liquidity, as evidenced by the rapid growth of the broad money aggregates, which was causing concern amongst Bank of England officials and others. The fear was that it might seek a home overseas, at least temporarily if a Labour victory appeared to be a realistic prospect, and spark a crisis. Calling an early election, when Labour was riding high in the opinion polls, would increase the chances of such a crisis. Within the ERM a realignment might prove necessary if a run on sterling transpired. Thatcher's assessment appears to have been that this would be more politically damaging than a depreciation of sterling outside the ERM. France, however, with the support of Germany and the other members, managed successfully to stave off a realignment until after the March 1986 election in France.

One could only speculate about whether an early election was being considered. Some of those given to speculation felt alternatively that an early election was not on the cards and that, following the April realignment of the French franc and the Deutschmark, the ERM was ready to receive sterling. With the UK assuming the six-monthly revolving Presidency of the EC in July 1986 and having bolstered its reserves in September 1986, they felt that the time had come for the UK to show its commitment to European integration, which many members believed it lacked, by joining the ERM—the ERM being one of the EC's most significant achievements and having been enshrined in the Treaty. The UK's Presidency however passed without sterling joining the ERM.

Roy Jenkins (1984), who was president of the European Commission at the time of the EMS's creation, has been a strong advocate of UK membership and again urged the UK to join the ERM in 1986.[23] Apart from purely domestic policy considerations, he argued that other compelling reasons for UK membership were that it would facilitate the development of a new international monetary system, and it would further advance the prospects of London as the dominant financial centre in the European time zone. The latter advantage cannot be easily overlooked by the government, which has been actively promoting London as a financial centre. Along with a growing number of economists and politicians, Jenkins believed that a tripartite agreement between the EMS, Japan and the US would be achieved. This would involve the development of three currency blocks with the major currencies, the yen, the dollar, and the Deutschmark or the ECU, fluctuating within target zones.[24] Jenkins argued that the UK should formally attach itself to the European currency block and that London should attempt to serve as its financial centre. Towards this end UK membership of the ERM and promotion of the ECU were essential. Continued independence would allow the Deutschmark to dominate, inhibit the development of the ECU, and possibly result eventually in the promotion of Frankfurt over London.

There have been numerous suggestions for furthering European monetary integration. For example, Alphandery and Fourcans (1984) suggested that integration and the development of the role of the ECU should proceed in three stages. Firstly the ECU should become a parallel currency alongside existing domestic currencies in all member states with its use initially restricted to that of private and official unit of account. The second stage would involve making the ECU an effective medium of exchange and therefore a real currency. This would require agreement between the member states to allow the creation of a European central bank which might emerge from the EMCF or from some other arrangement between the central banks of the member countries. The ECUs would be issued only in exchange for national currencies, so that the total European monetary stock would continue to depend on the monetary policies of each member country. The ECU would be allowed to float against the national currencies and exchange controls would need to be abolished so that the currencies of the most inflationary countries were not replaced too rapidly by the ECU and to ensure that anti-inflationary monetary policy was conditioned by market forces. Finally, the national currencies would be withdrawn from circulation. National central banks would then either be stripped of monetary policy responsibility or be required to cooperate in a manner akin to the Federal Reserve Banks in the US monetary system. It was proposed that the European Central Bank should have a status that ensured its independence *vis-à-vis* the political system.

Schokker (1980) has suggested that the functions of a European central bank would be: to coordinate a common internal monetary policy and a common external exchange rate policy, to issue money in ECU equivalents and to circulate it, possibly replacing domestic currencies completely, to act as banker to the community as well as to member states or their central banks, and to represent the community internationally in monetary and financial matters such as dealings with other central banks and the IMF.

Parkin (1978) also considers the future of the central banks of the members of the EC. He argues that the establishment of a European central bank would restrict their monetary policy-making, though not perhaps their operating, roles. The existing central banks might also retain their regulatory functions, he suggests, although the regulatory and supervisory systems would also be coordinated in the process of European cooperation. Parkin envisages a European Communities Reserve System with a European Communities Open Market Committee, with open market operations and rediscounting being undertaken by member central banks, especially those in the major financial centres such as London and Frankfurt. He also foresees the replacement of all EC member currencies by the Europa,[25] the supply of which would be controlled by the European Communities Reserve Board.

We noted, in Chapter 4, that in response to the 1977 EC banking directive,[26] and to the internationalisation of banking, progress has been made towards the harmonisation of EC banking law[27] and the regulatory and supervisory practices in the member countries under the purview of the EC Banking Advisory Committee. Full harmonisation of the banking system is still a long way off, and accounting and disclosure practices continue to differ greatly, making banking comparisons difficult. Whilst progress is being made in this area, attention has turned increasingly to the reduction of intracommunity restrictions on other financial services and on capital flows. We have already noted that the removal of capital market restrictions, and exchange controls in particular, are seen by many, including the Bundesbank, as a prerequisite for further European monetary integration and that progress is being made in this area. With the general breakdown of barriers between the sectors of the financial service industry in the member countries, the need for action to liberalise trade in traditionally non-banking financial services has become more urgent. The ultimate aim of financial integration is to secure the most efficient allocation of funds within the EEC, in order to promote the most productive activities. Integration should also ensure that the financial services industry develops efficiently, in a competitive environment, in order to be able to compete with the US and the increasingly competitive Japanese industries. In 1983 the European Commission issued a communication on financial integration assessing the reasons for lack of progress in the past, stating the case for a relaunching of efforts and making a number of practical proposals.[28] Underlying their arguments was the need to promote an efficient allocation of resources. In 1985, the EEC heads of government broadly endorsed the European Commission's proposals to achieve a fully free internal market by 1992.[29] The liberalisation of capital markets and the creation of a free market for financial services were designated as high priority areas. British government ministers seem particularly keen to promote a free market in financial services and the liberalisation of capital markets, believing that the UK financial services industry in general and the Stock Exchange and other City-based markets in particular, would benefit from such developments.

The economic experiences of the early 1980s have demonstrated the potential benefits of international cooperation through coordination of national fiscal and monetary policies.[30] The contrast between the mix of monetary and fiscal policy being pursued by the US and by the major European governments, especially following France's conversion to the European orthodoxy in 1983, became particularly stark. Meade (1984) outlined the New Keynesian principles of financial policy coordination for a full community of nations. He also envisaged the possibility, which is probably the most likely eventuality, that all free enterprise countries would not wish to join the full community. In this case, regional grouping might emerge and he outlined the principles of financial policy for such a group. The emergence of regional grouping is particularly likely if proposals to reform the world monetary system, to be discussed in Chapter 7, involving major currency zones are adopted. In this case the EMS might evolve as the vehicle for policy coordination amongst the EC member countries with the ECU acting as the zonal currency. Under Meade's proposals the member countries would rely on fiscal and wage-setting policies to maintain a high and stable level of real economic activity whilst containing inflation. Freely floating exchange rates, within agreed bands, would be adopted by the member countries with central targets for exchange rates set in terms of the ECU and targets would be set for the exchange rate between the ECU and outside currencies. These latter exchange rates would be announced and revised at frequent regular intervals. The community would decide on bands or zones with upper and lower limits on these exchange rates. It would continuously review the monetary and interest rate policies of its members to keep the exchange rates within the agreed bands. Central target exchange rates would be revised to accommodate the required fiscal deficits. Intervention in the exchange markets would be carried out by the agency managing the community currency pool. Thus, in an institution such as the EMS, each member country would be free to devise its own fiscal and wage-setting policy and institutions with a view to maintaining economic activity at low unemployment levels whilst containing inflation, but there would be extensive pooling of sovereignty in the case of monetary policy, covering interest rate setting, foreign exchange rates and official intervention on the exchange markets. Central target exchange rates would be agreed and continuously adjusted in a crawl to offset differences in rates of domestic inflation. National monetary policies would be jointly managed with the objective of keeping exchange rates within predetermined bands. The real central target rates of exchange would be jointly adjusted so as to relieve members of any undesirable large budget deficits or surpluses which might result from the domestic fiscal policies necessary for the maintenance of domestic equilibrum. Finally, all official interventions in foreign exchange markets would be undertaken by a community authority, such as the EMCF or the EMF, in order to avoid temporary perverse strains on the members' balances of international payments.

In May 1986, in pursuit of the achievement of further monetary integration, M. J. Delors, the European Commission's President, unveiled a two-phase plan to liberalise financial flows in the community. The first phase would concentrate on exchange controls and capital movements and was to be completed by 1992. The second phase would concentrate on liberalising all monetary and financial flows in the community, not just those related to commercial transactions. Phase one would have a major impact on France, Italy and the new members, Greece, Spain and Portugal, where exchange controls were still widely used and exemptions from EC rules have been greatest with respect to capital movements.

Fulfilment of the plan would go a long way towards removing the remaining German opposition to further monetary integration and the development of the ECU's role, as would UK participation in the ERM.

NOTES

1. *See* Kruse (1980) for a history of the evolution of European monetary integration.
2. Who joined the European Communities in January 1986, following a lengthy period of negotiations and preparations.
3. The Bank for International Settlements; *see* below.
4. In its 1985 and 1986 annual reports.

5. For further discussion of the development of the ECU and its future prospects *see* Allen (1986) and Mayer (1986).
6. *See* Bank for International Settlements *Annual Report*, June 1986, for details.
7. *See* Hirsch (1967, Chapter 2) for an account of the origins and membership of the BIS.
8. Such as ECU-denominated Euronotes and Eurobonds.
9. *See* Bank for International Settlements *Annual Report*, June 1985, pp.127–33.
10. *See* Dennis and Nellis (1984) and Lomax (1985) for example.
11. *See* House of Commons (Red Book) 1980.
12. *See* Chapters 5 and 7 for further discussion.
13. *See* Chapter 7 for further discussion.
14. *See* Dennis and Nellis (1984) for further discussion.
15. Since the US trade deficit proved slow to respond to the dollar's depreciation and Japan and Germany were unwilling to reflate their economies; *see* Chapter 7.
16. House of Commons Treasury and Civil Service Committee (1985).
17. Some controls had been lifted by the French socialist government in 1985 and the newly elected French conservative government removed some further controls in April 1986 and committed itself to a further relaxation in the future. The Italian government also relaxed some of its controls in the spring of 1986.
18. Through the Shadow Chancellor Roy Hattersley in July 1986.
19. In his Economic Viewpoint Column in the *Financial Times* in 1985 and 1986.
20. FRN = floating-rate note; *see* Chapter 3.
21. The alignment of EC member currencies that preceded the ERM; *see* Kruse (1980).
22. The reform of the UK Stock Exchange; *see* Chapter 2.
23. In the Sixth Mais Lecture given at the City University.
24. *See* Chapter 7 for further discussion.
25. Since Parkin's (1978) article the ECU has emerged, although if it is to circulate as a currency for consumer transactions a more attractive name, such as the Europa, might be given to it.
26. Commission of the European Communities (1977).
27. *See* Banker Research Unit (1981, Chapter 11), J. Welch (ed.) (1981, Chapter 11), and Cooper (1984) for details.
28. Commission for the European Communities (1983).
29. At their summit meeting in Madrid in June 1985.
30. *See* Chapter 7 for further discussion.

7 Reforming the International Monetary System

7.1 THE PROBLEMS

Since the breakdown of the Smithsonian Agreement[1] in 1973, following the second dollar devaluation in two years, a floating exchange rate (FER) system has been in operation. Under this system about a quarter of the currencies of the IMF member countries actually float freely, the remainder being pegged to a single currency (usually the dollar) to a basket of currencies (commonly the SDR)[2], or as an interconnected group of currencies, through the ERM of the EMS; see Chapter 6. The pegged currencies do, however, float against all the currencies that float against the currency or currencies to which they are aligned. The FER system replaced the fixed but adjustable exchange rate system that had operated since the 1944 Bretton Woods Agreement.[3] This agreement established the IMF as an organisation that would oversee a stable world financial system and monitor the system of fixed exchange rates. It also provided for the establishment of the IBRD or World Bank to provide development assistance. The IMF and the IBRD are specialised agencies of the United Nations. The founders of the IMF, forty-five nations led by the US and the UK, were concerned to prevent a return of the beggar-my-neighbour trade policies that had preceded the war. In this period of depression countries resorted to competitive currency depreciations in an attempt to reduce domestic unemployment. Under the Bretton Woods Agreement, each IMF member was required to establish a par value for its currency in terms of gold and hence the dollar, following the restoration of dollar–gold convertability after the war, and maintain an exchange rate within a 1 per cent band above or below the agreed fixed rate. This was to be achieved using gold and other currency reserves for intervention and by using monetary policies to manipulate the interest rates. The exchange rate could be changed only after seeking IMF approval, which was to be given only if the country's balance of payments was in 'fundamental disequilibrium'.[4] The IMF also stood ready to lend, under certain conditions, to member countries facing temporary balance of payments deficits, to enable them to make the necessary interventions to maintain their exchange rates. Under the system the onus tended to be upon the deficit countries to undertake the necessary adjustments through restrictive domestic policies and/or devaluation, despite the fact that in aggregate deficits and surpluses should cancel.[5] This asymmetry was one of the weaknesses of the system and it is one that persists to some extent in the FER system, as we noted in our discussion of the Latin American debt problem in Chapter 5.

In August 1971 the US found itself in 'fundamental disequilibrium' and severed the link between gold and the dollar. After four months of negotiations the finance ministers of the Group of Ten (G10)[6] met at the Smithsonian Institute and formulated the Smithsonian Agreement, which established a new set of fixed parities with wider temporary margins of 2.25 per cent above and below parity and the dollar remained inconvertible. By June 1972 the pound was under pressure and was 'temporarily' floated. In February 1973 there was a second dollar devaluation and by then the Swiss franc, the Italian lira and the Canadian dollar had joined sterling in floating and by March there was generalised floating. Since then the FER system has operated *de facto* between most major currencies, the most important exceptions being the currencies of the EC countries participating in the ERM, which has operated since March 1979, and the EEC 'snake in the tunnel' system that preceded it. These currencies float against non-member currencies, but maintain fixed exchange rates, within $2\frac{1}{4}$ per cent bands, between each other.

Under the FER system currencies have not been permitted to float completely freely since central banks have intervened in the currency markets in order to influence exchange rates. It is thus a 'dirty' or 'managed', rather than a 'freely', floating exchange rate system. Interventions have increasingly been made using reserve currencies rather than gold, and central banks have run down their gold reserves to some extent.[7] Gold no longer figures prominently in the international monetary system. The dollar is still the dominant reserve currency, although use of the Deutschmark, the yen and the Swiss franc as reserve currencies has increased.[8] Sterling's role declined throughout the postwar period but it has experienced periodic increases in popularity.[9] There is currently, therefore, a multi-currency reserve system (MCRS) in which the dollar dominates and the role of gold has diminished significantly.[10]

As a result of the growth in word trade and the internationalisation of banking and the capital and money markets,[11] the number and value of exchange rate transactions have increased rapidly since the breakdown of the Smithsonian Agreement. Twenty-four-hour trading in the foreign exchange markets through linkages between the major financial centres in the various time zones is now in operation. It has been estimated[12] that less than 10 per cent of currency dealings have a direct relationship to trade and long term capital flows and major currencies regularly fluctuate by 1 or 2 per cent in a single day and often change by up to 4 per cent. The growth in the value of exchange rate transactions has far outstripped the growth in central bank foreign currency reserves. Individual countries therefore find it virtually impossible to influence the exchange rates of their currencies in the face of adverse market sentiment. Instead they have found it necessary to act jointly through coordinated intervention involving their central banks. The weight of daily foreign exchange rate transactions is such that coordinated dealings, involving a small number of central banks, which have had some impact in the past, might now also have a limited impact. At the 1982 Versailles economic summit the issues of the capabilities and merits of exchange rate intervention were raised.[13] There were differences of opinion between the US and most of the European countries and Japan, with the UK tending to side with the US, which advocated non-intervention. Provision was, however, made for an international study of intervention to be completed in time for the 1983 Williamsburg summit. The report argued broadly that coordinated intervention might be beneficial in some cases but could not prevail against ingrained market sentiment. On the basis of this a compromise was reached at the 1983 summit and as a result coordinated intervention was promised where it was agreed that it would be helpful. As a result, since 1983 the US has proved more willing to intervene, though usually only in a small way. The consensus view on intervention was reflected in G30 policy pronouncements,[14] which broadly argue that: intervention to iron out short term fluctuations can be beneficial, intervention to influence medium term fluctuations can be occassionally useful, but intervention to alter longer term trend movements is futile. The art is to decide whether exchange rate movements are short, medium or long term in nature.

By September 1984 the Bundesbank judged the dollar to be significantly overvalued against the Deutschmark and intervened. Its policy was to hit the dollar whenever its appreciation faltered and the market seemed to be taking stock of the situation. A series of independent interventions followed. This policy aimed to create doubts in the minds of the speculators. It was not until February 1985, after the dollar had appreciated further against the yen and the major European currencies, that a number of other central banks shared the Bundesbank's view that the dollar was nearing its peak and that consequently the time was ripe for coordinated intervention. In late February the Bundesbank led a coordinated attack on the dollar which was followed by further smaller coordinated interventions over the next month or so, some of which involved the FRB in a limited way. Over the period eleven billion dollars' worth of reserves were committed but in the period that followed some of the dollars were repurchased leaving the central banks with healthy profits from the operation, which also seemed to have successfully helped the dollar to turn the corner. The key to the agreement on the intervention appeared to lie in the fact that in early 1985 it was generally accepted on both sides of the Atlantic and in Japan that the dollar was grossly overvalued, given the US's rapidly increasing balance of trade deficit, and must be nearing its peak. It only remained to wait for an opportunity where trading was thin and the market showed some signs of uncertainty so that intervention could have maximum impact on expectations.

Thus intervention is most likely to be successful when it anticipates changing market sentiment and reinforces it. It is unlikely to prove successful when it is undertaken in the face of entrenched expectations or tries to 'lean against the wind'. The policy of 'leaning with the wind' has to be delicately balanced, however, since there is a risk that the wind could be whipped up into a gale. The FRB's participation in the coordinated intervention was relatively minor, partly because its participation was restricted by the continued scepticism about the role of intervention expressed by the US administration. The FRB, like the other central banks, wished to see a gradual depreciation in the overvalued dollar or a 'soft landing', since rapid depreciation of the dollar would have been extremely disruptive both to the US economy, where its inflationary impact might be significant, and the world economy. Overzealous intervention by the FRB could have sparked a more rapid depreciation of the dollar leading to a 'hard' or 'crash' landing. The intervention seemed to have been well timed and the dollar depreciated fairly gradually, with a few fits and starts, in the subsequent period so that the soft landing appeared to be on. The alternatives to the coordinated intervention strategy were either to leave the currencies to the vagaries of the markets and to allow central banks to concentrate on the management of their currency reserve portfolios to maximise profits in order to contribute to their reserves and government revenues, or to encourage central banks to concentrate on individual intervention aimed at ironing out short term fluctuations only.

An important decision in favour of coordinated intervention was taken at the September 1985 meeting, in the Plaza Hotel New York, of the G5 finance ministers. They agreed to intervention in the exchange markets to bring the dollar down further at a time when market sentiment seemed to be turning decisively against the dollar. This was because of the growing US trade deficit and a run of economic data which indicated that US growth was slowing appreciably. The Plaza Agreement formally marked a significant change in attitude by the UK and the US officials. The intervention, by the central banks of the G5 which followed led to a sharp depreciation of the dollar, especially relative to the Deutschmark and the yen.

A free fall of the dollar was, however, averted and a new mood of uncertainty was created, inhibiting speculative trading on the foreign exchanges. The US communique to the IMF following the meeting also urged great convergence of economic policy amongst the major industrial nations. The impetus behind the new initiative seemed to have been the growing pressure on the US Congress to introduce protectionist legislation. It was hoped that the devaluation of the dollar would generate an expectation of reductions in the US trade deficit and the German, and, more especially, Japanese trade surpluses, and thereby reduce demands for protectionist legislation from within the US.

In subsequent meetings the G5 agreed to engineer coordinated interest rate cuts in order to stimulate growth in the major economies, which would both contribute to the resolution of the debt problem (see Chapter 5), and reduce protectionist pressures. In March 1986, the German monetary authorities led a round of interest rate reductions and were followed by Japan, the US, Holland and France. UK rates were cut later.

Towards the end of the first quarter of 1986, the dollar had depreciated significantly and there was uncertainty concerning the US view of the need for further falls. The Treasury and Trade Secretaries, James Baker and Malcolm Baldridge respectively, seemed to believe that further depreciation might be necessary to correct the trade balances rapidly enough to head off protectionist pressures. The Chairman of the FRB, Paul Volcker, was, however, concerned about the risk of inducing the dollar to fall too rapidly and causing it to overshoot its optimum level. He was also concerned about the inflationary effects of the depreciating currency because the resultant rise in import prices might rekindle inflationary expectations. In order to assess the potential of this effect he had to take account of the counterbalancing influence of falling oil and commodity prices. Also weighing against the FRB's tendency to advise caution was the fact that a further fall in interest rates seemed to be required to boost the flagging US economy and to help the US financial system (see Chapter 3) and the Latin American debtors (see Chapters 3 and 5) resolve their problems. Meanwhile the US money supply growth continued to exceed the FRB's targets.

In April 1986, it became clear that the Japanese authorities wanted to halt the appreciation of the yen. They wanted a period of consolidation to allow the Japanese economy to adjust to the effects of the yen's appreciation on the competitiveness of Japanese industry in their export markets. Disagreements amongst the G5 appeared to be emerging ahead of the IMF-IBRD spring meetings and the UK Chancellor, Nigel Lawson, called for a further rise in the yen, apparently with the tacit support fo the US authorities but much to the annoyance of the Japanese. The dollar's fall was, however, temporarily halted, largely as a result of the Libyan crisis, but it resumed in the latter half of April, when the US reduced its interest rates and was followed by Japan but not by Germany. Japan intervened to support the yen but the FRB and the Bundesbank did not participate in the action. There was, however, some evidence that the central banks of the major industrial nations did try to achieve some stability on the foreign exchanges ahead of the Tokyo economic summit in early May.

Following the Tokyo summit, it appeared that Japan and Germany, with some support from Paul Volcker, wanted a period of stability to allow consolidation whilst many US officials wanted a further fall in the dollar and their position was being supported by the UK. It was evident that trade balances had not adjusted and had indeed worsened, due to the J-shaped curve effect and because the fall in oil prices had benefited Germany and Japan to a greater extent than the US. Although an oil importer like Japan and Germany, the US also has a major oil sector. The J-curve effect results because depreciation reduces the price of exports and raises the price of imports. Until volumes of exports and imports adjust in response, which takes time due to outstanding contracts for example, the value of imports actually rises and the value of exports falls, leading to a worsening of the trade balance. Provided the price elasticities of exports and imports are sufficiently large, the trade deficit will eventually improve, however.

In June 1986, there appeared to be some evidence that the US deficit was at last beginning to decline and there was some mildly encouraging economic data. This supported arguments for consolidation. In July, however, the trade balances again worsened and some US officials suggested that a further 10 to 15 per cent depreciation of the dollar would be required. In June and July the Japanese authorities continued with their lone intervention, in order to prevent a large yen appreciation which would have been damaging to Prime Minister Yasuhiro Nakasone's party's election campaign, given the growing opposition to further yen appreciation by industrial and other lobby groups. The dollar, however, continued to depreciate.

Meanwhile protectionist pressures within the US continued to grow and a potentially restrictive Trade Bill was tabled by Congress in June 1986 only to be voted down in August following intense lobbying by President Reagan. Further evidence was accumulating to confirm the slowdown in US growth and doubts grew about the size of the rebound in growth that could be expected in the second half of 1986. Official growth forecasts, made in the optimistic light of falling oil prices, were revised downwards. The oil price fall was originally expected to have a major stimulatory effect, especially in the second half of the year. It grew evident, however, that the initial impact of the oil price fall on the world economy and on the US with its significant energy sector was perverse. Officially it was hoped that the oil shock would also have a J-curve effect, with the beneficial effects merely having been postponed until 1987. In the light of these economic prospects, there was renewed pressure on the FRB to reduce interest rates. Although reluctant to lead off in a further round of interest rate cuts, because of fears of causing a dollar free fall, the FRB duly obliged with a further $\frac{1}{2}$ per cent cuts in July and August 1986. Japan and Germany declined to follow. Japan had been reluctant to move until after the July elections and the Bundesbank had ruled out further interest rate cuts until its monetary growth had been brought back into its target range. It was also inhibited by the fact that following the April ERM realignment (see Chapter 6) the Deutschmark had been trading near to the bottom of its band.

Following the Japanese elections, and the return of Yasuhiro Nakesone and his party to power, no further interest rate cut was immediately forthcoming. The Bundesbank also declined to act in the light of more encouraging monetary figures and a movement of the Deutschmark towards the middle of its band in the latter half of July, and the upper end of its band in August 1986, despite promptings from France, which wished to reduce its interest rates, and the risk that another ERM realignment might be necessary especially in view of the weakness of the Danish krone. In order to head off protectionist pressures the US administration needed to be seen to be doing something to help restore a trade balance. It was widely felt within the US that elimination of the trade deficit would require rapid growth in US export markets and especially in the surplus countries, Japan and Germany. Because the full effect of the dollar's depreciation, which was, in July 1986, approaching 40 per cent against the yen since the first quarter of 1985, would take time to work through and might have perverse effects for some time due to the J-curve effect, complementary action was required. The US administration wanted Germany and Japan to undertake a fiscal expansion and to reduce interest rates further. Both countries were unwilling to comply because they were reasonably satisfied with their current policies and were fearful of the future demands of their ageing populations on government expenditure. In both countries interest rates stood at 3.5 per cent and their monetary authorities felt that not only was there little scope for a significant further reduction but also that a reduction would be more likely to stimulate inflation than growth, given the high levels of liquidity in their economies and the low levels of prevailing rates. Growth had, however, slowed markedly in both Japan and Germany and unemployment was high in the latter. The slowdown in growth was to be expected given the export bias of both economies and the declining US growth combined with the appreciation of their currencies, although there was evidence of a rebound in Germany in the second quarter of 1986, with encouraging rises in domestic consumption and investment.

In his half-yearly statement to the US Congress and the Senate Banking Committee in July 1986, Paul Volcker, Chairman of the FRB, argued that only increased economic policy coordination offered the prospect of a sustained non-inflationary world expansion. Neither faster US growth nor a rapid dollar depreciation were the answers. A more rapid US expansion would aggravate the international trade imbalances and possibly stimulate inflation, and the risk of a cascading depreciation remained. He reiterated recent comments which he and the Treasury Secretary, James Baker, had recently made, urging the US's trading partners to grow faster in order to reduce their trade imbalances. In particular he argued that countries like Japan and Germany should redirect their economies towards domestic growth and reduce their dependence on exports for expansion. He felt that this should be possible at a time of high unemployment when ample resources were being released by the export sector as the external stimulus faded. For its part the US needed to reduce its budget deficit, more or less in line with the reduction of the trade deficit, shift more resources into exports and reduce dependence on foreign capital inflows. The reduction in the budget deficit was necessary to avoid the danger of reigniting inflation and, although it would probably further reduce growth, this would be offset by the reduced trade deficit, which itself was causing a drag on growth.

If the US's major trading partners, and Japan and Germany in particular, prove unwilling to cooperate then the US will have little choice but to go it alone. The FRB declared that it would cut its interest rates in isolation again, as it subsequently did, if necessary. Such initiatives were clearly likely to induce a further depreciation of the dollar. Alternatively, the US administration might ultimately have to accede to protectionist pressures, which were likely to increase following the installation of a Democratic Party majority in the Senate as a result of the 1986 mid-term elections. The future prospects for further coordinated intervention, therefore, appeared to lie in the balance in mid 1986, and so too did the prospects for further economic policy coordination (see Chapter 8). More encouraging US economic data in September 1986 rekindled inflationary expectations in the light of the continuing rapid growth in monetary aggregates and the accommodative FRB policy. This led to a rise in short term interest rates and the dollar, raising the possibility that the next move in US interest rates could be upwards rather than downwards. This conflicted with the previously prevailing expectation that the annual meeting of the IMF and the IBRD in October would bring forth a further coordinated interest reduction.

The coordinated interest rate reduction did not transpire but there was a coordinated intervention to support the dollar in October 1986. Then, at the end of October, the US and Japan concluded an agreement to stabilise the yen–dollar exchange rate. For its part, Japan agreed to cut its interest rate by 0.5 per cent, to introduce a small reflationary fiscal package in the autumn and to consider reforming its tax system, whilst the US promised to continue with its efforts to reduce its budget deficit. This bilateral agreement put pressure on the Deutschmark and called into question Europe's, and particularly Germany's commitment to international economic cooperation. Germany remained unwilling to cut interest rates and to introduce a stimulatory fiscal package. Perhaps in a final effort to secure European support for international economic cooperation, Mr Baker arranged a series of meetings with key European Finance Ministers in December 1986. If these meetings prove unproductive, the US is likely to go it alone with the possible continued support of Japan if it is able to comply with future US policy initiatives.

The prevailing concensus appeared to be that, given the tendency in the current FER system for currencies to become over- or undervalued relative to exchange rates required to achieve balances of trade, some future intervention will be required to condition medium term movements.[15] Coordinated intervention needs to be well timed in order to have maximum impact on expectations, although fairly regular small scale interventions might also have the beneficial effect of reminding speculators of the reality of the risks involved in the game they are playing. Despite the success of recent coordinated interventions it seems likely that the FER system will lead some currencies to become significantly over- or undervalued in the future. The question has, therefore, arisen: can the exchange rate system be reformed in such a way that some of the flexibility inherent in the FER system is retained whilst the danger of overshooting is eliminated?

7.2 THE PROPOSALS

A return to some previously operating international monetary system, such as the gold standard or the Bretton Woods (BW) system, is clearly unlikely given that these were abandoned as unsatisfactory. A return to the BW system would result in inflexibility and the exchange rates would be hard to maintain in the face of the widely varying inflation rates currently prevailing in the various member countries of the IMF. Further, the BW system ultimately revolved around a single reserve currency, the dollar, and would not fit well with the emerging MCRS. If, however, the SDR could be developed into a widely acceptable reserve asset, akin to the Bancor proposed in the Keynes Plan,[16] which was rejected with the adoption of the White Plan,[17] which formed the basis of the BW Agreement, and the reserve asset advocated in the Triffen Plan,[18] then the MCRS could be replaced eventually. A return to a fixed-rate system, with perhaps wider bands or zones than adhered to under the BW system, could then be considered. It would have the advantage that reliance on the dollar, or any other domestic currency, would be eliminated. It would also overcome the problem of seigniorage accruing primarily to the US[19] since it would accrue to the issuing body, the IMF, and would benefit all participants.[20]

Alternatively, some sort of commodity standard could be developed. Historical examples are gold- and silver-based systems. France has from time to time proposed a return to some form of gold standard and the idea was apparently given some consideration by the Reagan administration in the US. The rigidity of the system, along with its implications for domestic monetary policies,[21] implies that such proposals are unlikely to find widespread support. Further, the reliance on gold supplies from Russia and South Africa, which are the major producers, makes the political acceptability of such a system dubious. A basket of other commodities chosen because of their widespread sources of supply and the stability of the overall price index could instead underly the system. The political and practical problems of choosing the appropriate basket would appear to be immense, however. The substantial fall in commodity prices in the first half of the 1980s would have made it virtually impossible to construct a stable index in that period, for example. Given the reliance on fiduciary issues in the domestic economies of the major currencies, not only is a commodity-based system outmoded but it would not work in the manner of the gold standard because under that system a country's gold reserves lay at the base of its money supply. It is also rather costly to run a monetary system that is based on commodities that require the use of resources to produce and transport to a place where they normally remain idle and necessitate further expenditure on storage and security.

A system which could potentially build on the merits of the fixed and floating exchange rate systems is one based on currency blocks. In such a system countries would form blocks by aligning their currencies to one of the major reserve currencies: the yen, the dollar and the Deutschmark. Alternatively in Europe the ECU could be further developed as a reserve currency to replace the Deutschmark. Fixed target rates with agreed bands would operate within the blocks and the exchange rates between the key reserve currencies would float freely or within agreed bands around target rates. When it became clear that the target rates were inappropriate phased adjustments to the targets could be made. The problem of choosing the optimal blocks would be a major one, though it would be conditioned by dominant trade flows and time zones to a great extent. It has been suggested that fairly natural blocks exist in western Europe, and perhaps even eastern Europe, south-east Asia and America. This would leave Africa, the rest of Asia and a number of other countries unallocated and without major reserve currencies. The way in which the blocks should operate internally is open to a number of suggestions. If they were to be modelled on the ERM[22] then ultimately the result would be that the participants would loose autonomy concerning monetary and interest rate policies, since convergence would be enforced. According to one's view of the working of the economy, this might also mean some *de facto* loss of control over fiscal policy. This would be especially true if one believed in the monetarist view currently dominant in Europe, which argues that control of the money supply requires control of the fiscal deficit. Alternatively, if one holds New Keynesian views then the blocks could be developed along the lines proposed by Meade[23] to preserve a greater degree of autonomy in fiscal policy. It is of course possible that each block might adopt a different internal arrangement.

In the absence of formal blocking it has been argued that the current system would benefit from less reliance on the dollar. The G30[24] advocates the promotion of the SDR to replace the dollar as the major reserve currency and the further development of the MCRS in the interim. The latter would require enhancing the roles of the Deutschmark and the yen, and perhaps the ECU. The West German authorities seem willing to go along with this development at present. In the 1970s the Bundesbank had opposed the extension of the Deutschmark's reserve currency role because it feared that it might restrict its ability to control the money supply. In addition the government feared that it would boost the Deutschmark with adverse trade effects. In the early 1980s the Deutschmark depreciated against the dollar and there were large capital outflows to the US. In this environment the West German authorities have taken measures[25] to promote actively the international currency role of the Deutschmark in order to stem the capital outflows and raise the value of the Deutschmark relative to the dollar without having to raise the interest rate appreciably and consequently risking a reduction in the economic growth rate. Japan was encouraged by the US, in the early 1980s, to reduce restrictions inhibiting the development of the yen as a reserve currency. The objective of the measures urged on Japan by the US was to increase the demand for, and hence the value of, the yen relative to the dollar, thus reducing the imbalance of trade between the two countries, which was growing rapidly in Japan's favour and was the major cause of the US's increasing trade deficit. By the mid 1980s the rate of the yen had increased substantially but it was felt that further liberalisation of the Japanese financial system (see Chapter 4) could add significantly to its attractiveness as an international currency. The G30 hopes that reduced reliance on the dollar, and eventually other domestic currencies with the promotion of the SDR, will help to insulate the world economy and exchange rate system from the domestic economic policies pursued by individual countries. The G30 was particularly critical of the historically high US fiscal deficit in the early 1980s, which conflicted with what it viewed as the basically sound monetary policy being pursued by the FRB, a view shared by the IMF, the OECD, the members of the EC and a number of economic commentators.[26]

In the light of the current problems associated with the functioning of the international monetary system, and in response to the promptings from France for an international conference to deal with the issue, the May 1983 Williamsburg economic summit declaration invited finance ministers, in consultation with the managing director of the IMF, to define the conditions for improving the international monetary system and to consider the part which might be played by a high level international monetary conference. The invitation was taken up by the finance ministers and the central bank governors of the G10 in Washington in September 1983 and, following a preliminary exchange of views on the conditions necessary to improve the functioning of the international monetary system, they instructed their deputies to meet in order to identify the areas in which progressive improvements might be sought. The deputies were requested to report to them in the next meeting, to be held in early 1984. The deputies requested background papers from the IMF, the OECD, the BIS and Commission of the EC. A progress report was considered by the finance ministers and central bank governors of the G10 in May 1984 and the deputies were urged to complete the final report, by May 1985, concentrating on the following areas: the functioning of the FER system and causes of volatility and trend movements in exchange rates, ways to strengthen multilateral surveillance, with a view to promoting greater policy coordination and exchange rate stability, and the management of international liquidity and the future role of the IMF.

In anticipation of the conclusions of the report the G10 ministers and governors issued a communique, in May 1984, asserting that the FER system had made a positive contribution to the maintenance of international trade and payments and to the adjustment process in a difficult economic environment, that a return to a generalised system of fixed parities was unrealistic at the present time, that given varying degrees of dissatisfaction with the present system it should be improved, that a greater degree of convergence in economic performance among nations was desirable, and that coordinated intervention to counter disorderly exchange market conditions could be beneficial. The communique also affirmed the need to strengthen multilateral surveillance over countries' policies, particularly within the context of the IMF. It noted that a number of questions in the area of international liquidity remained to be addressed, including: the process of creation, control and distribution of international liquidity; the role of the international financial markets; and the role of the SDR. It agreed on the need to maintain the monetary character of the IMF, supported the principle of making IMF financing available with appropriate conditionality and called for closer cooperation between the IMF and the IBRD.

The deputies' final report was transmitted to the ministers and governors of the G10 on 1 June 1985. Among its principal conclusions[27] were the following: the current FER system has shown weaknesses and should be improved; target zones for exchange rates, as advocated by France,[28] would not, however, be practical or desirable in current circumstances; the IMF should strengthen surveillance over members' policies; excessive swings in the availability of liquidity should be avoided; the SDR may still have a useful role in meeting the global need for reserves and the IMF should carry out a comprehensive review of its future role; the IMF should phase down the policy of enlarged access[29] and terminate it as soon as possible.

The ministers and governors of the G10 considered the report in June 1985 and in their communique endorsed the deputies' general conclusion that the basic structure of the present system, as reflected in the Articles of Agreement of the IMF, remained valid and required no major institutional change. They agreed that the system had shown weaknesses and that there was a need to improve its functioning. They acknowledged the desirability of actions to foster greater stability in exchange and financial markets and agreed that the strengthening of international surveillance could help achieve this goal. They argued that intervention could play only the limited role of countering disorderly market conditions and reducing short term volatility, adding that countries should occasionally be willing to engage in coordinated intervention. A majority of ministers and governors agreed with the report's opposition to a move to target zones in present circumstances. The report was to be transmitted to the IMF's Interim Committee,[30] where all of the IMF members are represented, to ensure that the developing countries as well as the industrial member countries had a chance to comment on it.

Thus no radical changes were proposed but coordination of domestic economic policies was to be pursued alongside multilateral surveillance by the IMF. It was hoped that if coordination could be achieved the tendency for currencies to become over- or undervalued in relation to the values consistent with trade balancing would be reduced considerably and the present FER system could be persevered with. Some proponents of exchange rate target zones, however, feel that they would actively promote international policy coordination, whilst advocates of the FER system argue that greater policy coordination is a prerequisite for exchange rate reform.[31]

In contrast to the G10 report, the G24 deputies report[32] on their August 1985 meeting, which was also transmitted to the Interim Committee, recommended the creation of a new international monetary system. It considered the earlier G10 deputies' report and recommended that an in-depth study of the two reports be undertaken by a subcommittee with representatives drawn from the Interim and Development Committees.[33] The G24 report advocated target zones, with improved policy coordination in the interim, and more intervention to stabilise exchange rates. It proposed that multilateral surveillance should involve two stages: multilateral negotiations conducted on a regular basis within the IMF framework, followed by bilateral consultations. It advocated that confidentiality should be maintained throughout. The G24 report demonstrated that the developing countries felt that reform of the international monetary system, the fight against protectionism, management of international liquidity and SDR issues, and the resolution of the debt problem were all interlinked.

At the annual meetings of the IMF and the IBRD in

October 1985 the Interim Committee decided to defer substantive consideration of the G10 and G24 deputies' reports until the spring meetings and asked the IMF's executive board to study the issues raised in the meantime.

The G24 communique to the spring meetings called for an international conference to discuss both the debt crisis and the transfer of resources to developing countries within the context of the reform of the international monetary system. It stressed the asymmetry of the adjustment process. Their views were seemingly finding favour with the US administration, which was becoming increasingly concerned about the onus being placed upon the US, as a deficit country, to adjust and the lack of cooperation forthcoming from the surplus countries. In his February 'State of the Union' message, President Reagan asked the US Treasury to explore the idea of an international monetary conference on the role and relationship of international currencies and to prepare a report for the autumn of 1986. The US administration seemed to be hoping that an initiative to reform the international monetary system might stave off protectionist pressures. The G24 communique also expressed concern at the lack of progress by the IMF's executive body towards reaching concrete programmes of action on the G10 and G24 reports. It reiterated their calls for a representative committee, reflecting the interests of both industrial and developing countries, perhaps drawn from the Interim and Development Committees, to examine the proposals, and for the convening of an international conference for which the subcommittee should prepare.

At the spring meetings, in April 1986, the Interim Committee reviewed the G10 and G24 reports.[34] It will be recalled that the G10 report basically argued that the FER system remained valid and that no major institutional changes were required, whilst acknowledging that the system had shown weaknesses and should be improved through greater cooperation and coordination in policy making. The G24 report, however, contested that the FER system was unsatisfactory and that a variety of improvements should be considered, including target zones and mechanisms to trigger consultations when economic indicators suggested that a realignment was required. The Interim Committee argued that the

FER system had proved sufficiently flexible to allow adjustment to major shocks, such as those to oil prices, and that long term misalignments remained a source of concern requiring policy convergence and coordination. It concluded that there was insufficient support for target zones. The G24 press release, following the meetings, renewed its call for the G10 and G24 reports to be considered by a representative committee.

Whilst no progress was made towards a system of target zones, the G10 and G24 moved closer on the development of multilateral surveillance. The G10 communique to the spring meetings advocated the study of the role of policy indicators in the development of policy coordination. The Interim Committee also considered the formulation of representative indicators to achieve policy consistency to be an approach worth exploring and recognised the importance of exchange rates as indicators of policy consistency.

At the Tokyo summit,[35] in May 1986, it was agreed that close and continuous policy coordination should be pursued. To facilitate this it was agreed that the G7[36] finance ministers should work together more closely in the period between the annual summit meetings. They were asked to meet at least once a year to review their individual economic objectives and forecasts collectively and to use a set of indicators of policy and performance to examine their mutual compatibility. The summit leaders also supported the launching of the new round of GATT negotiations in September 1986.

There was no announcement on target zones in the summit communique. In February, however, the Director of the French Treasury proposed a gradual move from coordinated intervention by central banks to a system of target zones. He suggested that initially the zones of reference should be kept confidential and should allow a wide margin, of say 5 to 10 per cent from the central values. The system should then be gradually institutionalised, following discussion within the IMF. A special conference was deemed unnecessary and it was judged that the UK and Japan would favour efforts to establish exchange rate stability, although potential German opposition was acknowledged. Ahead of the Tokyo summit in May, the US administration had attempted to build broader support for a conference on international monetary reform. The President of the Bundesbank, Karl Otto Poehl, however, firmly rejected the idea of exchange rate target zones. Poehl argued that monetary authorities would probably be unable to cope with the huge capital flows and that no industrial country was willing to allow exchange rate targets to condition their domestic fiscal and monetary policies. He did, however, comment favourably on attempts to coordinate policies. Ironically, the arguments used by Mr Poehl were the same as those used by those sceptical of the merits of creating the EMS and similar to those used by opponents of UK participation in the ERM of the EMS.[37] Further, the 1986 BIS annual report argued that target zones may not be achievable or even desirable. This was because it would be extremely difficult to agree on an equilibrium pattern of exchange rates, even within a wide margin. In addition target zones would force excessive reliance on monetary policy, which is the only policy instrument capable of responding quickly to changes in exchange rates. The end result could consequently be detrimental to domestic and international balance. The BIS cautioned that the model of the ERM of the EMS could not be generally applied because it linked the currencies of countries of similar size and structure which have a history of cooperation, it took years to establish, and it did not include the world's major currency. Coordinated policy making was, therefore, the only realistic option in the near future.

Bretton Woods delivered stable exchange rates with relatively free trade flows but restricted capital flows. The FER system, with increasingly freer capital flows, has led to creeping protectionism. To many it seems inappropriate to sacrifice free flows of real goods and services for financial freedom. In this light it has become necessary to coordinate macroeconomic, and probably microeconomic, policies to reduce the incentives inducing the huge capital movements. These large, and often speculative, capital flows have increasingly come to be viewed as the root cause of the prolonged misalignments of exchange rates that have contributed to trade imbalances and encouraged the growth in protectionism.

Progress towards cooperation and coordination has been

made since James Baker took over from Donald Regan as the US Treasury Secretary in 1985. There is, however, a real risk that the US may be forced back into the isolationist stance of the Regan era. A demonstration of commitment to systematic adjustment is thus urgently required from the countries with trade surpluses if the talk of policy coordination is not to prove vacuous.

Many authorities believe that the world is moving towards a *de facto* multicurrency system in which the Deutschmark, the yen and the dollar will dominate. At the annual international monetary conference,[38] the Chairman of the Bank of Tokyo argued that the Plaza Agreement implied the *de facto* ending of the dollar standard and the development of a MCRS in its place. The monetary system would in future revolve around the three major currencies and other currencies would align to one of the three, or perhaps to a basket comprising them. Policy coordination would be required to stem potentially massive shifts of funds and avert the consequent disruptive effects on exchange rates. He felt that the mutual surveillance of ten selected indicators, agreed at the Tokyo summit, should prevent the reoccurrence of serious misalignments. Similarly, Keegan (1986) concludes that the world is being driven inexorably towards a system of target zones.

Others are more sceptical about the natural development of a target zone system. They argue that the Plaza Agreement and the resulting interventions had the pragmatic purpose of reducing pressures for protectionist legislation by the US Congress. There had been little serious consideration of the framework being aimed for and many countries, especially Germany and the UK to a lesser extent, guarded their independence jealousy. When exchange rates had eventually stabilised and it was accepted that they were close to their equilibrium values, governments might be more disposed towards considering ways of maintaining them. That would be the time to hold an international monetary conference.

The question of how near the world is to such a situation arises. Many felt that the dollar would not fall much further, for a sustained period, than the levels reached in August 1986. A lot, however, hinged on the willingness of the surplus countries, especially Japan and Germany, to do their share of adjustment. In the end only time will tell whether the new cooperative approach to policy making will work and whether it will eventually lead to a replacement of the FER system with a target zone system. Such an outcome will require a considerable amount of political will and responsibility and recognition of the increasingly interdependent nature of the world economy. The new order would also have to be able to withstand changes of government in the major industrial countries. The French government elected in February 1986, for example, may prove less disposed towards encouraging international monetary reform than its predecessor had shown itself to be at the 1984 London and 1985 Bonn economic summits. An incoming UK Labour government might prove unwilling to submit to restrictions on its policy options. Perhaps most importantly, a change in the US administration, or even amongst its major officials, might lead to as big a shift in policy as that experienced following the replacement of Donald Regan by James Baker as US Treasury Secretary.

The downside risks are that the commitments to cooperation and coordination will prove vacuous. Significantly, recent commitments do not incorporate the term convergence, as early statements had done, and there were marked differences in the views held by the officials from the countries participating in the Tokyo summit on its significance, James Baker being the most and the German officials the least enthusiastic. Total convergence is, of course, inappropriate, because of the differing structural characteristics of the major economies. Progress is, however, unlikely to be made without some convergence, given the major imbalances that prevail, the trade imbalance between the US or Japan being one of the more important ones. The counterpart to this imbalance was the capital account imbalance. The US had become a major capital importer, especially from Japan. Behind these capital flows lays the large US budget deficit and the marked differences in the propensities to save and consume between the two countries. By international standards the US savings ratio remained low, making it difficult for the US to fund its budget deficit, which was not high as a proportion of its GNP by international standards but was nevertheless historically high. In contrast, Japanese savings were relatively high and the domestic economy was unable to absorb them. Interest differentials could theoretically have been adjusted to encourage US and discourage Japanese savings, but the room for manoeuvre was small given the adverse effects a rise in US rates would have had on the US economy and the fact that Japanese nominal rates, at 3.5 per cent, were already fairly low. The underlying macroeconomic problem required attention. The US budget and trade deficits both required reduction whilst the Japanese economy needed to be reoriented towards internal growth, as outlined in the Maekawa Report,[39] which was commissioned by Prime Minister Yasuhiro Nakasone and endorsed by the US administration. The report advocated a shift away from export-led and towards domestically generated growth in Japan. It contained little in the way of concrete prescriptions for the achievement of reform. The re-election of Prime Minister Nakasone and his party increased the prospects of action on the report but a large fiscal stimulus remained unlikely given the country's concern about its ageing population and the future government expenditure commitments this would entail. A small reflationary package was, however, introduced in Autumn 1986. Action to reduce the US budget deficit became more uncertain in July 1986 when a provision in the Gramm–Rudeman–Hollings Bill, for automatic government expenditure cuts whenever budget deficits exceeded preset norms, was ruled unconstitutional by the Supreme Court in the US. Without the automacy provision, budget deficit reductions would continue to depend on political will, which might well evaporate if evidence of a US economic slowdown accrues. Additionally, the tax systems in the two countries are very different. The US system, like the UK and European systems, tends to discourage savings by taxing interest, even though savings as part of income have already been taxed. Further it encourages consumption through generous, by UK and European standards, allowances on interest payments. Interest received on Japanese savings, especially through the popular postal system accounts, is, in contrast, largely untaxed and allowances on interest payments are much smaller. Many feel that tax reforms, aimed specifically at achieving fiscal neutrality between savings and consumption, should be a goal and that other micro and supply side measures will be necessary to achieve sufficient convergence to ensure worthwhile cooperation and coordination. Such measures are difficult to agree upon and to implement and could only be put on agenda for longer term cooperative agreements. The US tax reform legislation passed in August 1986 should, however, help to reduce imbalances. Tax allowances on interest payments and tax rates are to be significantly reduced. These measures should encourage saving and discourage consumption in the US. Target zones could of course exist during the process of convergence if the central rates were changed periodically and gradually.

If, however, the proposed coordination of policy comes to nothing and an international conference is not called, or fails, then the world risks a trade war and a return to the beggar-my-neighbour policies which, given the currently high unemployment rates, is likely to lead to a replay of the 1930s. Hopefully this will not be allowed to happen, especially when one remembers that the period ended in war. It is to be hoped that, having seemingly abandoned the pursuit of insular monetarist policies, the world's leaders will respond to Baker's more Keynesian initiatives. Whilst the onus of adjustment remains on the deficit countries, a problem that led to the breakdown of the Bretton Woods Agreement, there is little ground for optimism, however. Now that the US has become a major debtor and with its growth slowing it is incumbent upon the surplus countries, particularly Japan and Germany, to pick up the growth torch. If they do not, the trading system, on which their growth has been so heavily dependent, may collapse and the debt problem may return to crisis. Some way must be found to guarantee symmetry of adjustment. This will necessarily imply some loss of freedom of action by participants in the increasingly interdependent world economy, in which one country's actions necessarily affect other countries and each country should, therefore, be accountable for its own actions.

Meanwhile, the ERM of the EMS continues to function reasonably well and one of the currency blocks is, therefore, already in place. With the yen developing, howbeit slowly, as a prominent international currency and the dollar's importance declining relatively, the other blocks might naturally fall into place. An international conference might usefully speed things up, however, and would hopefully give the developing countries a bigger say in the formation of a new international monetary system which they feel to be part and parcel of the resolution of their interrelated debt, liquidity and trade problems. In particular it might help to stem protectionist pressures on the US Congress and the Reagan administration. President Reagan appears to hope that an international conference will have such an effect and might even result in the creation of a new world monetary system which would stand as a memorial to his presidency.

NOTES

1. *See* Grubel (1984, Chapter 7).
2. Special Drawing Rights; *see* Grubel (1984, Chapter 8) and Tew (1970, Chapter 10).
3. *See* Tew (1970, Chapters 6 and 7).
4. A disequilibrium on the balance of trade which is not expected to be self-correcting and which causes pressure for exchange rate adjustment; *see* Tew (1970, Chapter 8).
5. There has, however, been an increasing discrepancy, with the aggregate deficit exceeding the aggregate surplus due to accounting errors. The existence of an aggregate deficit may have imparted a deflationary adjustment bias.
6. The ten major industrial countries—Belgium, Canada, France, Germany, Holland, Italy, Japan, Sweden, the UK and the US—which established the IMF's General Agreement to Borrow (GAB) in October 1962.
7. The US Treasury, for example, held gold auctions intermittently between 1975 and 1979 and other major industrial countries also sold gold reserves in the 1970s.
8. *See* Kenen (1983) and Group of Thirty (1982a), and IMF and BIS annual reports and OECD publications.
9. Most recently in connection with: its petrocurrency status, developments in the City of London affecting its attractiveness as a financial centre, and the government's innovative funding programme.
10. *See* Kenen (1983), Group of Thirty (1980, 1982a), and Laney (1980).
11. *See* OECD (1983) for an account of the internationalisation of banking.
12. By the Banks of England and Japan and the FRB, following studies of foreign exchange transactions in London, Tokyo and New York, respectively, in March 1986. The studies confirmed that activity in the foreign exchange markets had increased extremely rapidly, especially in

London following the lifting of exchange controls in 1979. In London only 9 per cent of the daily turnover of $90bn was accounted for by transactions carried out directly with customers. Each transaction with a customer, however, sparks a string of other deals as banks and other dealers adjust their positions. Until the extent of these latter dealings are gauged it is impossible to estimate the extent of purely speculative activity.
13. Attended by the leaders of the governments of the seven most powerful industrial nations.
14. Group of Thirty (1982b).
15. *See* Lever (1985).
16. Command Paper 6437.
17. HMSO (1943).
18. *See* Triffen (1964).
19. Seigniorage was the name given to resources accruing to sovereign rulers who minted coins with a face value larger than the intrinsic metal value in the coin and the costs of their production and distribution. In this context the seigniorage accrues to the US because the only way that the rest of the world can acquire dollars is by running a balance of payments surplus, thus transferring real resources as claims on assets to the US.
20. Though the problem of its distribution would remain; *see* Grubel (1984, Chapter 8).
21. Which are essentially constrained by the need to set interest rates to maintain the gold parity of the currency in the light of international flows of gold in connection with balance of payments settlements; *see* Grubel (1984, Chapters 5 and 7) for further details.
22. *See* Chapter 6.
23. *See* Meade (1984) and Chapter 5 Section 2 for further discussion.
24. The Group of Thirty brings together leading academic economists and senior central and commercial bankers to explore problems in the functioning of the international economic system.
25. Such as the removal of 'withholding tax', which is a tax on interest paid to overseas investors in domestic securities.
26. *See* Dornbusch (1984) for example.
27. *See IMF Survey* 'Supplement on Group of Ten deputies report', July 1985.
28. At recent economic summits attended by the heads of government of the seven largest industrial nations.
29. The enlarged-access policy provides resources in much larger amounts and for longer periods than are available under its credit tranch policy and extended fund facility (*see* Barclays Bank 1984a). to members with serious balance of payments problems that are large in relation to their quotas.
30. *See IMF Survey*, 1 April 1985, for a review of the origins and achievements of the Interim Committee of the Board of Governors of the IMF.
31. *See* Bergstrand (1984) fur further discussion.
32. Entitled 'The functioning and improvement of the international

monetary system'; *see IMF Survey*, September 1986 for further details.
33. *IMF Survey*, 1 April 1985 also reviews the origins and achievements of the Development Committee.
34. These are compared and contrasted in the *IMF Survey*, 30 June 1986.
35. Of the leaders of the seven major industrial nations: the US, the UK, France, Germany, Japan, Canada and Italy.
36. i.e. the G5 finance ministers plus those of Canada and Italy.
37. *See* Chapter 6 for further discussion.
38. Held in Boston, US on 1 June 1986.
39. Published in April 1986 and taking its name from the Chairman of the Commission, Mr Haruo Maekawa, a former Governor of the Bank of Japan.

8 Do We Need A World Central Bank?

The Latin American debt crisis, discussed in Chapter 5, and its threat to the solvency of the international banking system raised the question of whether a world lender of last resort was needed. In the 1982 Mexican rescue, lender of last resort responsibility was shared by the US Treasury and FRB, the IMF, the BIS, and to some extent the commercial banks themselves, whose attention was drawn by the IMF and the FRB to their community of interest in the rescue. The rescue relied heavily on the US authorities to provide first line support. Whether or not they are willing to continue to shoulder this responsibility, which is to some extent unavoidable given the dominance of the dollar as an international currency, the political acceptability of this arrangement to Europe, let alone the Third World, seems questionable. The BIS is believed to have developed contingency plans to cover for possible future calls on lender of last resort facilities, especially in connection with the Euromarkets. These plans involve the mobilisation of the lender of last resort facilities of its member central banks. The FRB is, however, not a participating member of the BIS,[1] the US being represented by Citibank, which is a commercial bank. Further, the BIS's command over dollar reserves is small relative to those of the FRB, which issues the currency. There are, however, currency swap arrangements between the FRB and the BIS. It is conceivable that whilst the dollar remains the dominant reserve currency some institution such as the IMF or the BIS could build up large, normally idle, dollar reserves. This would be inefficient. It is far better for the currency-issuing authority to act as lender of last resort because there is no need for large idle stocks of reserves to be held. Under the multicurrency reserve system which seems to be gradually developing,[2] the responsibility would be shared between the issuers of the major currencies. This would, however, leave them in a politically dominant position which might ultimately prove unacceptable to the Third World countries.

The situation would be different if the SDR could be promoted to become the major world reserve asset since the issuing authority, the IMF, would then naturally act as lender of last resort and would become more like a world central bank. It would then be natural for the IMF to seek some control over world liquidity management and monetary policies in general, in order to ensure that its issuing policy was consistent with low and stable world inflation. This might ultimately lead it to condition the monetary policies pursued in the member countries. It is unlikely that the SDR would replace national currencies since the political obstacles to this are similar but greater than those involved in establishing a common currency for the EC.[3] The SDR might conceivably exist as a parallel currency, in which case monetary policy coordination involving the IMF and the member countries would be essential. The relationship between the IMF and the central banks of its member countries could take a variety of forms. It is unlikely that the central banks would cede all responsibility for monetary control to the IMF, but some form of close consultation involving regular meetings would be required. In the absence of the development of a reserve currency role for the SDR, the central banks of the major countries might form a coordinating committee to manage world liquidity, either independently or working within the IMF. This might evolve out of a reform of the international monetary system based on target zones and improved policy coordination.[4]

Responsibility for world liquidity management and the adoption of a world lender of last resort role would probably also lead the IMF to develop regulatory and supervisory powers over the financial system. This would be essential to prevent undue reliance on its lender of last resort facilities and the moral hazard this entails.[5] The IMF might be particularly active in coordinating the regulation and supervision of the international banking and financial markets, especially the currently unregulated Euromarkets.[6] It would also wish to promote widespread adoption of the supervisory initiatives of the Basle Committee,[7] to press for standardised accounting procedures and disclosure practices amongst financial institutions, and to improve information flows on country risks and the international banking system, perhaps in conjunction with the BIS and the IIF.[8]

The potential for developing the IMF into a world central bank, outlined above, is based on the assumption of a vastly extended role for the SDR. The G30 have suggested that this could come about through the establishment of a substitution account, which could be operated by the IMF. Participants would deposit foreign exchange, mainly dollars, into the account in return for SDR's denominated certificates.[9] Some of the IMF's gold holdings could be used to back the account and through it the IMF could gradually adopt the character of an SDR-issuing bank with capital (gold) assets, interest-earning assets and interest-bearing liabilities. Alternatives to gold backing are also considered by the G30. One advantage of this proposal is that it would give the IMF a much greater degree of financial independence, especially from the US on which it currently relies heavily for funding. Alternative means of achieving greater financial independence, whilst stopping short of the establishment of a substitution account, are also proposed by the G30. These involve allowing the IMF to raise funds from the private markets which, unlike the IBRD, it is not permitted to do. The US and other IMF members, especially the industrial countries, seem unwilling to grant the IMF financial independence. At the 1986 spring meetings of the IMF and the IBRD, the Interim Committee did, however, ask the IMF's executive board to study possible ways of improving the SDR's monetary characteristics to increase its attractiveness as a component of monetary reserves.[10]

In the absence of developments designed to promote the SDR, the international monetary system will, for some time, continue to be based on a dollar-dominated MCRS, even though the system might become more balanced, with the yen and Deutschmark assuming a greater role in the future. Under this system world central banking functions are currently shared by a number of institutions. The IMF and the OECD, for example, monitor economic and monetary policy. The OECD monitors the economic performance of the member countries and publishes reports.[11] These reports have not been overtly critical in the past, although some mild criticism was made of the US fiscal and monetary policy mix in the mid 1980s. It also provides a useful talking shop in which senior economic officials can exchange views and receive briefings from the OECD secretariat. It has not yet undertaken the role of actively trying to dissuade member countries from pursuing policies which adversely effect their neighbours or used its expertise to provide authoritative guidance on the technicalities of interdependence. The IMF, which has a much wider membership, has, however, been urged to extend its multilateral surveillance in order to promote policy coordination between nations.[12] Quite what this will entail is as yet uncertain. If it means publishing reports there is a risk that they may turn out to be as bland as those of the OECD, since lack of confidentiality in discussions involving senior officials of the member countries may restrict their scope. Without some conditioning force through the international monetary system, as provided under fixed exchange rate systems, policy coordination depends largely on the willingness of the participants. Thus, although policy cooperation and coordination might ultimately lead to an international monetary system based on target zones, as discussed in the previous chapter, more rapid development of such a system might itself encourage more coordination.

Other forums for promoting international cooperation and policy coordination include: the annual economic summits attended by the leaders of the seven major industrial powers, the Interim Committee,[13] the Development Committee,[14] the European Community, the BIS, the GATT,[15] the Groups of Five, Seven and Twenty-four,[16] the UNCTAD,[17] and the UN council itself. One of the main functions of the IMF is to monitor and give advice on balance of payments and exchange rate policies. The BIS and the IBRD monitor the international banking and capital markets and appraise country and exchange rate risks. The IIF also monitors the economic policies of debtor nations and helps to assess country risks on behalf of its member banks. Additionally, the IMF and the IBRD provide financial assistance to deficit countries and LDCs. Their activities have tended to overlap increasingly in recent years. Traditionally the IMF concentrates on short term macroeconomic adjustment and financial assistance to help restore balance of payments equilibrium. The IBRD traditionally concentrates on longer term financial assistance, and especially project leading, to encourage economic development and microeconomic policies. More recently the IBRD has supplemented its project lending, which still accounts for the majority of its total lending, with programme lending which is not tied to specific projects. Programme lending through structural adjustment loans is supposed to support structural adjustment in countries with short term foreign exchange problems. Meanwhile the IMF has been offering longer term assistance through its extended fund facility[18] and enlarged access policy[19] to help countries with more persistent balance of payments problems which require structural adjustment.

In the light of these developments, in 1984 the G10 urged the IMF to confine itself to its traditional duties and statements by finance ministers, and central bank governors of some of the major industrial nations indicated that they would like the IBRD to do the same. To the extent that their activities continue to overlap and to ensure that they complement each other the G10 ministers and central banks have urged that cooperation between them should be strengthened. The Baker Plan[20] seems to have marked a change of attitude since it urged the IMF, the IBRD and its affiliates, and the MDBs to increase their lending to developing countries without repeating calls which had emanated particularly from the US Congress for the IBRD and the IADB to restrict themselves primarily to project lending. The emphasis was rather the reverse. It suggested that the IBRD should promote growth by using its microeconomic expertise to help develop and sponsor policies designed to achieve adjustment and improved market efficiency. The IMF was to continue to exploit its expertise relating to macroeconomic policies and the two institutions were to work more closely together, to sponsor growth-oriented adjustment. It is unclear whether the Baker Plan will have a major impact on the roles of the IMF, the IBRD and its affiliates, and the development banks, especially the IADB, since Congress still holds the purse strings and no significant increase in funding has been forthcoming in the nine months that have passed since the announcement of the Baker Plan in October 1985. Some commentators have argued that some overlap is inevitable and that a merging of the IMF and the IBRD should be considered or alternatively a specific agency should be established to deal with structural adjustment finance.[21] Such an agency would take over some of the current responsibilities of the IMF and the IBRD, perhaps drawing on their expertise, and eliminate the overlap in their perceived roles.

The G10 countries, and the US in particular, seem keen to confine funding of these institutions to current sources.[22] They seem unwilling to allow them the increased independence that would be afforded by permitting them greater access to the private markets and to develop as banks. In particular they will not permit them to increase their gearing, so that the IMF is unable to adopt the character of a bank, lending on the basis of its capital assets. This would be a natural development of proposals for the establishment of an SDR substitution account. Further the IBRD, they feel, should not be permitted to lend more than its subscribed capital, reserves and retained earnings. The latter restriction is imposed by its Articles of Agreement and ensures a financially conservative ratio of loans to paid in and callable capital of 1:1. Given, however, that the IBRD must operate on the assumption that the unpaid portion of its capital base will not be called upon, the ratio of paid in capital, reserves, and retained earnings to loans is 25 per cent, which compares to an average capital to asset ration, or gearing of about 5 per cent for major US and UK commercial banks. By banking standards, therefore, the IBRD could potentially increase its gearing substantially. The risk is that a rise in the gearing ratio might reduce the IBRD's credit rating and increase the cost of its funding through the bond markets, thereby making its loans more expensive. With increased gearing, smaller donations would be required from the US and other major contributors to its funding. This benefit to the donors would have to be balanced against some loss of control over the IBRD's lending policies as a result of its greater financial independence.[23] The IMF and the Bank in their turn have stressed the need for adequate and reliable funding if they are to be able to plan effectively and to perform the functions expected of them successfully.

The BIS[24] acts as a central bankers' bank with the objectives of promoting the cooperation of central banks and of providing additional facilities for international financial operations. It acts as trustee or agent in regard to international financial settlements entrusted to it under agreement with the parties concerned. Broadly speaking it has four main functions. It provides a forum for central bankers to discuss problems with their counterparts from other countries. It engages in banking business on their behalf. It is a centre for international monetary and economic research and collects and collates monetary and economic data. Finally, it has important agency functions such as the handling of transactions for the EMCF of the EC.[25] Since most of its decisions and discussions are related to the technical business of central banking, finance ministers are excluded from its meetings. At the BIS, secret arrangements are believed to have been made for central banks to act as lenders of last resort to commercial banks in the event of a major international banking crisis and various central banking committees meet, such as the Cooke Committee on bank supervision.[26] As bankers' bank the BIS can intervene in the currency markets on behalf of a member central bank. This allows intervention to be carried out on a discreet basis and for central banks in different time zones, such as those of Japan and the US, to intervene outside normal business hours.

Martin (1970) argued that a world central bank was required to coordinate and manage world monetary policy. He noted that the IMF, the BIS, the OECD and GATT engaged in five main types of activity that would be associated with a world central bank. Through them advice is given to individual countries so that a constructive influence is provided from outside for the correction of balance of payments difficulties, mutlilateral consideration is given to ensure that proposed national policies are examined for their effects on other countries, agreed codes of behaviour in the fields of exchange rate practices, restrictions on trade, and capital movements are administered, financial help for countries with external payments difficulties is provided, and reserves are created to ensure an orderly growth of official reserves. These institutions influence the behaviour of individual nations through both moral suasion and the provision of credit. Martin saw the creation of the SDR as the most dramatic development so far in the process of evolution toward a world central bank and looked ahead to the development of a stabilisation function for the SDR, involving the IMF in world liquidity regulation. He also saw a role for the world central bank in supervising the Euromarkets and forecast the creation of a European federal reserve system and various other regional central bank groupings coordinated through some umbrella organisation, which might perhaps be the IMF. The main contribution of the world central bank would be to act as the restraining conscience on national governments, constantly reminding them of the need to consider the external effects of their policies and of the benefits from international cooperation and policy coordination.

In the previous chapter we noted that the 1986 Tokyo economic summit endorsed proposals for an expansion of the IMF's multilateral surveillance role as part of an initiative to promote greater economic policy coordination and co-operation between countries. If the IMF can fulfil this role it will have taken a major step towards becoming a world central bank. Given that some of the other functions of a central bank are currently being performed by other existing institutions, these activities might, in the future, be brought together in some way, so that further evolution towards a world central bank would occur. Real progress towards the development of a world central bank could be made if the role of the SDR was significantly expanded. Similarly progress towards a European central bank will be associated with the extension of the role of the ECU, as we noted in Chapter 6. If Martin is right, the ECU could be the first of a number of regional currencies and the European central bank that might emerge in the future the first, apart perhaps from the FRB, of a number of regional central banks. In connection with supervision, the world central bank might also provide deposit and perhaps asset insurance schemes as well as regulate the Euromarkets and other international interbank markets that might emerge, and coordinate national supervisory efforts.

Witteveen (1983), as we noted in Chapter 5, advocated the establishment of an insurance facility at the IMF. He suggested that this could be linked with an extension of the IMF's supervisory responsibilities and its powers to control international liquidity. The Governor of the Bank of England,[27] among others, has suggested that its powers in the latter direction should be extended in the future. To control bank lending, Witteveen suggests the imposition of variable reserve requirements on Eurodeposits and variable solvency requirements, which should be applied on a consolidated basis, on international lending. To control international liquidity he advocates the strengthening of the role of the SDR, using a dollar substitution account, so that it becomes the principal reserve asset. Its supply would remain under the control of the IMF. The introduction of reserve and solvency requirements would require coordinated action by central banks. The insurance facility would aid supervisory efforts since it could be linked to conditionality on debtor countries receiving IMF-insured loans, thus giving some backing to the current enhanced surveillance procedure,[28] which replaces conditionality once debtors are no longer borrowing from the IMF. Additionally, insurance could be restricted to banks in a country or debts of a country where the solvency ratios are applied and where reserve requirements on Eurocurrency liabilities are in force. This would impose some control over offshore banking centres and force them to cooperate.

The ultimate aim of the world central bank, in Martin's view, would be to encourage the harmonisation of national fiscal and monetary policies on a multilateral basis in order to maintain the international payments mechanism and facilitate international trade. This view was formulated prior to the inception of the FER system but, as noted in Chapter 7, there has in the mid 1980s been a growing realisation of the need for policy coordination as a result of increasing international interdependence and prolonged exchange rate misalignments. Whether or not a fully fledged world central bank is necessary to achieve policy coordination is debatable. The finance ministers and central bank governors of the G10 appear to think that the IMF and the OECD are sufficient and have urged the IMF to extend its multilateral surveillance role with a view to promoting policy cooperation and coordination. There is, however, pressure from the undedeveloped countries, as noted in Chapter 7, for an international conference on international monetary reform and for the development of an institutional framework giving them a greater say in policy formulation and coordination. If Martin is right, an evolutionary process towards the development of a world central bank is already in motion and further increases in international economic interdependence may well strengthen it. Whether or not the resulting world central bank would ever have a range of powers and reponsibilities to match those of national central banks is a moot point. This evolutionary process might conceivably need to be accelerated, however, if the problems facing the world's economy are to be resolved and a damaging reversion to protectionist isolationism is to be averted.

NOTES

1. *See* Hirsch (1969, Chapter 12) for an account of the origins and membership of the BIS.
2. *See* Chapter 7.
3. *See* Chapter 6.
4. *See* Chapter 7.
5. *See* Chapter 1.
6. The new regulatory and supervisory arrangements being developed in the City of London (*See* Chapter 2), where the Eurocurrency and Eurobond markets are predominantly based, will introduce some self-regulation to the Eurobond market. The Eurocurrency market will remain unregulated, however.
7. *See* Chapter 4.
8. The Institute of International Finance, which grew out of a meeting attended by the representatives from leading banks on 27 October 1982. The banks agreed to provide a forum through which individual borrowers could present lenders with information concerning their needs and smaller banks could be provided with country risk and economic performance assessments. The IIF came into being in June 1983 and commenced full operations in 1984.

9. *See* Group of Thirty (1980).
10. *See* Chapter 7.
11. The OECD was founded in 1961 to replace the thirteen-year-old Organisation for European Economic Cooperation, a byproduct of Marshall Aid, after President J. F. Kennedy had proposed US membership. Today it has twenty-four members, all industrial countries; its non-European members are the US, Australia, Canada, Japan and New Zealand.
12. *See* Chapter 7.
13. Which is the principal advisory committee of the IMF and has ministerial representation that reflects the composition of the Fund's executive board; *see* note 30, Chapter 7.
14. Which has the full title: 'Joint Ministerial Committee of the Bank and the Fund on the Transfer of Real Resources to Developing Countries'. See *IMF Survey*, 1 April 1985, for a review of its history and achievements.
15. The General Agreement on Trade and Tariffs is an international treaty signed in 1947 by twenty-three countries in order to set up an international trading organisation and direct policies towards the reduction of trade barriers. GATT is a specialist UN organisation based in Geneva and now has nearly ninety contracting partners, and a further thirty-one countries apply GATT rules *de facto*.
16. *See* Chapter 6.
17. UNCTAD is the United Nations Conference on Trade and Development.
18. The extended fund facility provides medium term assistance to help members with structural adjustment in their economies. Continued drawings are subject to the fulfilment of performance criteria included in the arrangements; *see* Barclays Bank (1984a) for further details.
19. *See* note 29, Chapter 7.
20. *See* Chapter 5.
21. *See* Bird (1983) and Midland Bank (1984), for further discussion.
22. *See* Barclays Bank (1984a and 1984b) for details and the funding of the IMF and the World Bank respectively. *See also* Group of Thirty (1983) on IMF funding.
23. *See* Barclays Bank (1984b), for further details on the World Bank's funding.
24. *See* Hirsch (1969, Chapter 12) on the origins of the Bank for international Settlements and The Banker (1979), on the widening role of the BIS.
25. *See* Chapter 6.
26. *See* Chapter 4.
27. *See* Bank of England (1984).
28. *See* Chapter 5 and *IMF Survey*, 15 July 1985, for further discussion of enhanced surveillance.

Appendix A The Secondary Banking Crisis[1]

The origins of the 'secondary banking crisis' lay in various structural developments in the banking system and in the economic context within which they occurred. Over a number of years, during which there had been a fairly clear demarcation between the activities of various types of bank and on other deposit-taking institutions, the Bank of England had developed an understanding, in fulfilling its supervisory role, with the institutions it recognised as banks. This relationship has been likened to a club arrangement.[2] Following some fairly isolated incidents, involving difficulties amongst non-bank financial intermediaries in the 1950s and early 1960s, the Protection of Depositors Act was passed in 1963. The Act drew a distinction between banks proper, which were exempt from the provisions of the Act, and other deposit takers. Later, in Section 123 of the 1967 Companies Act, powers were conferred on the Board of Trade to grant certificates to companies that could satisfy the Board, under the Money Lenders Acts of 1900 and 1927, that they were carrying out genuine banking business. Hence the banks granted certificates became known as 'Section 123 banks'. The Board of Trade was not equipped to carry out day to day supervision of these banks. The criteria used in granting Section 123 certificates had more to do with the type of business than its quality or the reputation of its management. Under Section 127, of the 1967 Companies Act, a modified list of recognised banks was formed; the responsibility for their supervision was to lie with the Bank of England.

In the late 1960s credit control by the Bank of England was

tight and it was the clearing banks and the finance houses which bore the brunt of the monetary policy. The consequence was that normal, reputable, banking business was diverted to the fringe banks, which made loans and granted credit secured on second mortgages. In order to eliminate these distortions, 'competition and credit control' (CCC) was introduced in 1971[3]. It aimed to modify monetary control procedures by making them more reliant on open market operations and provided for special deposits to be used as a back-up, and to generate more competition in banking. It was expected that the new regime would cause a contraction in fringe banking, as reputable business returned to normal banking channels, and that monetary policy would be more effectively executed. CCC can also be seen as a response to criticisms of the clearing bank cartel that had been aired in the Monopolies Commission Report on the proposed bank mergers involving Martins, Lloyds and Barclays[4] and by the National Board for Prices and Incomes.[5] Its effect in this connection was to end the interest rate setting agreement among the clearing banks.

In the event, economic conditions offset any influence CCC may have had on causing the fringe banking business to contract. From 1971, an expansionary policy was pursued by the government.[6] Investment was slow to respond but by the early 1970s the property market was ready for lift-off. This was because after the restrictions in force during the late 1960s new projects had dried up. By the early 1970s there was an inadequate supply of office property in particular, and rents were rising. Thus, with the economy awash with money, the property sector offered the best prospects and further, with rising inflation, property had the added attraction of being regarded as a good hedge. The recognised banking system was discouraged from financing property development by the Bank of England, which encouraged the banks to provide finance for industry in general and exporters in particular. The fringe banks, therefore, enjoyed a rapid rise in property business which more than offset the decline in their more traditional banking business after CCC. Given this ready and profitable outlet for funds, the fringe banks increasingly drew on the rapidly growing wholesale money markets, in which commercial companies and major institutional investors were major depositors. Additionally, the major clearing banks, being excluded from the property business and with industry still undemanding, also lent funds through the interbank market. The major clearers did, however, deal in the property business indirectly through the establishment of subsidiaries and the purchase of interests in fringe banks. The fringe banks were involved in a seemingly safe and profitable business but they were making medium and long term loans, for property development, and funding these operations largely through short term borrowing on the wholesale markets. They were thus taking risks through extensive exposure to one type of business and through extensive mismatching. In 1973 economic conditions deteriorated, sterling was in almost continuous crisis and the rate of interest was consequently raised whilst the 'corset'[7] was imposed on the clearing banks. In November 1973 London and County Securities (LCS), which held a Section 123 certificate, found itself short of liquidity because it was unable to renew deposits through the money markets. The risk involved in property business had become increasingly evident since December 1972, as a result of a freeze imposed on business rents and the rapid rise in interest rates. The effects of these changes were to raise the cost of liquid funds relative to the revenue from long term committed property loans and to reduce the profitability of the property firms doing the borrowing. When LCS's problems materialised, the supply of funds to companies similarly involved soon dried up. The Bank of England faced the problem that a number of deposit-taking institutions were in danger of imminent collapse and that this might lead to a more general crisis of confidence. This would have spread to the recognised banking sector because of their involvement with the fringe banks through subsidiaries, share interests and the interbank market. The clearing banks themselves were not in direct danger because funds withdrawn from the fringe banks tended to be deposited with them. There was, however, the more general risk of an international loss of confidence in the City of London and a withdrawal of funds from abroad could have had serious effects on both the value of the pound and future invisible earnings.

The Bank of England, therefore, recognised that it was

necessary to act promptly in accordance with its role as crisis lender of last resort to ease the liquidity crisis facing the fringe banks in order to protect the recognised banks and their depositors and the reputation of London as a financial centre. The Bank's response was to draw on the help of the major London clearing banks, the club, to deal with the first casualties in an *ad hoc* manner. Meanwhile a central committee was set up, which became known as 'the lifeboat', to deal with the wider ramifications of the problem. All deposit-taking institutions with known or anticipated liquidity difficulties were identified and investigated. Non-viable companies would be given no support. Companies related through shareholding or large debts to major financial institutions were to be supported by those institutions. The rest were to be supported by recycling the funds being withdrawn from the fringe banks and deposited with the clearing banks. The Committee determined the terms of the support and the Bank of England's contribution and share of the risks. Interest on support lending was charged at the commercial rate, based on the interbank rate with a margin added according to perceived risk. The aim was to maintain clearing bank profitability and to encourage borrowers to regenerate their funding capabilities as soon as possible. In some cases, however, concessionary rates had to be granted.

There were three distinct phases of development following the onset of the crisis. The first was from November 1973 to March 1974, in which the problem was primarily perceived as one of recycling the deposits accumulating with the clearing banks. The second was from March 1974 to December 1974, in which larger institutions sought help and the sums involved rose sharply due to the worsening economic climate[8] and their inability to compensate for losses on property business. Support by the clearers reached 40 per cent of their aggregate capital reserves and they felt that further lending through the 'lifeboat' arrangement would prejudice their own financial soundness ratings.[9] Thus any further funding or risk taking had to be undertaken by the Bank of England alone. At this time also the international situation was deteriorating, largely as a result of the 1973 oil price shock, and the international financial community was shaken by the collapse of the

German Bankhaus Herstatt because of its excessive foreign exchange exposure and losses. As a result, lines of credit extended through the Eurocurrency market to smaller banks were also withdrawn. Given the international edginess, the Bank was anxious to avoid a default by any UK banking institution on external obligations. This was because London's position as the centre of the Eurocurrency market could have been prejudiced. The Bank of England, therefore, acted as sole lender of last resort until the crisis began to recede and the liquidity difficulties seemed to have been overcome.

The third period began in January 1975. During this period attention moved from Europe to the USA, where the Comptroller of Currency announced that one hundred and fifty of the nation's banking institutions were under close scrutiny. Also during this period a major international recycling problem, caused by the 1973 oil price shock, emerged.[10] Against this background, the Bank of England continued its support outside the 'lifeboat'.

The 'lifeboat', therefore, involved the sharing of lender of last resort responsibilities, which were provided at a price by the clearing banks and the Bank of England. The banks, ultimately under threat from 'knock-on' or domino effects from the 'secondary banking crisis' and being in receipt of funds withdrawn from the fringe banks, recognised their community of interest with the Bank of England. They thereby reduced the need for the Bank to inject massive amounts of extra cash to prop up the secondary banking sector and prevented the shock waves spreading widely through the UK banking and financial system and perhaps beyond. Ultimately, however, the Bank of England showed that it was willing to assume the function of crisis lender of last resort alone. Outstanding lifeboat lending by the clearing banks and the Bank had only been halved by June 1978. The effects of the crisis, therefore, took a long time to unwind. The crisis ultimately induced an extension to the supervisory responsibilities of the Bank of England, which assumed responsiblility for licensed deposit-taking institutions as a result of the 1979 Banking Act.

NOTES

1. For fuller accounts of the origins, development and containment of the crisis *see* Bank of England (1978), Channon (1977) and Reid (1982).
2. *See* Revell (1975).
3. *See* Bank of England (1971).
4. Monopolies Commission (1968).
5. Command Paper 3292.
6. Which was a Conservative government. Edward Heath was Prime Minister and the resulting boom was dubbed the 'Barber Boom', after the Chancellor, Anthony Barber.
7. More formally known as the supplementary special deposit scheme (SSDS); *see* Brown (1982) or Bank of England (1982b) for a history of and details on the scheme.
8. The quadrupling of oil prices, instigated by OPEC at the end of 1973, had been followed by the miners' strike and the three-day week, a general election and a tough March budget with the promise of another budget later in the year.
9. Thus causing a rise in the costs of funding their operations.
10. The quadrupling of oil prices had led to significant rise in oil revenues for oil producers, and especially OPEC members. These countries, being sparsely populated, could not absorb the revenues internally. Consequently they explored overseas investment opportunities. They generally showed a preference for liquidity so that the money was handled largely by the banking system, which found ready lending opportunities in the deficit countries; *see* Cohen (1981).

Appendix B The Johnson Matthey Affair

On 1 October 1984 the Bank of England mounted a dramatic rescue of the Johnson Matthey Bank (JMB), which was the banking arm of the Johnson Matthey Company (JMC) and a major dealer on the gold bullion market, where it was one of the five bullion dealers. The Bank took control of JMB, purchasing it for £1 and injecting £100m of capital, and organised a £150m standby credit from twenty-five UK banks and members of the gold bullion market. The parent also agreed to contribute £50m to the bank's capital.

Officially, action was taken to head off a major crisis in the bullion market, over which the Bank had supervisory responsibility.[1] Dr Owen[2] subsequently criticised the Bank for failing to regulate the bullion and commodity markets adequately. JMC approached the Bank after an auditor's report showed major problems with JMB's commercial loans. The group calculated that the necessary provisions would wipe out the bank's capital and perhaps even jeopardise the group as a whole. JMB's problem stemmed from a few large loans rather than a number of small ones and JMB had exceeded the Bank's prevailing lending guidelines, which had no legal force and were flexible, but were supposed to prevent banks from lending more than an equivalent of 10 per cent of their capital to any one borrower without permission. In the search for rapid growth JMB had taken on not only large but risky loans.

It was feared that the JMB rescue would set a precedent and lead other banks to take more risks because they could expect the Bank to bail them out. Hard-liners argued that JMB should have been allowed to go into liquidation. The

Chancellor claimed that he was not consulted over the proposed rescue package, and the Deputy Governor of the Bank, whose role was central in the rescue, apparently instigated it without consulting the Governor.

A £150m package of indemnities to cover the exceptional losses of JMB was finally agreed between the Bank and a group of clearing banks, accepting houses and gold bullion houses on 8 November 1984, after tortuous negotiations. The indemnities were a contingency reserve against the possibility that JMB's losses might exceed its £170m worth of capital. The banks and bullion brokers put up £75m and insisted that the Bank put up a similar amount, rather than the £25m originally proposed. The clearing banks committed £35m, the four gold bullion brokers £30m and the accepting houses £10m. Thus the Bank put a significant amount of public money at risk.

The clearing banks provided indemnities under sufferance, arguing that they were not responsible for JMB's losses. They were bitter following the March 1984 budget,[3] feeling that the Bank should have protected their corner. The difficulty the Bank experienced in assembling the guarantee package highlighted the conflicts banks face between their desire to participate in regulation and supervision and their responsibilities to shareholders. They proved less cooperative in the JMB crisis than they had done in the secondary banking crisis a decade or so earlier. This change of attitude could have resulted from the fact that markets had become more competitive and their participants less segregated. The implication was that the Bank could not take cooperation for granted when it tried to launch a rescue operation in the future.

The Treasury and Bank Review Committee's report[4] provided additional information on the origins and causes of the JMB affair. JMB had failed to report that it had lent 115 per cent of its capital to two borrowers, both of whom were doubtful credit risks. Instead it reported a 72 per cent exposure. The Bank in its account of the crisis said that the collapse was due to bad management rather than fraud and that JMB had failed to identify the extent of its exposure due to inadequate internal controls.[5] In July 1985 JMB, now wholly owned by the Bank, issued a writ against Arthur

Young, alleging breach of contract and/or negligence in the firm's capacity as auditors and accountants of JMB. The Bank felt that Arthur Young should have drawn attention to the inadequate internal controls. Later in July 1985 Arthur Young decided to sue the Chancellor for libel in connection with his allegations that the Bank's report on the JMB affair raised questions about the role of the auditors. In March 1985, following the Bank's report and an investigation commissioned by the Bank into JMB by accountants Price Waterhouse, the Bank decided to call in the City Police Fraud Squad with a watching brief to clarify details on the events which led up to JMB's collapse. Additionally Mr Brian Sedgmore MP compiled a dossier on the JMB affair which he has submitted to the Chancellor and the Minister for Corporate and Consumer Affairs in support of his demand for an independent and exhaustive enquiry into the affair. The government, however, refused to commission such an inquiry, despite Mr Sedgemore's allegations and the fact that six months had elapsed between the Bank's rescue of JMB and its decision to call in the Fraud Squad.

In July 1985, eight months after the rescue, the Fraud Squad launched investigations into criminal offences after gaps in JMB's records had been discovered. The Bank, however, stressed that there was no evidence, contrary to Mr Sedgemore's allegations, of fraud by directors or staff. Rather, the fraud involved the bank's clients and the cause of the losses were serious shortcomings in JMB's management.

By July 1985 JMB's losses were estimated to be £248m, more than half of its £400m loan book. Losses were attributed to dubious shipping loans to the Imham brothers, whose total borrowings were £35m, and loans totalling £53m and £21m to the Sipra and Gomba groups of companies respectively. Loans to the Sipra group included shipping and trading loans. These trading loans, as well as those to the Imham brothers and other clients involved in trade with Nigeria, were the immediate cause of JMB's collapse, the January 1984 military coup in Nigeria having been followed by a suspension of overseas payments.

By September 1985 the feared losses had been revised downwards to £220m, as a result of the Bank recovering what it could and seeking security for some of the outstanding loans. Then in October 1985 the Bank called in the liquidators for the Gomba and Sipra groups. Growing evidence of fraud led to renewed pressure for an enquiry, following allegations by Mr Sedgemore that the Bank's staff were now implicated. The Chancellor refused an inquiry and absolved the Bank's staff and praised them for their handling of the affair. Pressure for an inquiry continued as it became evident in November 1985 that JMB had previously been defrauded in 1981. In December 1985 the Bank agreed a deal with the second largest debtors, the Imham brothers, who owed £35m. The Bank expected to recoup £5m in cash, £17m over a period of time, and write off £13m. Additionally in December the Fraud Squad uncovered frauds involving the smuggling of large sums of money out of Nigeria in exchange for bogus documents and it transpired that a client had previously been investigated in 1983 in connection with forged import documents. These frauds involved relatively small debtors. Then in February 1986 twelve people were arrested by Customs and Excise officers on suspicion of value added tax fraud in connection with £5m worth of gold bullion purchases by the bank. Gold has been smuggled into the UK and JMB had been presented with false documents. This raised suspicions about its previously untainted reputation as a bullion dealer, but it was stressed that the fraud did not involve JMB's present or former staff.

The affair began to draw to a close in April 1986 when the Bank sold JMB's bullion, treasury and foreign exchange business, as well as the viable part of its loan book, to Westpac, Australia's largest bank, for £67.5m. It had already sold its insurance broking business for £5.5m and its futures broking business for £1.8m. With other sales in prospect the Bank was reasonably hopeful of recouping its £100m capital injection. The Bank was left with the troubled loan portfolio, which had been written down to £25m, and hoped to recover more loans and to benefit from a negligence claim on JMB's auditors, Arthur Young. The indemnity package remained in place but drawings on it were likely to be significantly less than once feared. By May 1986, reduced estimates of JMB's losses implied that the Bank would be liable to contribute £27m as a result of its 50 per cent share in the indemnity agreement. Johnson Matthey, as parent company, carried a loss of about £150m and the banks, under the indemnity agreement, carried a loss of about £27m.

NOTES

1. *See* Committee to Review the Functioning of the Financial System (Wilson Committee) (1978).
2. Leader of the Social Democratic Party.
3. Which had made them liable to taxes on their leasing business.
4. Command Paper 9432, (1985).
5. Bank of England (1985).

Appendix C The Continental Illinois Crisis

In May 1984 Continental Illinois was rescued by the FDIC following rumours about its liquidity. These were largely unfounded but caused it to suffer a dramatic loss of credit over the space of a fortnight, threatening its solvency. It was the eighth largest US bank prior to the crisis and was well regarded, having capital ratios comparable to its rivals.

In order to contain the crisis, which could have had domino effects nationally and internationally, an aid package of $5.5bn was put together by a group of major commercial banks and the FDIC gave the bank a public vote of confidence. They hoped that by extending credit to solve the liquidity crisis the rumours would subside. They had a vested interest in doing so, since rumours could also have hit banks known or suspected to have dealings with Continental Illinois via the interbank market. Confidence was not, however, restored and the FRB and the FDIC took the unprecedented step of guaranteeing all deposits in an attempt to restore confidence whilst they sought a buyer for Continental Illinois. The large international depositors, whose withdrawal of deposits had been mainly responsible for the liquidity crisis, did not renew their lines of credit, despite the announcement of full deposit protection. Continental Illinois' deposits were much larger than FDIC's funds, hence the need for the FRB's backing. As well as extending credit, the larger banks and the FDIC injected $2bn of capital and Continental Illinois had to borrow $2bn from the Federal Reserve Bank of Chicago, its direct lender of last resort, and $4bn from the FRB.

Once it became clear, in July 1984, that no buyer was

forthcoming a rescue package was assembled. The FDIC bought $4.5bn of problem loans from Continental Illinois, which were mainly loans to the energy sector, and injected $1bn worth of capital, giving it an 80 per cent stockholding and effectively nationalising the bank. The $5.5bn commercial bank credit remained in place and the FRB lent the FDIC $3.5bn to help finance the rescue package. The FDIC strengthened the Continental Illinois management team and proceeded to shrink its balance sheet, with a view to future sale in order to recoup its capital injection. The $4.5bn of assets purchased had a book value of $5.1bn. The assets were to be purchased in two instalments: $3bn immediately and $1.5bn over three years. The total cost of the rescue to the FDIC was, therefore, $7.5bn,[1] which was more than double the amount banks had to put up to support Mexico in 1984. The FRB announced unlimited lender of last resort support to guarantee the rescue. The extent of the rescue's cost not surprisingly attracted criticisms of the supervisory system and raised questions about the prudence of allowing the deregulation of the banking system to proceed at the pace experienced in the early 1980s. Some members of the Senate and Congress banking committees called for retrenchment rather than increased permissiveness. In particular explanations were sought for why the crisis was not averted and why the FRB had not announced full lender of last resort support at an earlier date. An inquiry was set up and legislation which the bank supervisors had been seeking concerning deregulation was stalled.

The crisis and subsequent rescue confirmed that small banks are treated differently from large banks, which seemingly are not to be allowed to fail. The reason for this is that the domino effects of a large bank failure could lead to major repercussions affecting the whole domestic financial system and probably even the international banking system. Under the Basle Concordat[2] the US supervisors had responsibility for the solvency of Continental Illinois's merchant banking branch in London, for example. Also non-US banks were exposed to Continental Illinois via the Eurodollar market.

The rumours started because Continental Illinois was known to have a large energy loan portfolio and to be reliant on the wholesale market for funds. The increasingly common banking practice of liability management[3] was of necessity employed by Continental Illinois because of its narrow retail deposit base, which was the result of severe branching restrictions in the state of Illinois. The increase in liquidity that liability management, through wholesale funding, affords is clearly fragile and heavily dependent on confidence. Rumours can quickly lead to a withdrawal of credit lines, as the Continental Illinois case amply illustrated. The basis of the rumours, the high energy exposure, had, however, resulted from poor management control of loans. The Penn Square bank was allowed to fail in July 1982. It had grown rapidly due to overaggressive energy lending and its failure damaged confidence in other small banks and led to criticisms of the supervisors, even through the FDIC protected its depositors. Continental Illinois had dealings with Penn Square and had bought some of its energy loans. It had also engaged in, with hindsight, an overaggressive expansion of its own energy loans in the 1970s. The shockwaves from the Penn Square collapse hit other banks, some of them medium sized.[4] The Penn Square rescue was, however, played by the rules, the big depositors ultimately getting only 65 per cent of their uninsured claims.[5]

Despite it energy loan exposure, a result of conscious management decisions, Continental Illinois was doing reasonably well. Due to Illinois state branching restrictions, it was, however, largely Chicago based and relied on wholesale, rather than retail, deposits. Although more heavily reliant on wholesale funds than most US banks, and certainly than most major banks in other OECD countries, it is worth noting that banks in most major economies have become more reliant via liability management on wholesale funding.[6] The largely rumour-based problems experienced by Continental Illinois could, therefore, potentially apply to them. The heavy exposure to the energy sector became a liability when oil prices began to fall in the early 1980s and the problem was exacerbated by rising real interest rates, which increased the costs to borrowers of servicing the loans. This illustrates another problem. Although variable interest rates on loans can protect banks against interest rate risks[7] they can also add to the risk of default on loans if borrowers find it difficult to meet the higher interest payments. The spread of the practice of granting loans with variable interest rates through the banking systems of the world thus also exposes them to potential problems similar to those faced by Continental Illinois. The increasing proportion of bad and non-performing loans in Continental Illinois' portfolio locked in funds and ultimately sparked rumours of illiquidity which were exacerbated by the reactions on the wholesale market. There is clearly a question mark over the management for allowing the bank to get into such a position through its inadequate monitoring and control of loans, but the auditors and the supervisors, because they did not identify the problems and force the management to do something about it, are also implicated.

The Continental Illinois crisis is likely to have considerable repercussions for the US banks' regulatory and supervisory system. The supervisory system was already under view by a White House task force chaired by the Vice-President, George Bush, and bank regulations were under review by the Senate and Congress banking committees. The Continental Illinois crisis stalled legislation, pending the results of a full enquiry and consideration of its implications. In the hearings the FDIC in particular was severely criticised over its handling of the crisis, and the FRB did not escape without reproach.

First Chicago, the tenth largest US and second largest Chicago bank, was also the subject of rumours in July 1985 when it was hit by heavy losses.[8] Since October 1984, when it wrote off loans, largely due to exposure to the farming sector, it had been under scrutiny and had been ordered by its supervisors to raise its capital base. Consequently, it had sold and leased back its headquarters, one of its least liquid capital assets.[9] In First Chicago's case the rumours, however, proved unfounded and the bank moved back into the black in the third quarter of 1985. Also in this quarter Continental Illinois' results showed that it had dramatically reduced its 'safety net' borrowings from the FRB and the group of twenty-eight banks and had achieved operating net earnings. In October 1984 Continental Illinois' borrowings had exceeded $9bn but by the end of September 1985 they were below $1bn. Mainly as a result of Continental Illinois' expected long term dependence on its funds, the FRB had reduced its long term lender of last resort surcharge in 1984.

First Chicago had only broken even in the second quarter of 1985 following the Brazilian bank affair,[10] and it suffered from adverse market reaction. Despite the rumours, however, First Chicago was able to continue funding itself normally and did not suffer badly from large withdrawals. This was because it had a more diversified deposit base than Continental Illinois and because 23 per cent of its balance sheet consisted of liquid assets, making it the second most liquid bank in the US. It had a greater volume of core deposits than Continental Illinois because it is traditionally the largest savings bank in Chicago. As a result, the proportion of core deposits in its balance sheet was similar to that of the New York money centre banks. It had also made efforts to build up relationships with big depositors and was, therefore, less reliant on the interbank market than Continental Illinois. It had 3,200 corporate sector depositors and 92 per cent of its domestic liabilities were derived from this direct marketing effort. This practice of dealing directly with fund placers made its funding more costly but more stable. Like Continental Illinois, however, a significant proportion of its funds were raised overseas. But these funds were mainly placed by US corporations through its offshore branches. Its usage of the interbank market was kept as low as 2 per cent of the group's balance sheet and never exceeded 8 per cent. It therefore had much more stable and diversified sources of funding than Continental Illinois.

The unpredictability of First Chicago's performance, however, led to a significant downgrading of its credit rating,[11] making it more expensive for it to raise money and capital by issuing paper and debt than other major money centre banks.

NOTES

1. i.e. $2bn original + $1bn subsequent capital injection + $4.5bn worth of bad loans purchased.
2. An agreement on the allocation of supervisory responsibilities for the international banking system reached between central banks meeting at

the Bank for International Settlement in Basle in 1975 and revised in 1983.
3. Through which banks first seek loans and then raise the funds rather than raise deposits and then seek profitable loan business.
4. e.g. Seafirst (twenty-ninth largest), which was rescued by Bank America, which had also bought energy loans from Penn Square in a purchase and assumption transaction with the FDIC.
5. The FDIC officially only insures individual deposits up to a value of $100,000.
6. This has been a response to their shrinking share of aggregate retail deposits, which is due to the success of non-bank financial intermediaries such as 'thrifts' in the US and building societies in the UK in attracting savings deposits.
7. Which result from the costs of funds and the revenue from loans moving out of line.
8. As a result of its involvement with a failed Brazilian bank in which it had bought a 44.5 per cent stake in 1984.
9. As had a number of other US banks following general instructions in 1984 to raise capital ratios.
10. *See* note 8.
11. By the US credit rating agencies, Moody's and Standard and Poors', in 1985.

References

Allen, P. R. (1986), 'The ECU: birth of a new currency', *Group of 30 Occasional Papers* **30**, New York.
Alphandery, E. and Fourcans, A. (1984), 'How to create a single European currency', *Financial Times*, 20 June, p. 19.
Bagehot, W. (1873), *Lombard Street*, H. S. King & Co., London.
Bank of England (1971), *Competition and Credit Control*, May, London.
Bank of England (1978), 'The secondary banking crisis and the Bank of England's support operations', *Bank of England Quarterly Bulletin*, Vol. **18**, No. 2, June, pp. 230–99.
Bank of England (1980), 'The measurement of capital', *Bank of England Quarterly Bulletin*, September, pp. 324–9.
Bank of England (1981), 'Foreign currency exposure', *Bank of England Quarterly Bulletin*, June, pp. 235–7.
Bank of England (1982), 'The measurement of liquidity', *Bank of England Quarterly Bulletin*, September, pp. 399–402.
Bank of England (1982a), 'The role of the bank supervisor', *Bank of England Quarterly Bulletin*, December, pp. 547–52.
Bank of England (1982b), 'The supplementary deposit scheme', *Bank of England Quarterly Bulletin*, March, pp. 74–85.
Bank of England (1984), 'The role and future of international financial institutions', *Bank of England Quarterly Bulletin*, Vol. **24**, No. 4, December, pp. 503–10.
Bank of England (1985), *Report and Accounts*.
Bank of England (1986), 'Consolidated supervision of institutions authorised under the Banking Act 1979, *Bank of England Quarterly Bulletin*, March, pp. 85–9.
Bank for International Settlements (1985), *Fifty-Fifth Annual Report*, June, Basle, Switzerland.
Bank for International Settlements (1986), *Fifty-Sixth Annual Report*, June, Basle, Switzerland.

Bank for International Settlements (1986a), *Recent Innovations in International Banking*, April, Basle, Switzerland.

The Banker (1979), 'What the BIS stands for', *The Banker*, June, pp. 25-8.

The Banker (1986), *EFTPOS: Slow Progress*, February, pp. 75-84.

Banker Research Unit (1981), *Banking Structures and Sources of Finance in the European Communities*, 4th Edition, Chapter 11, EEC harmonization. The Financial Times Business Publishing Ltd, London.

Banking Federation of the European Community (1980), *The Use of the ECU in Banking Transactions*, Brussels.

Barclays Bank (1984a), 'The IMF—Its Financial Role', *Barclays Review*, February, pp. 8-13.

Barclays Bank (1984b), 'The World Bank—Its Role in Financing Development', *Barclays Review*, August, pp. 55-61.

Bergstrand, J. H. (1984), 'Bretton Woods revisited', *New England Economic Review*, September/October, pp. 22-33. Federal Reserve Bank of Boston, MA, USA.

Bird, G. (1983), 'Reforming the Fund', *The Three Banks Review*, December, No. 140.

Bispham, J. (1986), 'Growing public sector debt: a policy dilemma', *National Westminster Bank Quarterly Review*, May, pp. 52-67.

Brown, R. (1982), *A Guide to Monetary Policy*. Bank Information Service, London.

Budd, A. (1986) 'A book that changed an economist's mind', *Financial Times*, 26 March 1986, p. 25.

Chandavarkar, A. G. (1984), *The International Monetary Fund: Its Financial Organisation and Activities*, IMF Pamphlet Series No. 42, International Monetary Fund, Washington DC.

Channon, D. F. (1977), *British Banking Strategy*. Macmillan, London.

Cline, W. R. (1986), 'A programme that can work', *Financial Times*, 14 May 1986, p. 35.

Coghlan, T. (1980), *'The Theory of Money and Finance'*. Macmillan, London.

Cohen, B. J. (1981), *Banks and the Balance of Payments*, Allenheld, Osmun and Co., New Jersey.

Cohen, D. (1985), 'Reassessing Third World debt', *Economic Policy*, Vol. 1, No. 1 November, pp. 141-67.

Command Paper 3292 (1967), *National Board for Prices and Incomes Report*, No. 34 'Bank Charges', HMSO, London.

Command Paper 6437 (1943), *Proposals for an International Clearing Union*, HMSO, London.

Command Paper 9316 (1984), *Building Societies: A New Framework*, July. HMSO, London.
Command Paper 9432 (1985) *Financial Services in the UK: A New Framework for Investor Protection*, July. HMSO, London.
Command Paper 9550 (1985), *Report of the Committee Set Up to Consider the System of Banking Supervision*, July. HMSO, London.
Command Paper 9695 (1985), Banking Supervision, December HMSO, London.
Commission of the European Communities (1977), *First Council Directive*, OJ. No. L332, 17.12.1977.
Commission of the European Communities (1983), *Council Directive of 13 June on the Supervision of Credit Institutions on a Consolidated Basis*, (83/350/EEC), Brussels.
Commission of the European Communities (1983), *Financial Integration*, COM (83) 207 Final, 20 April, Brussels.
Committee on Banking Regulations and Supervisory Practices (1975), *The Basle Concordat*, December, Basle, Switzerland. See also 'Developments in co-operation among bank supervisory authorities', *Bank of England Quarterly Bulletin*, June 1981.
Committee on Banking Regulations and Supervisory Practices (1978), *Consolidation of Bank's Balance Sheets: Aggregation of Risk Bearing Assets as a Method of Supervising Bank Solvency*, October, Basle, Switzerland.
Committee on Banking Regulations and Supervisory Practices (1983), *Principles for the Supervision of Banks' Foreign Establishments*, May, Basle, Switzerland.
Committee on Banking Regulations and Supervisory Practices (1986), *The Management of Banks' Off Balance Sheet Exposures: A Supervisory Perspective*, March, Basle, Switzerland.
Committee to Review the Functioning of the Financial Institutions (Wilson Committee) (1978), *Second Stage Evidence*, Vol. **4**, 'The Stock Exchange, The Bank of England', HMSO, London.
Congdon, T. (1981), 'The first principles of central banking', *The Banker*, April, pp. 57–62.
Cooper, J. (1984), *The Mangement and Regulation of Banks*', Chapter 5. Macmillan, London.
Crawford, M. (1985), 'Third World debt is here to stay', *Lloyds Bank Review*, No. 155, January, pp. 13–31.
Dale, R. S. (1981), 'Prudential regulation of multinational banking: the problem outlined', *National Westminster Bank Quarterly Review*, February, pp. 14–24.
Dale, R. S. (1984), 'Continental Illinois: the lessons for deposit

insurance', *The Banker*, July, pp. 12–22 and 91.

Dale, R. S. (1984), *The Regulation of International Banking*. Woodhead-Faulkner, Cambridge.

Danielsen, A. L. (1982), *The Evolution of OPEC*. Harcourt Brace Jovanovich, New York.

Dennis, G. and Nellis, J. (1984), 'The EMS and UK membership: five years on', *Lloyds Bank Review*, No. 154, October, pp. 13–31.

Dornbusch (1984), 'The overvalued dollar', *Lloyds Bank Review*, No. 152, April, pp. 1–12.

Dunham, C. R. and Syron, R. F. (1984), 'Interstate banking—part II', *New England Bank Review*, May/June, pp. 11–28.

EEC (1973), 73/183/EEC, Council Directive of 24 July 1973 on 'The abolition of restrictions on the freedom of establishment and freedom to provide services in respect of self-employed activities of banks and other financial institutions'.

Federal Reserve (1984), 'The Federal Reserve position on restructuring of financial regulation responsibilities', *Federal Reserve Bulletin*, July, pp. 547–57.

Francis, J. C. and Archer, S. H. (1971), *'Portfolio Analysis'*. Prentice Hall, New Jersey.

Friedman, M. and Schwartz, A. J. (1963), *'A Monetary History of the United States, 1867–1960'*. National Bureau of Economic Research, New Jersey.

Goodhart, C. (1986), 'Has the time come for the UK to join the EMS?', *The Banker*, February 1986, pp. 26–9.

Group of Thirty (1980), *Towards a Less Unstable International Monetary System*, New York.

Group of Thirty (1982a), *Reserve Currencies in Transition*, New York.

Group of Thirty (1982b), *The Problem of Exchange Rates: A Policy Statement*, New York.

Group of Thirty (1983), *The IMF and the Private Markets*, New York.

Grubel, H. G. (1984), *The International Monetary System*, 4th Edition. Penguin Books, Harmondsworth, Middlesex.

Hirsch, F. (1969), *Money International*. Penguin Books, Harmondsworth, Middlesex.

Hirsch, F. (1977), 'The Bagehot problem', *The Manchester School*, Vol. **45** pp. 241–57.

HMSO (1943), *United States Proposals for a United and Associated Nations Stabilisation Fund*. HMSO. London.

House of Commons (Red Book) (1980), *Financial Statement and Budget Report 1980/81*. HMSO, London.

House of Commons Bill 95 (1985/6), *Building Society Bill*, HC95.
House of Commons Bill 238 (1985/6), *Financial Services Bill*, HC238.
House of Commons Treasury and Civil Service Committee (1985), *The Financial and Economic Consequences of UK Membership of the EEC: The European Monetary System*, 13th Report HC57/-IV, HMSO.
IMF, Bi-monthly Surveys, International Monetary Fund, Washington, DC.
Institute for International Economics (1985), *Bank Lending to Developing Countries: The Policy Alternatives*, April. MIT Press, Cambridge, MA.
Inter Bank Research Organisation (1982), *IBRO Research Brief*, October, London.
Jenkins, R. (1984), 'European Monetary System and sterling', *Midland Bank Review*, Summer, pp. 23-5.
Johnson, C. (1981), 'Should Britain join the EMS?', *The Banker*, April, pp. 65-9.
Keegan, W. J. (1986), 'Towards a new Bretton Woods?', *Royal Bank of Scotland Review*, No. 149, March, pp. 3-10.
Kenen, P. B. (1983), *The Role of the Dollar as an International Currency*, Occasional Paper 13. Group of Thirty, New York.
Kraft, J. (1984), *The Mexican Rescue*. Group of Thirty, New York.
Kruse, D. (1980), *Monetary Integration in Western Europe*. Butterworth, London.
Laney, L. O. (1980), 'Towards a multiple reserve system', *Euromoney*, September, pp. 127-39.
Leohnis, A. (1985), 'EMS: a central banking view', *The Banker*, Vol. 135, No. 714, pp. 18-21.
Lever, H. (1983), 'The international debt threat: a concerted way out', *The Economist*, Vol. **288**, 9 July, pp. 14-16.
Lever, H. (1985), 'The dollar and the world economy: the case for concerted management', *Lloyds Bank Review*, No. 157, July, pp. 1-12.
Lever, H. and Sarnet, M. (1972), *'Investments and Portfolio Analysis'*. Wiley, New York.
Lever, H. and Huhne, C. (1985), *Debt and Danger*. Penguin Special, Penguin Books, Harmondsworth, Middlesex.
Lomax, D. F. (1983), 'Prospects for the European Monetary System', *National Westminster Bank Quarterly Review*, May, pp. 33-50.
Lomax, D. F. (1985), 'Would EMS membership help sterling?', *The Banker*, February, pp. 27-33.

Lomax, D. F. (1986), *The Developing Country Debt Crisis*. Macmillan, London.

McCarthy, I. (1979), 'Offshore banking centres: benefits and costs', *Finance and Development*, December, pp. 45-8.

Maisel, S. J. (ed.) (1981), *Risk and Capital Adequacy in Commercial Banks*. National Bureau of Economic Research (NBER), University of Chicago Press.

Makin, J. (1986), 'How to defuse the Mexican debt crisis', *Financial Times*, 14 May, p. 35.

Marris, S. (1986), 'Don't freeze out fiscal policy', *Financial Times*, 7 July, p. 31.

Martin, W. M. (1970), *Toward A World Central Bank*, 1980 Per Jacobsson Lecture. IMF, Washington DC.

Mayer, H. W. (1986), 'Private ECUs: potential macro-economic policy dimensions', *BIS Economic Papers*, No. 16, April. Bank for International Settlements, Monetary and Economic Department, Basle, Switzerland.

Meade, J. E. (1984), 'A New Keynesian Bretton Woods', The Three Banks Review, No. 142, June, pp. 8-25.

Micossi, S. (1985), 'The intervention and financial mechanisms of the EMS and the role of the ECU, *Banca Nazionale Del Lavoro Quarterly Review*, No. 155, December, pp. 327-46.

Midland Bank (1984), 'International Lenders and World Debt' *Midland Bank Review*, Winter, pp. 17-22.

Monopolies Commission (1968), *'Barclays Bank Ltd, Lloyds Bank Ltd and Martins Bank: A Report on the Proposed Merger'*. HMSO, London.

National Consumer Council (1983), *Banking Services and the Consumer: A Report by the National Consumer Council*. Metheun, London.

Nunnenkamp, P. (1986), *The International Debt Crisis of the Third World: Causes and Consequences for the World Economy*. Wheatsheaf Books, Brighton.

OECD (1983), *see* Peccioli, R. M. (1983).

Parkin, M. (1978), 'In search of a monetary constitution for the European communities', Chapter 8 in Fratiani, M. and Peeters, T. (eds.) *One Money for Europe*. Macmillan, London.

Peccioli, R. M. (1983), *The Internationalisation of Banking: The Policy Issues*. OECD, Paris.

Reid, M. (1982), *The Secondary Banking Crisis, 1973-1975*. Macmillan, London.

Revell, J. (1975), *Solvency and Regulation of Banks*, Bangor Occasional Papers in Economics, No. 5. University of Wales Press, Cardiff.

Ryrie, Sir W. (1986), 'Increasing the flow of risk capital to developing countries', *The Royal Bank of Scotland Review*, No. 150, June, pp. 3–16.

Schokker, E. (1980), 'The central bank and the state in the light of European integration', *Societe Universitaire Europeene de Recherches Financieres (SUERF)*, Netherlands.

Shipley, W. V. (1985), 'The right way to re-stabilise the US banking industry', *The Banker*, February, pp. 16–19.

Solomon, A. M. (1985), 'LDC debt: where do we go from here?', *The Banker*, Vol. **135**, No. 714, pp. 14–17.

Spraos, J. (1984), 'IMF conditionality—A better way', *Banca Nazionale Del Lavoro Quarterly Review*, No. 151, December, pp. 411–22.

Sumner, M. T. and Zis, G. (eds.) (1982), *European Monetary Union: Progress and Prospects*. Macmillan, London.

Syron, R. F. (1984), 'The New England experiment in interstate banking', *New England Bank Review*, March/April, pp. 5–17.

Tew, B. (1970), *International Monetary Co-operation 1945–70*. Hutchinson, London.

Tobin, J. (1963), 'Commercial banks as creators of credit', in Carlson, D. (ed.), *Banking and Monetary Studies*. Irwin, Homewood, Ill.

Triffen, R. (1964), 'The Evolution of the International Monetary System: Historical Reappraisal and Future Perspectives', Princeton.

Triffen, R. (1980), 'The future of the international monetary system', *Banco Nazionale Del Lavoro Quarterly Review*, March, No. 132, pp. 29–55.

Triffen, R. (1982), 'The European Monetary System and the dollar in the framework of the world monetary system', *Banco Nazionale Del Lavoro Quarterly Review*, September, No. 142, pp. 492–7.

Wallich, H. C. (1984), *Insurance of Bank Lending to Developing Countries*, Group of Thirty Occasional Paper No. 15, New York.

Wallich, H. C. (1984a), 'US bank deregulation: the case for orderly progress', *The Banker*, May, pp. 25–8.

Walters, A. A. (1986) *Britain's Economic Renaissance: Margaret Thatcher Reforms 1979–84*. Oxford University Press.

War on Want (1985), *Profits out of Poverty: British Banks and the Latin American Debt Crisis*. War on Want Campaigns Ltd, London.

Welch, J. (ed.) (1981), *The Regulation of Banks in the Member States of the EEC*, 2nd Edition, Chapter 11, EEC. Martinus Nijhoff, The Hague.

Witteveen, H. J. (1983), *Developing a New International Monetary System: A Long Term View*, 1983 Per Jacobsson Lecture. IMF, Washington DC.

Index

asset
  insurance 6, 98, 172–3
  management 15
  see also loans, insurance
auditors and auditing 19–24 *passim*, 40, 43, 190
Austral Plan 77, 103
adverse selection 8, 9

Bagehot problem 10
Baker Plan 85–95 *passim*, 102–8 *passim*, 170
balance of payments
  fundamental disequilibrium 139
  difficulties 171
  see also trade
bank(s) and banking
  Act (UK 1979) 12, 19–21, 24, 53–4
  authorisation or licencing 12, 22
  Bill 22
  central 2–4, 14, 15, 59, 81, 85, 93–7, *passim*, 100, 114, 116, 133, 140, 142, 152, 165–6, 169, 171,
    world 166, 172
  clearing 25
  club 3, 4
  commercial 33, 37, 67, 70–2, 78, 80, 90–2 95, 98, 100, 106
  concentration 30
  crisis 5, 9, 17
    see also secondary banking crisis
  energy 27, 29, 40, 46, 48
  failures 27–8
  farm 27–9, 40, 45–8 *passim*
  holding companies 38, 42
    Act (US) 36–7
    Douglas Amendment 36
  interdependence 16, 43
  investment 25, 37
    see also securities-houses legislation
  limited service or non-bank 14, 36, 41
  local 30
  merchant 25
  national 36–7
    Act (US) 36
  profits 46
  recognised 2, 12, 20–2
  regional 27, 29, 34
  surveys 31
  secondary or fringe
    see also secondary banking crisis
  secrecy 53, 61
  state 36–7
  supervision 19, 24, 59
  universal 25
  White Paper 22–4
Bank for International Settlements 51, 55, 58–9, 69, 73, 89, 97–8, 109, 115, 118, 152, 165–8 *passim*
Bank of England 10, 14–24 *passim* 57–62 *passim*, 65, 125, 129–31, 180
Bank Supervisory

201

Committee 23–5
Deputy Governor 25
Governor 22–4
Basle or Cooke
Committee 15, 23, 51, 54–5, 58–60, 171
Concordat 13, 51–5, 62, 65
Big Bang 13, 25, 60, 62, 130
see also Stock Exchange
bipolarity 125
Board of Bank Supervisors 22–4
Bradley Plan 103–4, 108
Branching 25, 55
defacto 36
nationwide 33
restrictions 5, 6, 30, 40, 45
Bretton Woods Agreement 138, 149, 161
Budget
1984 16
deficit (US) 75, 108, 147
building societies 23, 25
Bundesbank 92, 114, 119–21, 125–6, 129, 130, 141, 144–5
Bush or White House Taskforce 38, 42, 190

Capital
adequacy 7, 33, 42, 52
risk related 45
definition of 59
exports 75
flight 70–1, 77, 89, 98, 104–7 *passim*
flows 80, 140, 157, 159
measurement 13
ratio 10, 13–16 *passim*, 41–2, 48, 54, 81
gearing 14
risk asset 14
requirements 15, 16, 55, 63, 81
Chancellor of the Exchquer 16, 22–3, 129, 130, 144
Cartagena
Agreement 72
group 76, 80, 94
Cofinancing 92, 94–5, 99

commodity
prices 68, 74, 80, 85, 94, 143, 149
standard 149, 150
Controller of Currency 36
Office of 37
Confederation of British Industry (CBI) 122, 126
Congress (US) 36, 41, 45, 47, 88, 95, 105, 145–6, 158, 162, 169, 170, 190
consolidated
accounting 52
supervision 12–14, 20, 51
Contact Committee 53
Continental Illinois, Appendix C, 5, 8–10, 27, 30–1, 36–40 *passim*, 46–8, 73
Cooke Committee
see Basle
coresponsibility 87, 93
cross-selling 42
Cruzado Plan 77, 92, 103

Department of Trade and Industry (DTI) 19, 24, 63
deposit(s)
demand 43
see also insurance
protection 1, 2, 4
scheme
dual 44
time 43
Depositary Institutions Deregulations and Monetary Control Act 32
depreciation – *see* devaluation
deregulation 12, 20, 24, 30, 39, 57, 63
product 30, 32, 41
geographic 41
see also branching
devaluation 76, 117, 139
dollar 124, 143–7, 158
disclosure 5, 16, 21, 59
requirements 43
diversification
portfolio 1, 2, 14, 43–4

domino or knock-on effects 1, 44, 47, 180, 188

economic
  growth 67, 72
    export led 74
    gap 79
    US 79, 82, 86, 146, 160
    world 85–6, 143, 145
  policy
    convergence 120, 125, 143, 150, 159–61
    cooperation 148, 168, 173
    coordination 118, 143, 146, 166, 154–161 *passim*, 166, 168, 173
    indicators 136
  summits
    1982 140
    1983 140, 152
    1984 78–9, 94, 159
    1985 78–9, 159
    1986 156
  see also marketing, fiscal, and exchange
European
  central bank 114, 119, 128, 133
  Commission 134, 152
    president 117, 136
  Communities (EC) 113, 117, 118, 121, 139 166, 171
    Banking Advisory Committee 54–5
    Banking Federation 114
    Council of Ministers 118
    Directives 12, 13, 19, 54, 134
    Presidency 131–2
  Currency unit (ECU) 93, 113, 114 119–121, 132–6 *passim*, 150
    accounts 115
  Economic Community (EEC) 115, 134, 139
  Monetary
    Cooperation Fund (EMCF) 113, 115–18 *passim*, 122, 136, 171
    Fund (EMF) 113, 117, 136
    System (EMS) 113–21 *passim*, 126, 7, 135, 138, 157, 161
    Union (EMU) 113, 116
Exchange
  controls 63, 70, 76, 119, 128, 133–4, 136
  rate 93, 168
    coordinated intervention 140, 147–8
    fixed 150
    floating 135, 138–9, 148, 150–9 *passim*
      dirty 139
      free 139
    mechanism (ERM) 113, 116–32 *passim* 136, 138, 157, 161
    misalignments 157–8, 173
    policy 125
    realignments 87
    target zones 115–18, 132, 135, 153–9, 166, 168
export
  revenues 69, 73–4, 77, 80, 83–4
exposures
  country 102
  energy loan 34
  foreign currency 13, 30
  Latin America 30, 35, 69
  loan 22
  over 23, 39, 40
  see also risk(s)

Federal
  Deposit Insurance Corporation (FDIC) 7, 27, 29, 37–8, 44, 47, 188–90
  Deposit Insurance Scheme (FDIS) 8, 38–9, 42
  Federal Credit System (FFCS) 28
  Home Loans Bank Board (FHLBB) 31–3
  National Mortgage Assosiation (FNMA) 31
  Open Market Committee (FOMC) 37
  Reserve
    banks 36, 133
    Board (FRB) 10, 37–8, 53, 55,

69–75 *passim* 82, 87–93 *passim*, 141, 145, 147, 152, 165, 188–91 *passim*
   System (FRS) 3, 36–7, 114
   Savings and Loan Insurance Corporation (FSLIC) 31–4
financial
   conglomerates 20, 23, 40
   efficiency 59
   innovations 15, 57–9
   Services Bill 25, 56, 63
fiscal
   policy 75, 135, 157
   stimulous 160
   targets 76
floating rate notes (FRNs) 19, 100, 115, 129
   market 16
   perpetual 11, 16
foreign currency
   see reserves
fraud 20, 56, 61
   Investigation Group (FIG) 24
   Squad 24
free riders 7

General Agreement on Trade and Tariffs (GATT) 79, 86, 103, 108, 168, 171
Glass-Steagall Act 37, 41, 81
globalisation 17, 57, 59
gold
   reserves 140, 167
   standard 149–50
Group of
   Five (G.5) 144, 168
   Seven (G.7) 168
   Ten (G.10) 59, 129, 152–5, 169, 170, 174
   Twenty-Four (G.24) 80, 94, 104, 154–5, 168
   Thirty (G.30) 141, 151–2, 162
growth
   see economic growth

inflation 70, 82, 85, 100, 103, 117, 131, 143, 147, 149, 166

insider dealing 61
insurance
   deposit 1, 6, 172
      scheme 4, 35, 38, 128
      defacto 34, 38–9, 43, 97
      private 31, 33
      wholesale 6
   premium(s) 34, 36
      risk related 34, 46
   see also asset
Institute
   for International Finance (IIF) 87, 167–8
   of International Economics (IIE) 93, 100
Inter-American Development Bank (IADB) 79, 83, 87–8, 94–5, 99, 169, 170
Interest rate(s) 28, 68, 73, 80, 82, 85, 94, 98, 131, 143, 145, 147
   capitalisation 88, 100
   conditional 102
   capping 94, 100
   ceilings 94, 100
   coordination 142
   deregulation 32
   payments 68–70, 101, 106
International Association
   of Securities, Commissions (IASC) 61
   Bank for Reconstruction and Development (IBRD) or World Bank 75, 80–3, 87, 89, 98–109 *passim*, 138, 144, 147, 153–4, 161–71 *passim*
   Development Committee 14, 168
   Finance Corporation (IFC) 99
   Monetary Fund (IMF) 67–72 *passim* 78–83 *passim*, 87–109 *passim*, 138–54 *passim*, 166–74 *passim*
   Advisory Committee 78–9
   Compensator Finance Facility 100, 103
   Conditionality 96–8, 153
      Executive Board 155
      Interim Committee 13, 154, 168

Meetings 81–2
programme 75–9, 90
Structural Adjustment Loans 68, 76, 100, 169
surveillance
  enhanced or extended 78–80, 98, 173
  multilateral 152–5, 174
internationalisation 25
investor protection 1, 2, 4, 23, 25, 28, 42

J - curve 85, 144–6
Johnson Matthey Bank, A, B, 4, 10

Keynes Plan 149
Knock-on-effects
  see domino effects

Latin American debt
  boycott 73
  crisis 14–18, 25, 58, 165
  default 72–3, 87, 107
    sanctions 72–3, 107
  fatigue 88
  overhang 99, 101
  problem 139, 143, 154, 161
  refinancing 98
  rescheduling 98, 75, 78, 87, 97, 101
    see also Multi-Year Rescheduling Agreements
  restructuring 78, 99
  see also Paris Club
lender of last resort 5–10, 17, 38, 44, 46, 53, 59, 64, 69, 93, 97, 109, 115, 171, 187
  lifeboat
    see Appendix A
  world 53, 76, 98, 166, 171
  level playing field 58, 63–4
letters
  of comfort 22, 53
  of intent 69, 70, 76
liability
  contingent 15, 51, 58
  management 4–7

licensed deposit takers (LDTs) 2, 12, 20–2
liquidity 4
  adquacy 52
  crisis 9, 102
  guidlines 12
  international 152–4, 166, 172
  problems 5
  ratios 12
  requirements 55
Lloyds insurance market 17
loans and lending
  contingent 91
  forced 78, 88, 95
  insurance 96–9
  project 83, 169
  variable rate 40, 68, 189, 140
  syndicated 15, 72, 83, 88, 91

McFadden Act 36
market(s)
  discipline 5–6, 42–3, 46
  Euro 25, 43, 54, 56, 165–6, 172
    bond 1, 56, 58, 98
    currency 1, 47, 50, 77, 98
    dollar 188
    interbank 1, 4, 7, 43, 54, 172, 187
    wholesale 5, 40, 188, 190
Medium Term Financal Strategy (MTFS) 122, 125
Ministry of Finance
  Japanese 62, 64
monetary
  aggregate 9, 14, 147
  base 9, 13
  control 7, 9, 120
  policy 38, 59, 74, 118–19, 125, 127, 133–6 *passim*, 149–51, 157, 168
    convergence 114
  targets 76
money
  at call 13
  supply 150–1
  see also monetary
moral hazard 6, 7, 10, 97, 166–7
multi currency reserve system (MRRS) 140, 149, 151, 158, 166–7

Multi-Year Rescheduling
  Agreement (MYRA) 73–80, 84,
  88–9, 94, 100
Multilateral Investment Guarantee
  Agency (MIGA) 99
Multinational Development Banks
  (MDBs) 82–3, 88, 169
  see also Inter-American
  Development Bank (IADB)

note issuance facilities (Nifs) 57, 60

offshore
  banking centres 25, 50, 52, 57, 86,
  173
  Group of Bank Supervisors 55
oil
  price 29, 84–9 passim, 91, 94, 99,
  102, 106, 123–4, 130, 143, 145,
  155
  revenues 90
Organisation for Economic
  Cooperation and Development
  (OECD) 9, 30, 108–9, 152, 168,
  171, 174
Organisation of Petroleum
  Exporting Countries (OPEC)
  67–9, 83–6, 122–3
  surplus recycling 40, 67, 81, 86

Paris Club 78–9, 87
payments system 8, 38
Plaza Agreement 81, 85, 123, 141,
  158
policy
  see economic
population
  ageing 146, 160
  growth 74, 80, 90
portfolio diversification
  see diversification
protectionism 74, 79–81, 86–7,
  121–4 passim, 145–7, 154, 157–8
  174
provisions
  loan loss or bad debt 15, 18, 41–2,
  5, 48, 81, 101–2

  general 18
  specific 18

re-regulation 33, 56
reciprocity 62–4
recycling
  see organisation of Petroleum
  Exporting Countries (OPEC)
regulation(s)
  over 56
  product range 41
  self 35, 56
  under 56
reserve(s)
  asset 115, 116
  currency 72, 124, 151
restrictive practices 25
retail
  base 40
  deposits 5
risk(s)
  asset ratio (RAR) 14
  country 14, 77
  credit 58
  exchange rate 58
  insolvency 4, 6, 9
  interest rate 58, 189
  measurement 7
  mismatching 7
  off balance sheet 15, 45, 55, 58–9,
  65
  overconcentration 5, 14
  overexposure 14
  pooling 1, 12, 42
  portfolio 44
  premium 44
  see also diversification

Savings and Loan Associations
  (SLAs) 31–2
  see also thrifts
Secondary Banking Crisis Appendix
  A, 10, 19, 24, 185
Securities
  and Exchange Commission (SEC)
  4, 38, 61
  and Investment Board 2

houses 41, 62
    see also banks investment
securitisation 15, 25, 43, 59, 71, 101, 106
seigniorage 149
shareholder protection 1, 2
Smithsonian Agreement 1, 138, 139
solvency
    see capital
Special Drawing Rights (SDRs) 93, 94, 150–1, 154, 166–7, 172
    substitution account 167, 170
sterling crisis 130–1
Stock Exchange 13, 17, 25, 61
    see also Big Bang
structural adjustment loans
    see International
    Monetary Fund (IMF)
Surveillance
    see International Monetary Fund (IMF)
swaps
    currency 165
    debt for equity 99, 104–5

target zones
    see exchange rate
technological innovation 120
thrifts 28, 30, 32–4, 37, 40–1, 45, 48, 74
    see also Savings and Loan
    Association (SLAs)
trade balance 68

deficits 69, 74, 141
flows 150
free
    imbalances 67, 87
    liberalisation 104
    regulations 108
    sanctions 107
    war 108, 161
    see also protectionism and
    General Agreement on Trade
    and Tarriffs (GATT)
transparency problem 43
Treasury
    UK 24, 124–5
    and Bank Review
        Committee 21–2
    US 34, 69, 94, 99, 143, 165
    Secretary 4, 147, 155, 158–9
Triffen Plan 149

United Nations (UN)
    Conference on Trade and
        Development (UNCTAD) 107, 168
    General Assembly 104

White Plan 149
witholding tax 63
World Bank
    see International Bank for
    Reconstruction and
    Development (IBRD)